THE

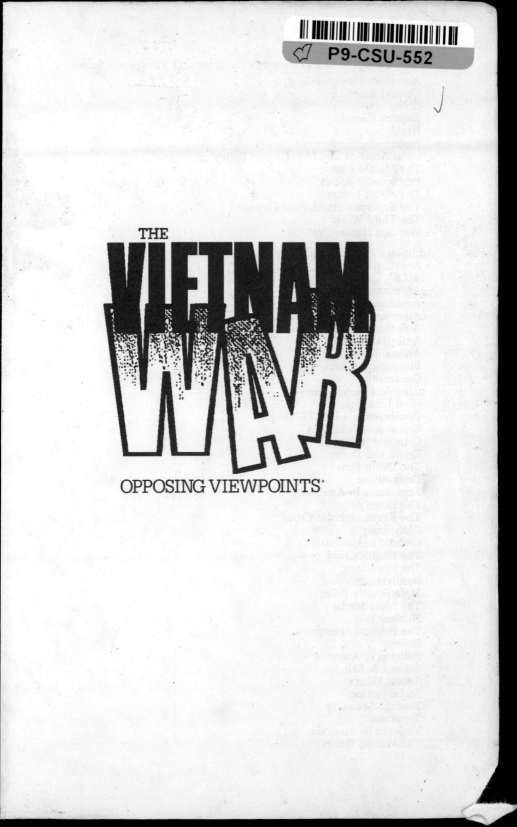

VIETNAM WAR

OPPOSING VIEWPOINTS

Other Books of Related Interest in the Opposing Viewpoints Series:

American Foreign Policy
Central America
China
Eastern Europe
Israel
Japan
Latin America and U.S. Foreign Policy
The Middle East
Problems of Africa
The Soviet Union
The Superpowers: A New Detente
The Third World
War and Human Nature

Additional Books in the Opposing Viewpoints Series
Abortion
AIDS
American Government
American Values
America's Elections
America's Future
America's Prisons
Animal Rights
Biomedical Ethics
Censorship
Chemical Dependency
Civil Liberties
Constructing a Life Philosophy
Crime and Criminals
Criminal Justice
Death and Dying
The Death Penalty
Drug Abuse
Economics in America
The Elderly
The Environmental Crisis
Euthanasia
Genetic Engineering
The Health Crisis
The Homeless
Immigration
Male/Female Roles
The Mass Media
Nuclear War
The Political Spectrum
Poverty
Religion in America
Science & Religion
Sexual Values
Social Justice
Teenage Sexuality
Terrorism
Violence in America
The War on Drugs

THE VIETNAM WAR

OPPOSING VIEWPOINTS®

David Bender & Bruno Leone, *Series Editors*

William Dudley & David Bender, *Book Editors*

OPPOSING VIEWPOINTS SERIES ®

Greenhaven Press, Inc.   PO Box 289009   San Diego, CA 92198-0009

Library of Congress Cataloging-in-Publication Data

The Vietnam war : opposing viewpoints / William Dudley and David Bender, editors.
     p.   cm. — (Opposing viewpoints series)
   Includes bibliographical references and index.
   Summary: Presents opposing viewpoints on various aspects of the Vietnam War, including the reasons for American involvement, the failure of United States policy there, and the effects on veterans.
   ISBN 0-89908-453-2 (pbk.). — ISBN 0-89908-478-8 (lib. bdg.)
   1. Vietnamese Conflict, 1961-1975.   [1. Vietnamese Conflict, 1961-1975.]   I. Dudley, William, 1964-   .   II. Bender, David, 1936-   .   III. Series: Opposing viewpoints series (Unnumbered)
DS557.7.V5667   1990   90-39794
959.704'3—dc20   CIP
                                                                  AC

Second Edition
Revised

Chapter 3: What Are the Legacies of Vietnam?

Chapter 4: How Has the Vietnam War Affected Veterans?

Chapter 5: What Should U.S. Policy Be Toward Indochina?

Why Consider Opposing Viewpoints?

"It is better to debate a question without settling it than to settle a question without debating it."

Joseph Joubert (1754-1824)

The Importance of Examining Opposing Viewpoints

The purpose of the Opposing Viewpoints Series, and this book in particular, is to present balanced, and often difficult to find, opposing points of view on complex and sensitive issues.

Probably the best way to become informed is to analyze the positions of those who are regarded as experts and well studied on issues. It is important to consider every variety of opinion in an attempt to determine the truth. Opinions from the mainstream of society should be examined. But also important are opinions that are considered radical, reactionary, or minority as well as those stigmatized by some other uncomplimentary label. An important lesson of history is the eventual acceptance of many unpopular and even despised opinions. The ideas of Socrates, Jesus, and Galileo are good examples of this.

Readers will approach this book with their own opinions on the issues debated within it. However, to have a good grasp of one's own viewpoint, it is necessary to understand the arguments of those with whom one disagrees. It can be said that those who do not completely understand their adversary's point of view do not fully understand their own.

A persuasive case for considering opposing viewpoints has been presented by John Stuart Mill in his work *On Liberty*. When examining controversial issues it may be helpful to reflect on this suggestion:

The only way in which a human being can make some approach to knowing the whole of a subject, is by hearing what can be said about it by persons of every variety of opinion, and studying all modes in which it can be looked at by every character of mind. No wise man ever acquired his wisdom in any mode but this.

Analyzing Sources of Information

The Opposing Viewpoints Series includes diverse materials taken from magazines, journals, books, and newspapers, as well as statements and position papers from a wide range of individuals, organizations, and governments. This broad spectrum of sources helps to develop patterns of thinking which are open to the consideration of a variety of opinions.

Pitfalls to Avoid

A pitfall to avoid in considering opposing points of view is that of regarding one's own opinion as being common sense and the most rational stance, and the point of view of others as being only opinion and naturally wrong. It may be that another's opinion is correct and one's own is in error.

Another pitfall to avoid is that of closing one's mind to the opinions of those with whom one disagrees. The best way to approach a dialogue is to make one's primary purpose that of understanding the mind and arguments of the other person and not that of enlightening him or her with one's own solutions. More can be learned by listening than speaking.

It is my hope that after reading this book the reader will have a deeper understanding of the issues debated and will appreciate the complexity of even seemingly simple issues on which good and honest people disagree. This awareness is particularly important in a democratic society such as ours where people enter into public debate to determine the common good. Those with whom one disagrees should not necessarily be regarded as enemies, but perhaps simply as people who suggest different paths to a common goal.

Developing Basic Reading and Thinking Skills

In this book, carefully edited opposing viewpoints are purposely placed back to back to create a running debate; each viewpoint is preceded by a short quotation that best expresses the author's main argument. This format instantly plunges the reader into the midst of a controversial issue and greatly aids that reader in mastering the basic skill of recognizing an author's point of view.

A number of basic skills for critical thinking are practiced in the activities that appear throughout the books in the series. Some of the skills are:

Evaluating Sources of Information. The ability to choose from among alternative sources the most reliable and accurate source in relation to a given subject.

Separating Fact from Opinion. The ability to make the basic distinction between factual statements (those that can be demonstrated or verified empirically) and statements of opinion (those that are beliefs or attitudes that cannot be proved).

Identifying Stereotypes. The ability to identify oversimplified, exaggerated descriptions (favorable or unfavorable) about people and insulting statements about racial, religious, or national groups, based upon misinformation or lack of information.

Recognizing Ethnocentrism. The ability to recognize attitudes or opinions that express the view that one's own race, culture, or group is inherently superior, or those attitudes that judge another culture or group in terms of one's own.

It is important to consider opposing viewpoints and equally important to be able to critically analyze those viewpoints. The activities in this book are designed to help the reader master these thinking skills. Statements are taken from the book's viewpoints and the reader is asked to analyze them. This technique aids the reader in developing skills that not only can be applied to the viewpoints in this book, but also to situations where opinionated spokespersons comment on controversial issues. Although the activities are helpful to the solitary reader, they are most useful when the reader can benefit from the interaction of group discussion.

Using this book and others in the series should help readers develop basic reading and thinking skills. These skills should improve the reader's ability to understand what is read. Readers should be better able to separate fact from opinion, substance from rhetoric, and become better consumers of information in our media-centered culture.

This volume of the Opposing Viewpoints Series does not advocate a particular point of view. Quite the contrary! The very nature of the book leaves it to the reader to formulate the opinions he or she finds most suitable. My purpose as publisher is to see that this is made possible by offering a wide range of viewpoints that are fairly presented.

David L. Bender
Publisher

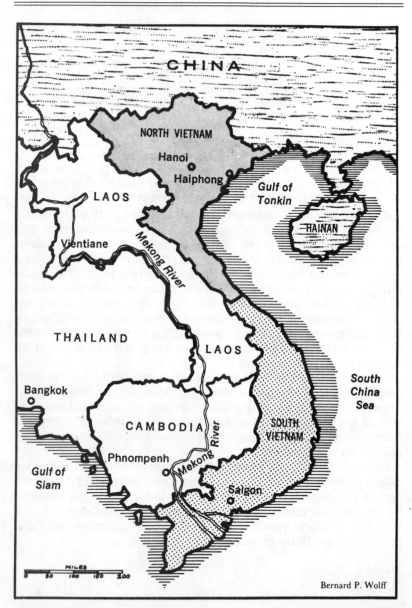

The 1954 Geneva agreements ended 60 years of French occupation and temporarily partitioned Vietnam at the 17th parallel.

Introduction

"Woe to the statesman whose reasons for entering a war do not appear so plausible at its end as at its beginning."

Otto von Bismarck (1815-1898)

In July 1962, Nikita Khrushchev, premier of the USSR, re-marked to the American ambassador Llewellyn Thompson: "In South Vietnam, the United States has stumbled into a bog. It will be mired down there a long time." Khrushchev's words clearly moved beyond prophecy as the United States ultimately found itself involved in an Asian land war which it could nei-ther seem to win nor honorably abandon. What began as a very limited effort to check Communist expansion in South Vietnam, ended over a decade later with more than 200,000 American soldiers killed or wounded. And beyond this calamitous legacy in human lives, what remains is perhaps the most disfigured chapter in American military and diplomatic history.

U.S. involvement in Vietnam began during the administration of Dwight D. Eisenhower (1953-1961). Vietnam, a former French colony, had been partitioned in 1954 into a Communist-dominated regime in the north and an anti-Communist regime in the south. North Vietnam, under the leadership of the skilled guerrilla fighter Ho Chi Minh, was lending military sup-port to a group of Communist insurgents in the south who were attempting to overthrow the South Vietnamese government. Under Eisenhower, several hundred military advisors were sent, along with economic aid, to strengthen the forces of anti-communism. As the insurgency began making consequential inroads, however, Eisenhower's successor, John F. Kennedy (1961-1963), decided to commit American support troops to South Vietnam.

Growing Involvement

In 1962, 4,000 troops were sent. Moreover, the United States began involving itself directly in the political affairs of South Vietnam, at first supporting and then contributing to the over-throw of the repressive regime of President Ngo Dinh Diem in 1963. From that point on, events moved swiftly as U.S. inter-vention mushroomed both politically and militarily. In 1964, President Lyndon B. Johnson (1963-1968) ordered U.S. air

13

strikes against North Vietnam. By 1965, these air strikes had become an almost daily part of the war. The number of American ground troops also increased significantly. In 1966, 200,000 U.S. soldiers were fighting in Vietnam. That number grew annually until by 1969, over a half-million troops were committed to the Vietnam enterprise.

Initially, most Americans backed Washington's Vietnam policy. Government reports depicted the Viet Cong (the name given the Communist insurgents) as a Communist guerrilla movement which employed terror and coercion to force the hapless peasantry of South Vietnam into submission. Moreover, the North Vietnamese, who were underwriting the efforts of the Viet Cong with troops and armaments, were receiving a steady supply of war materials and monies from Communist-bloc nations, especially the People's Republic of China. A dangerous situation seemed to be developing, one which the U.S. government referred to as the "domino theory": If South Vietnam were allowed to fall to communism, so eventually would the rest of Southeast Asia. Given these circumstances, aiding the government of South Vietnam appeared both honorable and consistent with America's best interests. But as the war dragged on and a military victory appeared more and more elusive, these arguments were rapidly becoming moot. Much weightier arguments were evolving, namely the cost in American and Vietnamese lives and in American dollars. Americans began questioning the credibility of those factors allegedly motivating their government's involvement.

A National Debate

The final outcome was a national debate unlike any other debate in American history. The war prompted many to examine the ultimate sources of American democracy. For the first time, the morality and designs of an American military involvement were seriously questioned on a large and telling scale. Throughout the nation, from all quarters, the same questions were being asked with growing regularity. Was the cause of freedom at home and in the world really being served in Vietnam or had the government created a self-serving illusion? Did America possess the economic and military resources to oversee world freedom; and, more basically, did it hold the moral right? As a final scathing indictment, was American intervention abroad anything but hypocritical so long as the nation continued to ally with, and even actively support, dictatorial regimes whose dubious saving grace was their opposition to communism? In less than a decade, Vietnam, a nation which in 1960 was practically unknown to most Americans, succeeded in generating the greatest amount of domestic unrest experienced in the United States since the Civil War.

14

Predictably, Vietnam became the primary focus of attention during the presidential election of 1968. In an apparent effort to induce the North Vietnamese to join the U.S. in negotiating a settlement to the war, President Johnson announced that he would not seek re-election. His vice president, Hubert H. Humphrey, became the Democratic nominee and was defeated by Richard M. Nixon (1969-1974) who claimed to have a "secret plan" for honorably disengaging American troops. However, Nixon's "secret plan," which amounted to a greater South Vietnamese troop involvement in concert with a gradual American pullout, in many respects succeeded only in intensifying the conflict.

U.S. Defeat

U.S. participation in the war ultimately ended in March 1973 following several years of peace negotiations. However, America's reaction to the new-found peace was more of pain than relief as North Vietnam quickly and decisively exploited the void left by the United States. The Communists persisted with a new tenacity as hamlet after hamlet, city after city, methodically fell to their forces. Gerald Ford (1974-1976), who succeeded Richard Nixon when the latter resigned in the wake of the Watergate scandal, attempted unsuccessfully to secure additional military aid from Congress for South Vietnam. Congress and the nation were little disposed toward repeating what were perceived as past errors. Finally, in April 1975, Communist forces captured Saigon, the capital of South Vietnam, and renamed it Ho Chi Minh City after North Vietnam's late and revered leader. What remained was the stinging realization that a dozen years of American financial and military might had accomplished little more than prolonging the inevitable.

Ironically, world events following the Vietnam War failed to fulfill the dire predictions people thought would result from U.S. defeat. The predicted "domino effect" did not materialize. Only Vietnam and two small neighboring countries, Laos and Cambodia, became Communist. These three nations soon fell behind their Southeast Asian neighbors in their economic development and standard of living. U.S. power and prestige continued to be highly respected in Asia. China and the U.S. normalized relations in 1978, while China and Vietnam ended their alliance and resumed their historical standing as bitter enemies, notwithstanding their shared Communist ideology. The Soviet Union gained the use of military bases in Vietnam, but this did not lead to the ultimate defeat of the U.S. In fact, the USSR has since faced dire economic problems, defeat in Afghanistan, and declining influence in Asia and the world.

The Vietnam War, however, remains a controversial topic

within the U.S. Divisions still exist today between supporters and protesters of the war, between those who served in Vietnam and those who stayed home, and between those who believed the war was winnable and those who did not. In his 1989 inaugural address President George Bush called for the U.S. to put the Vietnam War behind, stating that "the final lesson of Vietnam is that no great nation can long afford to be sundered by memory." Robert Drinan, a former congressman and Jesuit priest, responded to Bush's call by writing that "on the contrary, a truly great nation would ask itself why it is divided and 'sundered' by Vietnam."

Topics Debated

The Vietnam War: Opposing Viewpoints, like the 1984 volume it replaces, traces the Vietnam War from the earliest days of U.S. involvement to the present. This revised and updated edition features many new viewpoints and introduces several new topics, including chapters on Vietnam veterans and postwar U.S. policy in Southeast Asia. The following topics are debated: Why Did the U.S. Become Involved in Vietnam? Why Did U.S. Policy Fail in Vietnam? What Are the Legacies of Vietnam? How Has the Vietnam War Affected Veterans? What Should U.S. Policy Be Toward Indochina? The debates in this book indicate that the Vietnam War remains an important and controversial topic today as the United States struggles both to honor those who served in Vietnam and to define its proper role in the world.

CHAPTER 1

Why Did the U.S. Become Involved in Vietnam?

Chapter Preface

Why did the U.S. become involved in Vietnam, a small country thousands of miles away? Three important factors in the world situation following World War II provide some explanations.

The first factor was the end of colonialism. The European countries, weakened by the war, were unable to deny the growing demands for independence in their African and Asian colonies. In Vietnam, for example, an independence movement under the leadership of Ho Chi Minh rose to challenge French rule. The United States helped France, its World War II ally, by giving financial and military aid.

Ho Chi Minh was also a Communist, and thus part of the second factor: the rise of communism as a perceived threat to the United States. America's fears of communism grew when Communists came to power in China in 1949. U.S. foreign policymakers determined to "contain" communism and resolved that America's top priority should be preventing other countries in Asia and the rest of the world from becoming Communist. When Ho Chi Minh defeated the French in 1954 and seemed poised to take over Vietnam, U.S. leaders felt they had to act.

The third factor was the rise of the U.S. as a world power. In sharp contrast to the end of World War I when the U.S. more or less withdrew from international affairs, following World War II the victorious U.S. continued to play an active and dominant role in world diplomacy. The U.S. helped rebuild Europe and Japan, and set up alliances such as the North Atlantic Treaty Organization (NATO) to ward off communism and protect U.S. interests. With other countries in ruins from World War II, American power, wealth, and prestige were preeminent. Most American leaders thus not only felt obliged to become involved in faraway Vietnam, but were very confident that the U.S. would be successful in its endeavors. The prospect of the U.S. losing a war to a small country like Vietnam was unthinkable.

All three of these factors help to explain U.S. decisions concerning Vietnam. The three pairs of viewpoints in this chapter recall debates made by U.S. leaders at the beginning, middle, and closing of U.S. involvement in the Vietnam War.

"If the Communist forces won uncontested control over Indochina or any substantial part thereof, they would surely resume the same pattern of aggression against other free peoples in the area."

The U.S. Must Stop Communist Expansion (1954)

John Foster Dulles

John Foster Dulles served as Secretary of State from 1953 to 1959 under President Dwight Eisenhower. One of the primary architects of America's foreign policy following World War II, he regarded communism as a moral evil to be forcefully opposed. He supported the Nationalist Chinese against Communist China and was a strong backer of the South Vietnamese government of Ngo Dinh Diem. In the following viewpoint, Dulles argues that if the U.S. does not act to stop communist aggression in Vietnam, the Soviets and their allies will take over all of Southeast Asia.

As you read, consider the following questions:

1. What is the communists' plan for Indochina, according to Dulles?
2. How does Dulles suggest communist control of Indochina would affect the interests of the U.S. and its allies?

John Foster Dulles, from a speech delivered to the Overseas Press Club of America, New York, March 29, 1954.

Indochina is important for many reasons. First—and always first—are the human values. About 30 million people are seeking for themselves the dignity of self-government. Until a few years ago, they formed merely a French dependency. Now, their three political units—Vietnam, Laos and Cambodia—are exercising a considerable measure of independent political authority within the French Union. Each of the three is now recognized by the United States and by more than 30 other nations. They signed the Japanese Peace Treaty with us. Their independence is not yet complete. But the French Government in July 1953 declared its intention to complete that independence, and negotiations to consummate that pledge are actively under way.

The United States is watching this development with close attention and great sympathy. We do not forget that we were a colony that won its freedom. We have sponsored in the Philippines a conspicuously successful development of political independence. We feel a sense of kinship with those everywhere who yearn for freedom.

The Communist Plan

The Communists are attempting to prevent the orderly development of independence and to confuse the issue before the world. The Communists have, in these matters, a regular line which Stalin laid down in 1924.

The scheme is to whip up the spirit of nationalism so that it becomes violent. That is done by professional agitators. Then the violence is enlarged by Communist military and technical leadership and the provision of military supplies. In these ways, international Communism gets a strangle hold on the people and it uses that power to "amalgamate" the peoples into the Soviet orbit. "Amalgamation" is Lenin's and Stalin's word to describe their process.

"Amalgamation" is now being attempted in Indochina under the ostensible leadership of Ho Chi Minh. He was indoctrinated in Moscow. He became an associate of the Russian, Borodin [Mikhail Markovich Grusenberg], when the latter was organizing the Chinese Communist Party which was to bring China into the Soviet orbit. Then Ho transferred his activities to Indochina.

Those fighting under the banner of Ho Chi Minh have largely been trained and equipped in Communist China. They are supplied with artillery and ammunition through the Soviet-Chinese Communist block. Captured materiel shows that much of it was fabricated by the Skoda Munition Works in Czechoslovakia and transported across Russia and Siberia and then sent through China into Vietnam. Military supplies for the Communist armies have been pouring into Vietnam at a steadily increasing rate.

Military and technical guidance is supplied by an estimated 2,000 Communist Chinese. They function with the forces of Ho Chi Minh in key positions—in staff sections of the high command, at the division level and in specialized units such as signal, engineer, artillery and transportation.

In the present stage, the Communists in Indochina use nationalistic anti-French slogans to win local support. But if thcy achieved military or political success, it is certain that they would subject the people to a cruel Communist dictatorship taking its orders from Peiping and Moscow.

The Scope of the Danger

The tragedy would not stop there. If the Communist forces won uncontested control over Indochina or any substantial part thereof, they would surely resume the same pattern of aggression against other free peoples in the area.

Grave View of Communist Aggression

The President, in his April 16, 1953, address, and I myself in an address of Sept. 2, 1953, made clear that the United States would take a grave view of any future overt military Chinese Communist aggression in relation to the Pacific or Southeast Asia area. Such an aggression would threaten island and peninsular positions which secure the United States and its allies.

If such overt military aggression occurred, that would be a deliberate threat to the United States itself. The United States would, of course, invoke the processes of the United Nations and consult with its allies. But we could not escape ultimate responsibility for decisions closely touching our own security and self-defense.

John Foster Dulles, speech, June 11, 1954.

The propagandists of Red China and Russia make it apparent that the purpose is to dominate all of Southeast Asia.

Southeast Asia is the so-called "rice bowl" which helps to feed the densely populated region that extends from India to Japan. It is rich in many raw materials, such as tin, oil, rubber, and iron ore. It offers industrial Japan potentially important markets and sources of raw materials.

The area has great strategic value. Southeast Asia is astride the most direct and best developed sea and air routes between the Pacific and South Asia. It has major naval and air bases. Communist control of Southeast Asia would carry a grave threat to the Philippines, Australia and New Zealand, with whom we have treaties of mutual assistance. The entire Western Pacific area, including the so-called "offshore island chain," would be strategically endangered.

21

President Eisenhower appraised the situation when he said that the area is of "transcendent importance."

The United States has shown in many ways its sympathy for the gallant struggle being waged in Indochina by French forces and those of the Associated States. Congress has enabled us to provide material aid to the established governments and their peoples. Also, our diplomacy has sought to deter Communist China from open aggression in that area.

President Eisenhower, in his address of April 16, 1953, explained that a Korean armistice would be a fraud if it merely released aggressive armies for attack elsewhere. I said in September 1953 that if Red China sent its own Army into Indochina, that would result in grave consequences which might not be confined to Indochina.

Recent statements have been designed to impress upon potential aggressors that aggression might lead to action at places and by means of free-world choosing, so that aggression would cost more than it could gain.

The Chinese Communists have, in fact, avoided the direct use of their own Red armies in open aggression against Indochina. They have, however, largely stepped up their support of the aggression in that area. Indeed, they promote that aggression by all means short of open invasion.

A Threat to the Free Community

Under all the circumstances it seems desirable to clarify further the United States position.

Under the conditions of today, the imposition on Southeast Asia of the political system of Communist Russia and its Chinese Communist ally, by whatever means, would be a grave threat to the whole free community. The United States feels that that possibility should not be passively accepted, but should be met by united action. This might involve serious risks. But these risks are far less than those that will face us a few years from now, if we dare not be resolute today.

The free nations want peace. However, peace is not had merely by wanting it. Peace has to be worked for and planned for. Sometimes it is necessary to take risks to win peace just as it is necessary in war to take risks to win victory. The chances for peace are usually bettered by letting a potential aggressor know in advance where his aggression could lead him.

> *"To pour money, materiel, and men into the jungles of Indochina without at least a remote prospect of victory would be dangerously futile and self-destructive."*

The U.S. Must Be Cautious (1954)

John F. Kennedy

John F. Kennedy was president of the United States from 1961 until he was assassinated in November 1963. Although Kennedy eventually sent several thousand advisory troops to Vietnam during his presidency, he argues for caution and restraint in the following viewpoint. The viewpoint is excerpted from a speech Kennedy made when he was a U.S. senator. Kennedy warns against the folly of military involvement in the jungles of Indochina.

As you read, consider the following questions:

1. Why does Kennedy argue for a closer examination of the Indochina situation before the U.S. becomes involved?
2. Why is the author critical of optimistic U.S. statements concerning French military success in Indochina?
3. What is the primary reason Kennedy gives for claiming that American military assistance would be useless?

John F. Kennedy, speech to the U.S. Senate, April 6, 1954.

The time has come for the American people to be told the blunt truth about Indochina.

I am reluctant to make any statement which may be misinterpreted as unappreciative of the gallant French struggle at Dien Bien Phu and elsewhere; or as partisan criticism of our Secretary of State just prior to his participation in the delicate deliberations in Geneva. Nor, as one who is not a member of those committees of the Congress which have been briefed—if not consulted—on this matter, do I wish to appear impetuous or an alarmist in my evaluation of the situation. But the speeches of President [Dwight] Eisenhower, Secretary [John Foster] Dulles, and others have left too much unsaid, in my opinion—and what has been left unsaid is the heart of the problem that should concern every citizen. For if the American people are, for the fourth time in this century, to travel the long and tortuous road of war—particularly a war which we now realize would threaten the survival of civilization—then I believe we have a right—a right which we should have hitherto exercised—to inquire in detail into the nature of the struggle in which we may become engaged, and the alternative to such struggle. Without such clarification the general support and success of our policy is endangered.

The Geneva Negotiations

In as much as Secretary Dulles has rejected, with finality, any suggestion of bargaining on Indochina in exchange for recognition of Red China, those discussions in Geneva which concern that war may center around two basic alternatives:

The first is a negotiated peace, based either upon partition of the area between the forces of the Viet Minh and the French Union, possibly along the 16th parallel; or based upon a coalition government in which Ho Chi Minh is represented. Despite any wishful thinking to the contrary, it should be apparent that the popularity and prevalence of Ho Chi Minh and his following throughout Indochina would cause either partition or a coalition government to result in eventual domination by the Communists.

The second alternative is for the United States to persuade the French to continue their valiant and costly struggle; an alternative which, considering the current state of opinion in France, will be adopted only if the United States pledges increasing support. Secretary Dulles' statement that the "imposition in southeast Asia of the political system of Communist Russia and its Chinese Communist ally . . . should be met by united action" indicates that it is our policy to give such support; that we will, as observed by *The New York Times*, "fight if necessary to keep southeast Asia out of their hands;" and that we hope to win the support of the free countries of Asia for united action against communism in Indochina, in spite of the fact that such nations have pursued since the war's inception a policy of cold neutrality. . . .

Certainly, I, for one, favor a policy of a "united action" by many nations whenever necessary to achieve a military and political victory for the free world in that area, realizing full well that it may eventually require some commitment of our manpower.

Dangers of Intervention

If the present primarily military approach is persisted in, we are likely to be drawn ever more deeply into a Korean-type war, fought under political and military conditions much more unfavorable than those that prevailed in Korea and in the world a decade ago. Such a war cannot be won quickly, if it can be won at all, and may well last, like its Greek and Malayan counterparts, five or ten years, perhaps only to end again in a stalemate, as did the Korean war. . . .

The choices before us are not between intervention and non-intervention, but between an intervention which serves our political interests and thereby limits our military commitments, and an intervention which supports to the bitter end the powers-that-be, even if their policies, by being counterproductive, jeopardize the interests of the United States.

Hans J. Morgenthau, *Commentary*, May 1962.

But to pour money, materiel, and men into the jungles of Indochina without at least a remote prospect of victory would be dangerously futile and self-destructive. . . .

In February 1954, Defense Secretary Charles Erwin Wilson said that a French victory was "both possible and probable" and that the war was going "fully as well as we expected it to at this stage. I see no reason to think Indochina would be another Korea." Also in February, Under Secretary of State Smith stated that:

> The military situation in Indochina is favorable. . . . Contrary to some reports, the recent advances made by the Viet Minh are largely "real estate" operations. . . . Tactically, the French position is solid and the officers in the field seem confident of their ability to deal with the situation.

In later March, Admiral Arthur Radford, Chairman of the Joint Chiefs of Staff, stated that "the French are going to win." And finally, in a press conference some days prior to his speech to the Overseas Press Club in New York, Secretary of State Dulles stated that he did not "expect that there is going to be a Communist victory in Indochina"; that "in terms of Communist domination of Indochina, I do not accept that as a probability."...

Despite this series of optimistic reports about eventual victory, every Member of the Senate knows that such victory today appears to be desperately remote, to say the least, despite tremendous amounts of economic and material aid from the United States, and despite a deplorable loss of French Union manpower. The call for either negotiations or additional participation by other nations underscores the remoteness of such a final victory today, regardless of the outcome at Dien Bien Phu. It is, of course, for these reasons that many French are reluctant to continue the struggle without greater assistance; for to record the sapping effect which time and the enemy have had on their will and strength in that area is not to disparage their valor....

Intervention in a War of Colonialism

I am frankly of the belief that no amount of American military assistance in Indochina can conquer an enemy which is everywhere and at the same time nowhere, "an enemy of the people" which has the sympathy and covert support of the people. As succinctly stated by the report of the Judd Subcommittee of the House Foreign Affairs Committee in January 1954:

> Until political independence has been achieved, an effective fighting force from the associated states cannot be expected. . . . The apathy of the local population to the menace of Viet Minh communism disguised as nationalism is the most discouraging aspect of the situation. That can only be overcome through the grant of complete independence to each of the associated states. Only for such a cause as their own freedom will people make the most heroic effort necessary to win this kind of struggle.

This is an analysis which is shared, if in some instances grudgingly, by most American observers. Moreover, without political independence for the associated states, the other Asiatic nations have made it clear that they regard this as a war of colonialism; and the "united action" which is said to be so desperately needed for victory in that area is likely to end up as unilateral action by our own country. Such intervention, without participation by the armed forces of the other nations of Asia, without the support of the great masses of the peoples of the associated states, with increasing reluctance and discouragement on the part of the French—and, I might add, with hordes of Chinese Communist troops poised just across the border in anticipation of our unilateral entry into their kind of battleground—such intervention, Mr. President, would be virtually impossible in the type of military situation which prevails in Indochina.

"It is preposterous to maintain that we should reduce our effort and lessen our commitment to the great struggle of our century."

The U.S. Must Maintain Its Commitments (1965)

Thomas J. Dodd

Thomas J. Dodd was a Democratic senator from Connecticut and a supporter of President Lyndon B. Johnson's Vietnam policy. The following viewpoint is excerpted from a speech he delivered to the U.S. Senate in 1965. In it, Dodd describes the dangers of "the new isolationism" and states his belief that the United States must maintain its long-time stance of aiding people who are trying to defend or maintain liberty.

As you read, consider the following questions:

1. How does Dodd define "the new isolationism"? Why does he see this view as being potentially disastrous?
2. According to Dodd, why would it be wrong for the U.S. to withdraw from Vietnam?
3. What is the disease that Dodd says we are resisting in Vietnam? What are its dangers, in his view?

Thomas J. Dodd, speech to the U.S. Senate, February 23, 1965.

There has been developing in this country in recent years a brand of thinking about foreign affairs which, I believe, can aptly be described as "the new isolationism." This internal phenomenon is, in my opinion, potentially more disastrous in terms of its consequence than the major external problems that confront us.

Its background is a growing national weariness with Cold War burdens we have been so long carrying, a rising frustration with situations that are going against us in many places, a long-simmering indignation over the fact that our generosity and sacrifice have too often been met abroad, not just with indifference and ingratitude, but even with hostility and contempt.

Its political base seems to be to the Left of center, although it forms as yet a distinct minority there.

Its scareword is "escalation"; its cure-all is "neutralization."

Its prophets include some of my colleagues in the Congress, influential spokesmen in the press, and leading figures in the academic world. Some are new volunteers in this cause of retrenchment; they regard themselves as pragmatists. Others are old hands at Pollyanna-ism, those unshakable romantics who were disillusioned by Moscow at the time of the Hitler-Stalin pact, disillusioned by Mao when they discovered that he was not really an agrarian reformer, disillusioned by Castro when they learned he was not a cross between Thomas Jefferson and Robin Hood—and who, having again dusted themselves off, now look for new vistas of adventure. . . .

The Premise of the New Isolationism

The basic premise of the new isolationism is that the United States is overextended in its attempt to resist Communist aggression around the world, overcommitted to the defense of distant outposts, and overinvolved in the murky and unintelligible affairs of remote areas.

The corollaries of the new isolationism are many. It is contended that we should de-emphasize the Cold War and reverse our national priorities in favor of domestic improvements; that we should withdraw from South Viet-Nam; that we should cease involvement in the Congo; that we should relax the so-called rigidity of our Berlin policy; that foreign aid has outlived its usefulness and should be severely cut back; that our Military Establishment and our C.I.A. [Central Intelligence Agency] organizations that seem particularly suspect because they are symbols of world-wide involvement, should be humbled and "cut down to size" and stripped of their influence in foreign policy questions.

In my judgment all of these propositions have one thing in common. Each of them would strike at the heart of our national effort to preserve our freedom and our security; and collectively they add up to a policy which I can describe by no other name than "appeasement," subtle appeasement, unintentional appeasement, to be sure, but appeasement nonetheless.

My purpose, then, is to oppose these propositions and to enlist Senators' opposition against them—for the new isolationism is as bankrupt as the old.

U.S. Not Overextended

First of all—to tackle the main premise—I reject the assumption that the United States is overextended, or overcommitted, or overinvolved.

We are enjoying a spectacular growth in every index of national strength. Our population, our wealth, our industrial capacity, our scientific potential, our agricultural output, all are enjoying great upward surges. We were informed that our Gross National Product was again up in January 1965, and the trend seems ever upward.

Commitment of Honor

I want to say that these advocates of retreat, defeat, surrender, and national dishonor have not been doing the country any good when they went before a television network suggesting that this Nation was not committed to fighting aggression in this area. The Senate voted for the resolution in 1965, and Senators voted that this country would help that country resist aggression, and specifically authorized the President to take whatever steps he felt necessary to resist further aggression. We are committed. We have more than 200,000 men there. We have at stake our national honor. We are committed to resisting Communist aggression. That is what this is all about.

Russell Long, *Congressional Record*, February 16, 1966.

Far from overextending ourselves in the Cold War, we are actually in a period of declining defense budgets, of steadily lowered draft calls, of sharply reduced foreign aid, of one tax cut after another.

Let me emphasize this: In every basic resource, we have greater capacity today than in the early 1960s, by every military or economic standard, we are stronger; and by every physical measurement, the percentage of our resources going into the Cold War is lower. Why then should we talk of weariness or overcommitment?

We are not even straining ourselves. We are actually pursuing today a policy not only of both guns and butter, but of less guns and more butter.

So far as our resources go, we are capable of indefinite continuation and even intensification of our present efforts, if need be. It is only our mental, and perhaps our moral, resources which seem to be feeling the strain.

We would, of course, prefer to live in a world in which it were possible for us to have no commitments, a world in which we could devote all of our energies to the task of perfecting our society at home and enriching the lives of our people.

War of Survival

But we must face the world as it is. And the basic fact of our world is that Western civilization, itself terribly rent and divided, both politically and philosophically, has been forced into a twilight war of survival by a relentless and remorseless enemy.

It is incontestable, in terms of people enslaved and nations gobbled up over the past twenty years, that we have not been holding our own. And each year, the world Communist movement is committing more and more of its resources to the task of subjugating our allies, all around the perimeter of freedom.

Against this background it is preposterous to maintain that we should reduce our effort and lessen our commitment to the great struggle of our century.

Yet, according to *Time* magazine, it is the widespread sentiment of the academic world that we have overreached ourselves and ought to pull back. Walter Lippmann, the well-known columnist, for whom I have great respect, says that "the American tide will have to recede."

It has been argued that we would be in a "precarious situation" if we were attacked on several fronts. Of course we would, but does anyone believe that we can solve the problem by abandoning our commitments and defensive alliances? Would the loss of these countries be any the less disastrous because they were given up undefended?

On the contrary, if we are not strong enough to honor our commitments today, then we should solve the problem, not by reducing our commitments, but by becoming stronger, and by aiding our allies to become stronger.

Delicate Balance

The defense of the free world rests on a very delicate balance. The key elements in that balance are American power and American determination. If we lack the power to maintain that balance, then certainly all is lost. If we reveal that we lack the determination, if we, for instance, allow ourselves to be pushed out of Viet-Nam, such a humiliation may indeed be the second shot heard around the world; and a dozen nations might soon throw in the sponge and make whatever accommodation they could with an enemy that would then seem assured of victory.

In 1961, after a visit to Southeast Asia, I said on the floor of the Senate:

> If the United States, with its unrivaled might, with its unparalleled wealth, with its dominion over sea and air, with its heritage as the champion of freedom—if this United States and its free-world allies have so diminished in spirit that they can be laid in the dust by a few thousand primitive guerrillas, then we are far down the road from which there is no return.
>
> In right and in might, we are able to work our will on this question. Southeast Asia cannot be lost unless we will it to be lost; it cannot be saved unless we will it to be saved.
>
> This problem, seemingly so remote and distant, will in fact be resolved here in the United States, in the Congress, in the administration, and in the minds and hearts of the American people.

The passage of four years has not diminished my belief in this course. . . .

Responsible Support

No responsible world leader suggests that we should withdraw our support from Vietnam. To do so would unhinge a vast and vital area, thereby committing to Communist domination its resources and its people. This we cannot do. Therefore, we need the dedication and the courage to face some hard and unpleasant facts. We are at war in Vietnam and we must have the will to win that war. . . .

This nation must back up its resolve with whatever manpower, equipment, and weaponry it may take, first to stem the Communist advance in Laos and Vietnam, and then to help these countries, along with their neighbors in Thailand, to create conditions of stability and freedom in Southeast Asia. The security of all Asia hinges on this crucial battle.

Barry Goldwater, *Where I Stand*, 1964.

Twenty-five years ago, our country, comparatively new and untried among the great nations of the earth, through passage of the Lend-Lease Act, described by Winston Churchill as "the most unsordid act of recorded history," embarked irrevocably upon the path that has brought us to our present posture in history. Through that act, we affirmed the preservation and expansion of liberty as our highest goal; we acknowledged that freedom was insecure everywhere so long as tyranny existed anywhere; and we assumed the burden, and the glory, of being the champion and defender of man's highest aspirations.

Since that embattled hour, when the light of freedom was but a flicker in the dark, our journey across the pages of history has been fantastic and unprecedented: tragic, to be sure, in its mistakes and naiveties, but heroic in its innovations and commitments, prodigious in its energy and power, gigantic in its generosity and good will, noble in its restraint and patience, and sublime in its purpose and in its historic role.

We have not realized the high goals we set for ourselves in World War II.

But we have preserved freedom and national independence in more than half the earth; we have prevented the nuclear holocaust; we have restored Western Europe; we have helped friend and foe to achieve prosperity, freedom and stability; we have launched a world-peace organization and have kept it alive; we have offered the hand of friendship and help to the impoverished and backward peoples of the world if they will but take it.

Irresponsible Isolationism

It may be said of our country today, as of no other in history, that wherever people are willing to stand up in defense of their liberty, Americans stand with them.

We cannot know at this hour whether our journey has just begun or is nearing its climax; whether the task ahead is the work of a generation, or of a century. President Kennedy said, in his Inaugural Address, that the conflict would not be resolved in our lifetime.

The Chief of Staff of the Army recently told the Congress that it might well take ten years to decide the issue in Viet-Nam alone. And Viet-Nam is only one symptom of the disease, the epidemic, we are resisting.

Against this somber background, how foolish it is to talk of de-emphasizing the Cold War, of pulling out of Viet-Nam, of abandoning the Congo to Communist intrigue, of slashing the defense budget by 10 percent, or of any of the other irresponsibilities of the new isolationism.

"The true fact is that the United States has had no obligation to South Viet-Nam or anyone else under the SEATO treaty to use its own armed forces in the defense of South Viet-Nam."

The U.S. Has No Binding Commitments (1965)

Don R. Larson and Arthur Larson

Don R. Larson was director of the U.S. Information Agency under President Dwight Eisenhower. Arthur Larson was a professor of political science who served as the first head of the Department of Public Administration at the University of Punjab in Lahore, West Pakistan. In the following viewpoint, the authors disagree with the contention that the U.S. is committed by treaty to continuing the war in Southeast Asia. They believe this contention is based on faulty interpretation of treaty agreements.

As you read, consider the following questions:

1. According to the authors, on what two documents was the U.S. commitment to South Vietnam based?
2. What do the Larsons say is our one obligation?

Don R. Larson and Arthur Larson, from *Vietnam and Beyond*, Rule of Law Research Center, Duke University, 1965. Reprinted with permission of Arthur Larson.

The point of no return is rapidly being approached in Viet-Nam. The Marines have landed. Our planes and our men are engaged in almost daily bombing of a foreign land and people. The sending of ground forces in division strength is hinted at by the Army Chief of Staff. The committing of as many as 250,000 American troops is in the short-range contingency planning. The prospect of thousands of American men laying down their lives in a war on the Asiatic mainland looms larger with every day that passes.

Why?

Every time President Johnson is asked this question—and he now says that he has answered it over fifty times—the first reason he gives is always the same: We must do what we are doing to honor the commitments we have made to the Vietnamese people ever since 1954.

President Johnson bases his statement on two documents: the letter of President Eisenhower to President Diem of October 23, 1954, and the Southeast Asia Collective Defense treaty and protocol ratified in February 1955.

Eisenhower Letter

To understand the purpose of the Eisenhower letter, one must recall that it followed directly upon an agreement with France that "economic aid, budgetary support, and other assistance" would thereafter be furnished directly to Laos, to Viet-Nam, and Cambodia, rather than through France. Pursuant to this understanding, President Eisenhower wrote to President Diem to open discussion of this possibility. After a brief introduction and reference to our aid with the refugee problem, he said:

> We have been exploring ways and means to permit our aid to Viet-Nam to be more effective and to make a greater contribution to the welfare and stability of the Government of Viet-Nam. I am, accordingly, instructing the American Ambassador to Viet-Nam to examine with you in your capacity as Chief of Government, how an intelligent program of American aid given directly to your Government, can serve to assist Viet-Nam in its present hour of trial, provided that your Government is prepared to give assurances as to the standards of performance it would be able to maintain in the event such aid were supplied.
>
> The purpose of this offer is to assist the Government of Viet-Nam in developing and maintaining a strong, viable state, capable of resisting attempted subversion or aggression through military means. The Government of the United States expects that this aid will be met by performance on the part of the Government of Viet-Nam in undertaking needed reforms. It hopes that such aid, combined with your own continuing efforts, will contribute effectively toward an independent Viet-

Nam endowed with a strong government. Such a government would, I hope, be so responsive to the nationalist aspirations of its people, so enlightened in purpose and effective in performance, that it will be respected both at home and abroad and discourage anyone who might wish to impose a foreign ideology on your free people.

That is all. . . .

Where in this highly tentative, highly conditional opening of negotiations and statement of hopes is the "commitment," the "obligation," the pledging of our word? Even if we seem to have indicated a willingness to do something to help, what is that something—beyond aid in developing a strong, viable state?

Eisenhower Aid

The actual assistance program during the Eisenhower Administration confirms this concept. Of total aid from 1953 to 1961, less than one-fourth was classified as military, and more than three-fourths economic. Some idea of the relatively small size of the military side may be seen from the announcement on May 5, 1960, that the Military Assistance and Advisory Group would be increased by the end of the year from 327 to 685.

In short, the nearest thing to a commitment at this stage was an indicated willingness, subject to some stiff (and as yet unsatisfied), conditions and understandings, to provide economic and technical assistance, including military advisers, material, and training.

The other document allegedly imposing an obligation on us to fight to defend South Viet-Nam is a legal instrument, the SEATO [Southeast Asia Treaty Organization] treaty signed in September, 1954, and ratified in February, 1955. . . .

The true fact is that the United States has had no obligation to South Viet-Nam or anyone else under the SEATO treaty to use its own armed forces in the defense of South Viet-Nam. . . .

The specified events calling for direct action have not occurred.

The two operative defense provisions of the SEATO treaty occur in Article IV. They are set in motion by two different kinds of events, and call for two entirely different kinds of action by the parties.

Paragraph 1 comes into play when there is "aggression by armed attack." The obligation on each party is "to meet the common danger in accordance with its constitutional processes."

Paragraph 2 applies when "the territory or the sovereignty or political independence of any (covered area) . . . is threatened in any way other than by armed attack or is affected or threatened by any fact or situation which might endanger the peace of the area." In this event, the only obligation is that "the Parties shall

35

consult immediately in order to agree on the measures which should be taken for the common defense.". . .

The Real Policy of the U.S.

If the first type of "overt military aggression" occurred, Secretary of State John Foster Dulles said:

> The United States would of course invoke the processes of the United Nations and consult with its allies. But we could not escape ultimate responsibility for decisions closely touching our own security and self-defense.

But as to the second type of situation he said:

> The situation in Indochina is not that of open military aggression by the Chinese Communist regime. Thus, in Indochina, the problem is one of restoring tranquility in an area where disturbances are fomented from Communist China, but where there is not open invasion from Communist China.

And now note the pointblank statement of how *not* to deal with this problem:

> This task of pacification, in our opinion, cannot be successfully met merely by unilateral armed intervention.

Which is precisely what we are attempting today.

He goes on to say:

> Some other conditions need to be established. Throughout these Indochina developments, the United States has held to a stable and consistent course and has made clear the conditions which, in its opinion, might justify intervention. These conditions were and are (1) an invitation from the present lawful authorities; (2) clear assurance of complete independence to Laos, Cambodia, and Viet-Nam; (3) evidence of concern by the United Nations; (4) a joining in the collective effort of some of the other nations in the area; and (5) assurance that France will not itself withdraw from the battle until it is won.
>
> *Only if these conditions were realized could the President and the Congress be justified in asking the American people to make the sacrifices incident to committing our Nation, with others, to using force to help to restore peace in the area.* (Italics supplied).

There, in plainest terms, was the real policy of the United States in 1954. It bears little resemblance to the present policy, which claims to have continued unchanged from that time to this. Present policy ignores the peacekeeping role of the United Nations, tries to achieve pacification by unilateral armed intervention, and disregards all of Dulles' five conditions except the first, that of invitation—and there are even those who would disregard the first. Most conspicuously, there has been no significant joining in the collective effort by other nations of the area, and as for France staying in the battle until it is won—the less said about that the better.

"As South Vietnamese forces become stronger,
the rate of American withdrawal can become
greater."

Vietnamization Will Shorten the War (1969)

Richard M. Nixon

Richard M. Nixon was elected president of the United States in
1968 and 1972. He remained in office until August 8, 1974,
when he resigned under pressure resulting from his involvement in the cover-up of illegal activities during the 1972 political campaigns. The following viewpoint is taken from a speech
Nixon delivered on national television at a time when the nation
was in conflict. Nixon explains that his policy is to strengthen
the South Vietnamese army so that those troops can gradually
replace Americans. Nixon argues that such a policy will eventually allow the U.S. to pull its troops out of Vietnam without con-
ceding to the Communists.

As you read, consider the following questions:

1. What does Nixon argue is the main obstacle to peace?
2. What is the Nixon Doctrine?
3. Why does the author think that Vietnamization is the only
   sound way to reduce U.S. involvement in Vietnam?

Richard M. Nixon, speech delivered on national television, November 3, 1969.

In 1954, North Vietnam, with the logistical support of Communist China and the Soviet Union, launched a campaign to impose a Communist government on South Vietnam by instigating and supporting a revolution.

In response to the request of the government of South Vietnam, President Eisenhower sent economic aid and military equipment to assist the people of South Vietnam in their efforts to prevent a Communist takeover. In 1962, President Kennedy sent 16,000 military personnel to Vietnam as combat advisors. In 1965, President Johnson sent American combat forces to South Vietnam. . . .

For these reasons, I rejected the recommendation that I should end the war by immediately withdrawing all our forces. I chose instead to change American policy on both the negotiating front and the battlefront. . . .

Obstacle to Peace

It has become clear that the obstacle in negotiating an end to the war is not the President of the United States. And it is not the South Vietnamese.

The obstacle is the other side's absolute refusal to show the least willingness to join us in seeking a just peace. It will not do so while it is convinced that all it has to do is to wait for our next concession, and the next until it gets everything it wants.

There can now be no longer any question that progress in negotiation depends only on Hanoi's deciding to negotiate, to negotiate seriously.

I realize that this report on our efforts on the diplomatic fronts is discouraging to the American people, but the American people are entitled to know the truth—the bad news as well as the good news, where the lives of our young men are involved.

Now let me turn, however, to a more encouraging report on another front.

At the time we launched our search for peace I recognized we might not succeed in bringing an end to the war through negotiation. I, therefore, put into effect another plan to bring peace—a plan which will bring the war to an end regardless of what happens on the negotiating front.

The Nixon Doctrine

It is in line with a major shift in U.S. foreign policy which I described in my press conference at Guam. Let me briefly explain what has been described as the Nixon Doctrine—a policy which not only will help end the war in Vietnam, but which is an essential element of our program to prevent future Vietnams.

We Americans are a do-it-yourself people. We are an impatient people. Instead of teaching someone else to do a job, we like to do it ourselves. And this trait has been carried over into our foreign policy.

In Korea and again in Vietnam, the United States furnished most of the money, most of the arms, and most of the men to help the people of those countries defend their freedom against the Communist aggression.

Honorable Peace

The operation has demonstrated that the Vietnamization program, designed to enable us to eventually remove our combat forces from South Vietnam, is progressing at an even more rapid rate than I had imagined. The operation has undoubtedly hastened the time when our objective of attaining an honorable peace can be achieved. . . .

I know that all Americans are tired of the war in Southeast Asia. I know the Congress and the administration is tired of the war. I am tired of the war. But I believe that most Americans would like to extricate ourselves in a manner which will encourage a stable peace. We should not leave a vacuum to be filled by Communists.

We must follow a responsible course. Vietnamization is such a course. I am convinced that the Cambodian operation has helped hasten Vietnamization and has helped to insure its success.

John Tower, *St. Paul Pioneer Press,* June 14, 1970.

Before any American troops were committed to Vietnam, a leader of another Asian country expressed this opinion to me when I was traveling in Asia as a private citizen. He said, "When you are trying to assist another nation to defend its freedom, U.S. policy should be to help them fight the war but not to fight the war for them."

Well, in accordance with this wise counsel, I laid down in Guam three principles as guidelines for future American policy toward Asia:

First, the United States will keep all of its treaty commitments.

Second, we shall provide a shield if a nuclear power threatens the freedom of a nation allied with us or of a nation whose survival we consider vital to our security.

Third, in cases involving other types of aggression, we shall furnish military and economic assistance when requested in accordance with our treaty commitments. But we shall look to the nation directly threatened to assume the primary responsibility of providing the manpower for its defense.

After I announced this policy, I found that the leaders of the Philippines, Thailand, Vietnam, South Korea, and other nations which might be threatened by Communist aggression, welcomed this new direction in American foreign policy.

The defense of freedom is everybody's business—not just America's business. And it is particularly the responsibility of the people whose freedom is threatened. In the previous Administration, we Americanized the war in Vietnam. In this Administration, we are Vietnamizing the search for peace.

The policy of the previous Administration not only resulted in our assuming the primary responsibility for fighting the war but even more significantly did not adequately stress the goal of strengthening the South Vietnamese so that they could defend themselves when we left.

The Vietnamization Plan was launched following Secretary Melvin Laird's visit to Vietnam in March 1969. Under the plan, I ordered first a substantial increase in the training and equipment of South Vietnamese forces.

In July, on my visit to Vietnam, I changed General Creighton W. Abrams' orders so that they were consistent with the objectives of our new policies. Under the new orders, the primary mission of our troops is to enable the South Vietnamese forces to assume the full responsibility for the security of South Vietnam.

Our air operations have been reduced by over 20 percent.

And now we have begun to see the results of this long overdue change in American policy in Vietnam.

After five years of Americans going into Vietnam, we are finally bringing American men home. By December 15, 1969, over 60,000 men will have been withdrawn from South Vietnam—including 20 percent of all of our combat forces.

The South Vietnamese have continued to gain in strength. As a result they have been able to take over combat responsibilities from our American troops.

A Plan for Withdrawal

Two other significant developments have occurred since this Administration took office.

Enemy infiltration, infiltration which is essential if they are to launch a major attack, over the last three months is less than 20 percent of what it was over the same period last year.

Most important—United States casualties have declined during the last two months to the lowest point in three years.

Let me now turn to our program for the future.

We have adopted a plan which we have worked out in cooperation with the South Vietnamese for the complete withdrawal of all U.S. combat ground forces, and their replacement by South Vietnamese forces on an orderly scheduled timetable. This withdrawal will be made from strength and not from weakness. As South Vietnamese forces become stronger, the rate of American withdrawal can become greater.

I have not and do not intend to announce the timetable for our program. There are obvious reasons for this decision which I am sure you will understand. As I have indicated on several occasions, the rate of withdrawal will depend on developments on three fronts.

One of these is the progress which can be or might be made in the Paris talks. An announcement of a fixed timetable for our withdrawal would completely remove any incentive for the enemy to negotiate an agreement.

Supporting Vietnamization

The best way for the United States to extricate itself from Vietnam with honor is to train the South Vietnam army and to equip it with modern weapons.

As these troops assume responsibilities which are now ours, our soldiers should be brought home as the military situation permits, remembering that we still have 50,000 troops in Korea 17 years after the armistice.

Mark W. Clark, *The New York Times*, 1970.

They would simply wait until our forces had withdrawn and then move in.

The other two factors on which we will base our withdrawal decisions are the level of enemy activity and the progress of the training program of the South Vietnamese forces. I am glad to be able to report tonight progress on both of these fronts has been greater than we anticipated when we started the program in June 1969 for withdrawal. As a result, our timetable for withdrawal is more optimistic now than when we made our first estimates in June. This clearly demonstrates why it is not wise to be frozen in on a fixed timetable.

We must retain the flexibility to base each withdrawal decision on the situation as it is at that time rather than on estimates that are no longer valid.

Along with this optimistic estimate, I must—in all candor —leave one note of caution.

If the level of enemy activity significantly increases we might have to adjust our timetable accordingly.

However, I want the record to be completely clear on one point.

At the time of the bombing halt in 1968, there was some confusion as to whether there was an understanding on the part of the enemy that if we stopped the bombing of North Vietnam they would stop the shelling of cities in South Vietnam. I want to be sure that there is no misunderstanding on the part of the enemy with regard to our withdrawal program.

We have noted the reduced level of infiltration, the reduction of our casualties, and are basing our withdrawal decisions partially on those factors.

If the level of infiltration or our casualties increase while we are trying to scale down the fighting, it will be the result of a conscious decision by the enemy.

Hanoi could make no greater mistake than to assume that an increase in violence will be to its advantage. If I conclude that increased enemy action jeopardizes our remaining forces in Vietnam, I shall not hesitate to take strong and effective measures to deal with that situation.

This is not a threat. This is a statement of policy which as Commander-in-Chief of our Armed Forces I am making in meeting my responsibility for the protection of American fighting men wherever they may be.

Only Two Choices

My fellow Americans, I am sure you recognize from what I have said that we really only have two choices open to us if we want to end this war.

I can order an immediate, precipitate withdrawal of all Americans from Vietnam without regard to the effects of that action.

Or we can persist in our search for a just peace through a negotiated settlement if possible, or through continued implementation of our plan for Vietnamization if necessary—a plan in which we will withdraw all of our forces from Vietnam on a schedule in accordance with our program, as the South Vietnamese become strong enough to defend their own freedom.

I have chosen the second course.

It is not the easy way.

It is the right way.

It is a plan which will end the war and serve the cause of peace—not just in Vietnam but in the Pacific and in the world.

In speaking of the consequences of a precipitate withdrawal, I mentioned that our allies would lose confidence in America.

Far more dangerous, we would lose confidence in ourselves. The immediate reaction would be a sense of relief that our men were coming home. But as we saw the consequences of what we had done, inevitable remorse and divisive recrimination would scar our spirit as a people.

We have faced other crises in our history and have become stronger by rejecting the easy way out and taking the right way in meeting our challenges. Our greatness as a nation has been our capacity to do what had to be done when we knew our course was right.

"The Vietnamization policy is based on the same false premises which have doomed to failure our previous military efforts in Vietnam."

Vietnamization Will Extend the War (1970)

George S. McGovern

George S. McGovern, one of the first Congressional critics of American military intervention in South Vietnam, was a Democratic senator from South Dakota. In 1972, he ran for president but was defeated by Richard M. Nixon. The following viewpoint is taken from a statement he made during the hearings before the Senate Committee on Foreign Relations. In it he argues that Vietnamization is simply an excuse the Nixon government uses to keep American troops in Indochina. McGovern contends that the South Vietnamese will never be able to take over the fighting being done by U.S. troops because its government is unpopular, corrupt, and abuses human rights.

As you read, consider the following questions:

1. Why does McGovern believe that the U.S. government should stop supporting the Thieu-Ky regime?
2. Why does he believe that Vietnamization cannot work as a means of disengaging the U.S. from Vietnam?
3. What does McGovern mean when he says that the U.S. should encourage the Vietnamization of the government?

George S. McGovern, statement before U.S. Senate Committee on Foreign Relations, February 4, 1970.

Mr. Chairman, and members of the committee, the resolution that I have submitted with the cosponsorship of Senators Frank Church, Alan Cranston, Charles Goodell, Harold Hughes, Eugene McCarthy, Frank Moss, Gaylord Nelson, Abraham Ribicoff, and Stephen Young of Ohio calls for the withdrawal from Vietnam of all U.S. forces, the pace to be limited only by these three considerations: the safety of our troops during the withdrawal process, the mutual release of prisoners of war, and arrangements for asylum in friendly countries for any Vietnamese who might feel endangered by our disengagement. (I have recently been advised by the Department of Defense that the 484,000 men we now have in Vietnam could be transported to the United States at a total cost of $144,519,621.)

This process of orderly withdrawal could be completed, I believe, in less than a year's time.

Such a policy of purposeful disengagement is the only appropriate response to the blunt truth that there will be no resolution of the war so long as we cling to the Thieu-Ky regime. That government has no dependable political base other than the American military presence and it will never be accepted either by its challengers in South Vietnam or in Hanoi.

We can continue to pour our blood and substance into a never ending effort to support the Saigon hierarchy or we can have peace, but we cannot have both General Thieu and an end to the war.

Barrier to Peace and Healing

Our continued military embrace of the Saigon regime is the major barrier, both to peace in Southeast Asia and to the healing of our society. It assures that the South Vietnamese generals will take no action to build a truly representative government which can either compete with the NLF [National Liberation Front] or negotiate a settlement of the war. It deadlocks the Paris negotiations and prevents the scheduling of serious discussions on the release and exchange of prisoners of war. It diverts our energies from critical domestic needs. It sends young Americans to be maimed or killed in a war that we cannot win and that will not end so long as our forces are there in support of General Thieu.

I have long believed that there can be no settlement of the Vietnam struggle until some kind of provisional coalition government assumes control in Saigon. But this is precisely what General Thieu will never consider. After the Midway conference in June 1969 he said, "I solemnly declare that there will be no coalition government, no peace cabinet, no transitional government, not even a reconciliatory government."

Although President Nixon has placed General Thieu as one of

the two or three greatest statesmen of our age, Thieu has brushed off the suggestion that he broaden his government and has denounced those who advocate or suggest a negotiated peace as pro-Communist racketeers and traitors. A coalition government means death, he has said.

Prescription for Endless War

Mr. Chairman, let us not delude ourselves. This is a clear prescription for an endless war, and changing its name to Vietnamization still leaves us tied to a regime that cannot successfully wage war or make peace.

When administration officials expressed the view that American combat forces might be out of Vietnam by the end of 1970, General Thieu called a press conference and insisted that this was an "impossible and impractical goal" and that instead withdrawal "will take many years."

Tragic Hoax

"Vietnamization" has now been fully revealed for a tragic hoax. . . .

It is now clear that the President has not abandoned the disastrous objective of the last tragic decade. It is *military victory* that he seeks—the perpetuation of whatever anticommunist government can be found—however corrupt, unpopular, or undemocratic, and however little they will fight to defend themselves, by whatever military means are necessary. It is a policy which seeks to preserve an American bridgehead on the Mainland of Southeast Asia. . . .

We cannot have it both ways. We cannot have both disengagement and escalation. We cannot hold to a goal of peace, disengagement, and a "political solution" while expanding the war and seeking the total destruction of the enemy.

Walter F. Mondale, speech, May 19, 1970.

And yet there is wide currency to the view that America's course in Southeast Asia is no longer an issue, that the policy of Vietnamization promises an early end of hostilities. That is a false hope emphatically contradicted not only by our ally in Saigon but by the tragic lessons of the past decade.

As I understand the proposal, Vietnamization directs the withdrawal of American troops only as the Saigon armed forces demonstrate their ability to take over the war. Yet a preponderance of evidence indicates that the Vietnamese people do not feel the Saigon regime is worth fighting for. Without local support, "Vietnamization" becomes a plan for the permanent deployment of American combat troops, and not a strategy for disengagement. The President has created a fourth branch of the American Government by giving Saigon a veto over American foreign policy.

If we follow our present policy in Vietnam, there will still be an American army, in my opinion, of 250,000 or 300,000 men in Southeast Asia 15 or 20 years hence or perhaps indefinitely. Meanwhile American firepower and bombardment will have killed more tens of thousands of Vietnamese who want nothing other than an end of the war. All this to save a corrupt, unrepresentative regime in Saigon.

Any military escalation by Hanoi or the Vietcong would pose a challenge to American forces which would require heavier American military action and, therefore, heavier American casualties, or we would be faced with the possibility of a costly, forced withdrawal.

False Premises for Vietnamization

The Vietnamization policy is based on the same false premises which have doomed to failure our previous military efforts in Vietnam. It assumes that the Thieu-Ky regime in Saigon stands for freedom and a popularly backed regime. Actually, the Saigon regime is an oppressive dictatorship which jails its critics and blocks the development of a broadly based government. Last June 20, the Saigon minister for liaison for parliament, Von Huu Thu, confirmed that 34,540 political prisoners were being held and that many of those people were non-Communists who were guilty of nothing more than advocating a neutral peaceful future for their country. In proportion to population the political prisoners held by Saigon would be the equivalent of a half million political prisoners in the United States.

The Thieu-Ky regime is no closer to American ideals than its challenger, the National Liberation Front. Indeed self-determination and independence are probably far stronger among the Vietnamese guerrillas and their supporters than within the Saigon Government camp.

I have never felt that American interest and ideals were represented by the Saigon generals or their corrupt predecessors. We should cease our embrace of this regime now and cease telling the American people that it stands for freedom.

I should like to make clear that I am opposed to both the principle and the practice of the policy of Vietnamization. I am opposed to the policy, whether it works by the standard of its proponents or does not work. I oppose as immoral and self-defeating a policy which gives either American arms or American blood to perpetuate a corrupt and unrepresentative foreign regime. It is not in the interests of either the American or the Vietnamese people to maintain such a government.

I find it morally and politically repugnant for us to create a client group of Vietnamese generals in Saigon and then give them murderous military technology to turn against their own people.

Vietnamization is basically an effort to tranquilize the conscience of the American people while our Government wages a cruel and needless war by proxy.

An enlightened American foreign policy would cease trying to dictate the outcome of an essentially local struggle involving various groups of Vietnamese. If we are concerned about a future threat to Southeast Asia from China, let us have the common sense to recognize that a strong independent regime even though organized by the National Liberation Front and Hanoi would provide a more dependable barrier to Chinese imperialism than the weak puppet regime we have kept in power at the cost of 40,000 American lives and hundreds of thousands of Vietnamese lives.

A Cruel Hoax

Even if we could remove most of our forces from Vietnam, how could we justify before God and man the use of our massive firepower to continue a slaughter that neither serves our interests nor the interests of the Vietnamese.

The policy of Vietnamization is a cruel hoax designed to screen from the American people the bankruptcy of a needless military involvement in the affairs of the Vietnamese people. Instead of Vietnamizing the war let us encourage the Vietnamization of the government in South Vietnam. We can do that by removing the embrace that now prevents other political groups from assuming a leadership role in Saigon, groups that are capable of expressing the desire for peace of the Vietnamese people.

Recognizing Ethnocentrism

Ethnocentrism is the attitude or tendency of people to view their own race, religion, culture, group, or nation as superior to others, and to judge others on that basis. An American, whose custom is to eat with a fork or spoon, would be making an ethnocentric statement when saying, "The Vietnamese custom of eating with chopsticks is stupid."

Ethnocentrism has promoted much misunderstanding and conflict. It emphasizes cultural and religious differences and the notion that one's national institutions or group customs are superior.

Ethnocentrism limits people's ability to be objective and to learn from others. Education in the truest sense stresses the similarities of the human condition throughout the world and the basic equality and dignity of all people.

Most of the following statements are taken from the viewpoints in this book. Some have other origins. Consider each statement carefully. *Mark E for any statement you think is ethnocentric. Mark N for any statement you think is not ethnocentric. Mark U if you are undecided about any statement.*

If you are doing this activity as a member of a class or group, compare your answers with those of other class or group members. Be able to defend your answers. You may discover that others will come to different conclusions than you. Listening to the reasons others present for their answers may give you valuable insights in recognizing ethnocentric statements.

E = ethnocentric
N = not ethnocentric
U = undecided

1. People of different cultures have many things in common.
2. Vietnam represents the cornerstone of the Free World in Southeast Asia.
3. God has marked America as a chosen nation.
4. Nations of the world must develop the ability to cooperate.
5. The Vietnamese are incapable of governing themselves without American help.
6. Americans are incapable of understanding the rich and complex culture of the Vietnamese.
7. Western civilization has been forced into a twilight war of survival by a relentless and remorseless enemy.
8. The defense of the Free World rests on a very delicate balance. The key elements in that balance are American power and American determination.
9. Wherever people are willing to stand up in defense of their liberty, Americans stand with them.
10. We Americans are a do-it-yourself people. We are an impatient people. Instead of teaching someone else to do a job, we like to do it ourselves.
11. Our greatness as a nation has been our capacity to do what had to be done when we knew the right course.
12. Chinese communism is superior to other brands of communism.
13. The Vietnamese people are unable to resist the advance of communism without U.S. help.
14. The current American political system is more democratic than the current Vietnamese political system.
15. The United States is the only revolutionary nation which has truly maintained its ideal of freedom for all.
16. Many Americans believe that communism and freedom cannot coexist.
17. A wise American foreign policy would cease trying to dictate the outcome of a local struggle involving various groups of Vietnamese.
18. Advocates of retreat, defeat, and surrender disgrace America when they say this nation is not willing to fight for freedom in Vietnam.

Periodical Bibliography

The following articles have been selected to supplement the diverse views presented in this chapter.

Robert McAfee Brown "U.S. Cannot Act as the World's Policeman," *Christianity & Crisis*, May 23, 1975.

J.L. Collins "What We're Doing in Vietnam," *U.S. News & World Report*, March 4, 1955.

Commonweal "New Vietnam Commitment," February 23, 1962.

John Foster Dulles "The Goal of Our Foreign Policy," *Vital Speeches of the Day*, December 15, 1954.

William H. Hunter "A Way Toward Peace in Indochina," *The New Republic*, April 16, 1962.

Gilbert Jonas "Southeast Asia: The Genesis of U.S. Policy," *Vital Speeches of the Day*, April 15, 1962.

John F. Kennedy "America's Stake in Vietnam," *Vital Speeches of the Day*, June 1, 1956.

Martin Luther King Jr. "A Prophecy for the 80s," *Sojourners*, January 1983.

Joseph Kraft "A Way Out in Viet-Nam," *Harper's Magazine*, December 1964.

Sidney Lens "How It 'Really' All Began," *The Progressive*, June 1973.

Gale W. McGee "Vietnam: A Living Example for Implementing the American Spirit," *Vital Speeches of the Day*, May 1, 1960.

R.P. Martin "New Tactics or Endless War?" *U.S. News & World Report*, July 30, 1962.

Hans J. Morganthau "The Realities of Containment," *The New Leader*, June 8, 1964.

Hans J. Morganthau "Vietnam—Another Korea?" *Commentary*, May 1962.

Bill Moyers "Vietnam: What Is Left to Conscience?" *Saturday Review*, February 13, 1971.

R.D. Murphy "Guiding Principles in United States Foreign Policy," *Department of State Bulletin*, June 10, 1957.

The Nation "Non-War and the Constitution," February 17, 1962.

Why Did U.S. Policy Fail in Vietnam?

Chapter Preface

The Vietnam War was the first war the U.S. ever decisively lost. In World Wars I and II, American military might eventually prevailed. Even the Korean War (1950-1953), which ended in a stalemate and a divided Korea, was a partial victory for the U.S. In contrast, the Vietnam War ended with North Vietnam sweeping into South Vietnam while Americans and some South Vietnamese who had worked closely with them frantically evacuated via helicopter.

This humiliating defeat made many Americans ask if their military forces could have won in Vietnam. The answers still diverge sharply today. Many conservatives, such as columnist Jeffrey Hart, believe the U.S. could have won. Hart blames U.S. leaders for not using America's full military capacity to bomb and destroy North Vietnam. "Having defeated Germany and Japan, it is nonsense to say that we could not have defeated, destroyed, a third-rate third world military power like North Vietnam. We could have done so over a weekend," he writes.

It was this sort of thinking, according to journalist David Halberstam, that contributed to U.S. defeat. "In Vietnam," he writes, "we made the most serious mistake a power can make. We were not respectful of the enemy. . . . The Viet Cong were both tough and brave. They had a political system that provided endless recruits and they had brilliant leadership from top to bottom." According to Halberstam, the United States lost not because of limited effort (the U.S. dropped more bombs on Vietnam than they used in World War II), but because they were fighting a tough determined people intent upon driving the foreigners out of their land.

The viewpoints in this chapter offer several answers to the troubling question of why the U.S. mission failed in Vietnam.

1

VIEWPOINT

"The failure to declare war in Vietnam drove a wedge between the Army and large segments of the American public."

U.S. Failure to Declare War Caused Defeat

Harry G. Summers Jr.

Colonel Harry G. Summers Jr. is a military scholar and Vietnam veteran. Best known for *On Strategy*, his 1982 study of the U.S. strategy in the Vietnam War, Summers is now a columnist and editor of *Vietnam*, a magazine on the Vietnam War. In the following viewpoint, Summers argues that the U.S. failed in Vietnam because of the strategic errors of its leaders. One of the key errors, according to Summers, was the lack of a declaration of war which could have rallied the American public behind the military, and given the U.S. a clear reason for involvement in Vietnam.

As you read, consider the following questions:

1. Why did President Johnson fail to declare war against North Vietnam in 1964, according to the author?
2. Why does Summers think the failure to declare war put the army in a dangerous position?
3. What does William F. Buckley claim is an important result of declaring war, according to Summers?

Reprinted with permission from *On Strategy: A Critical Analysis of the Vietnam War* by Harry G. Summers Jr. Published 1982 by Presidio Press, 31 Pamaron Way, Novato, California.

One of the continuing arguments about the Vietnam war is whether or not a formal declaration of war would have made any difference. On the one hand there are those who see a declaration of war as a kind of magic talisman that would have eliminated all of our difficulties. On the other hand there are those who see a declaration of war as a clear statement of *initial* public support which focuses the nation's attention on the enemy. (Continuation of this initial public support is, of course, contingent on the successful prosecution of war aims.) As we will see, it was the lack of such focus on the enemy and on the political objectives to be obtained by the use of military force that was the crux of our strategic failure.

A Declaration of War

Further, a . . . declaration of war makes the prosecution of the war a shared responsibility of both the government and the American people. Without a declaration of war the Army was caught on the horns of a dilemma. It was ordered into battle by the Commander-in-Chief, the duly elected President of the United States. It was sustained in battle by appropriations by the Congress, the elected representatives of the American people. The legality of its commitment was not challenged by the Supreme Court of the United States. Yet, because there was no formal declaration of war, many vocal and influential members of the American public questioned (and continue to question) the legality and propriety of its actions. . . .

The requirement for a declaration of war was rooted in the principle of civilian control of the military, and the failure to declare war in Vietnam drove a wedge between the Army and large segments of the American public.

It is not as if we did not know better. We knew perfectly well the importance of maintaining the bond between the American people and their soldiers in the field, and that this bond was the source of our moral strength. . . .

President Johnson could probably have had a declaration of war in August 1964 after the Gulf of Tonkin incidents when two American destroyers were attacked by North Vietnamese patrol boats. Instead of asking for a declaration of war, however, President Johnson asked Congress for a resolution empowering him to "take all necessary measures to repel an armed attack against the forces of the United States and to prevent further aggression." This Southeast Asia Resolution (better known as the Gulf of Tonkin Resolution) passed the Senate by a vote of 88-2, and the House by a unanimous voice vote of 416-0. . . .

When the President could have had it he didn't think he needed it, and when he needed it he couldn't have it. As the distinguished historian Arthur M. Schlesinger, Jr. commented,

"[President] Johnson could certainly have obtained congressional authorization beyond the Tonkin Gulf resolution for a limited war in Vietnam in 1965. He might even, had he wished (but no one wished), have obtained a declaration of war." The reason why neither the President nor the Congress (nor the military either, for that matter) seemed to think a declaration of war was necessary, and why the President deliberately did not seek to mobilize public support for such a proposal was that initially no one envisioned a 10-year war, the massive commitment of American ground troops, nor the ground swell of American opposition. It was hoped that the use of US tactical air power in South Vietnam, the "Rolling Thunder" air campaign against North Vietnam, and the limited use of US troops to protect air bases and logistics installations would cause the North Vietnamese to halt their aggression.

Presidential Error

President Johnson erred in relying on the Gulf of Tonkin resolution as his authority from the Congress to do what he deemed necessary in Southeast Asia. When dissent developed in 1966 and 1967, he would have been well advised to have gone back to the Congress for reaffirmation of the commitment to South Vietnam, a vote either of confidence or rejection. . . . President Johnson . . . should have forced the Congress to face its constitutional responsibility for waging war.

Harry G. Summers Jr., *On Strategy: A Critical Analysis of the Vietnam War*, 1982.

By the spring of 1965 it was obvious that such a limited response was not effective, and the decision was made to commit US ground combat troops to the war. Rather than go back to the Congress and ask for a declaration of war, writes Herbert Y. Schandler in *The Unmaking of a President: Lyndon Johnson and Vietnam*, "efforts were made to make the change as imperceptible as possible to the American public. . . ." In retrospect this was a key strategic error. Failure to make this crucial political decision led to fear of making the political decision to mobilize the reserves. Failure to mobilize the reserves led to failure of the military leadership to push for strategic concepts aimed at halting North Vietnamese aggression and led to campaigns against the symptoms of the aggression—the insurgency in the South—rather than against the aggressor itself. . . . For now we will limit our analysis to the question of why a declaration of war was not requested prior to the commitment of US ground combat forces.

One reason was that it would have seemed ludicrous for a great power like the United States to declare war on a tiny country like North Vietnam. War sanctions, both foreign and domestic, were deemed too massive to be appropriate. Another reason was the desire not to risk a Korea-style intervention by threatening Chinese security. There was also the danger that a formal declaration of war against North Vietnam might have triggered the implementation of security guarantees by China and the Soviet Union. Yet another reason may have been the fear that Congress would not approve such a declaration. This refusal would have caused an immediate halt to US efforts in South Vietnam (a preferable result, given the final outcome). A final reason may have been our use of the enemy's terminology to describe the nature of the war. In his analysis of our failure to declare war, University of California Professor Chalmers Johnson commented:

> [The label "People's War"] made it harder for a counterinsurgent state, such as the United States, to clarify for its own citizens exactly whom it was fighting when it defended against a people's war. Steeped in the legalistic concept that wars are between states, the American public became confused by its government's failure to declare war on North Vietnam and thereby identify the *state* with which the United States was at war. . . .

Instead of seeking further congressional support for the war, President Johnson took the opposite tack and fell back on his authority as President. In March 1966, the Legal Advisor to the Department of State told the Senate Committee on Foreign Relations:

> There can be no question in present circumstances of the President's authority to commit US forces to the defense of South Vietnam. The grant of authority to the President in article II of the Constitution extends to the actions of the United States currently undertaken in Vietnam.

Emphasizing this point in a news conference on 18 August 1967, President Johnson said, "We stated then, and we repeat now, we did not think the [Gulf of Tonkin] resolution was necessary to do what we did and what we're doing."

The only other time a declaration of war was politically feasible was when Richard M. Nixon assumed the Presidency in January 1969. He could have demanded that Congress either affirm our commitment with a declaration of war, giving him authority to prosecute the war to its conclusion, or reject the commitment, allowing him to immediately withdraw all American troops from Vietnam. But President Nixon had foreclosed this option with his campaign promises to bring the war to a close. Within weeks after assuming office, "Johnson's war" had become "Nixon's war." Like President Johnson, he fell back on his position as Commander-in-Chief as authority to prosecute the war.

Commenting on this, the Senate Committee on Foreign Relations said:

> The issue to be resolved is the proper locus within our constitutional system of the authority to commit our country to war. More, perhaps, than ever before, the Executive and Congress are in disagreement as to where that authority properly lies. It is the Executive's view, manifested in both words and action, that the President, in his capacity as Commander in Chief, is properly empowered to commit the Armed Forces to hostilities in foreign countries. It is the committee's view—*conviction* may be the better word—that the authority to initiate war, as distinguished from acting to repel a sudden attack, is vested by the Constitution in the Congress and in the Congress alone. . . .

Into this so-called "legal vacuum" fell the US Army, caught in the middle between the executive and the legislative branches. This was a dangerous position for both the Army and for the Republic. It was dangerous for the Army because in failing to mobilize the national will, the United States lost what Karl von Clausewitz called the strength of the passions of the American people strengthening and supporting us, the more vocal and passionate voices were too often raised in support of our enemies. . . .

An Untenable Position

In the later stages, when the Vietnam war became a partisan political issue, the Army was placed in the untenable position of becoming involved in domestic politics solely because it was obeying its orders. As General William Westmoreland observed:

> I recognized that it was not the job of the military to defend American commitment and policy. Yet it was difficult to differentiate between pursuit of a military task and such related matters as public and congressional support and the morale of the fighting man, who must be convinced that he is risking death for a worthy cause. The military thus was caught in between.

This impasse continued as long as US troops were committed to Vietnam. It was not until November 1973 that Congress, over the President's veto, passed the War Powers Resolution in an attempt to increase congressional control. The purpose of the Resolution was:

> . . . To fulfill the intent of the framers of the Constitution of the United States and insure that the collective judgment of both the Congress and the President will apply to the introduction of United States Armed Forces into hostilities, or into situations where imminent involvement in hostilities is clearly indicated by the circumstances, and to the continued use of such forces in hostilities or in such situations.

The Resolution requires the President to consult with the

Congress before military forces are committed. Military involvement can continue for 60 days, and for another 30 days thereafter if the President certifies in writing that the safety of the force so requires. Unless Congress specifically authorizes it by a declaration of war, resolution or legislation, the involvement cannot be continued beyond the 90 days. As one observer noted:

> The law forces Congress to make a decision after two or at the most three months of confrontation. A vote to continue operations signifies the sharing of responsibility with the Executive; a vote to terminate signifies an assumption of responsibility by Congress alone.

Although the War Powers Resolution is a step toward solving the legal issues involved, it does not necessarily solve the moral and psychological issues so important to the Army. It raises the appalling specter of taking soldiers into combat and then being forced to disengage under fire because congressional approval was not forthcoming. . . .

Effect of Declaration of War

We saw earlier that the congressional safeguard of a declaration of war had fallen out of fashion after World War II. But fashions change. Testifying before the Senate Foreign Relations Committee in March 1980 on the Iranian crisis, the distinguished scholar and diplomat George F. Kennan argued that the correct US response should have been a declaration of war. Not only would it have given the President clear-cut military authority, but it also would have provided nonmilitary options—e.g., internment of Iranian citizens, seizure of funds, US public concern would have been fixed and focused, and a clear signal would have been sent to the international community.

As columnist William F. Buckley observed:

> To declare war in this country would require a researcher to inform the President and Congress on just how to go about doing it. Declaring war is totally out of style. The post-Hiroshima assumption being that the declaration of war brings with it the tacit determination to use every weapon necessary in order to win that war. Thus we didn't go to war against North Korea, North Vietnam, or Cuba. But. . .
>
> To declare war is not necessarily to dispatch troops, let alone atom bombs. It is to recognize a juridically altered relationship and to license such action as is deemed appropriate. It is a wonderful demystifier . . . [leaving] your objective in very plain view.

One of the primary causes of our Vietnam failure was that we did not keep our "objective in very plain view." If a declaration of war could have accomplished that one task it could have been worth the effort.

"If the United States had not invested the situation in Vietnam with rivalry with Communist powers, the tragedy might have been avoided."

U.S. Pride Caused Defeat

Walter H. Capps

Walter H. Capps is professor of religious studies at the University of California in Santa Barbara. He has written and edited many books. In the following viewpoint, Capps argues that the U.S. lost in Vietnam because its leaders clung to outdated beliefs. America's leaders believed that they were locked in struggle with communism and that only America was capable of guaranteeing a stable world order. These beliefs led the U.S. to commit itself to Vietnam, Capps maintains, while pride prevented the U.S. from abandoning these beliefs and pulling out when it became obvious that the U.S. would not win the war.

As you read, consider the following questions:

1. How does Capps define what he terms the Armageddon mentality and the Eden mentality?
2. In the author's opinion, did the U.S. become involved in Vietnam for selfish reasons? How did its reasons change?
3. Why does Capps believe U.S. involvement was "confutable from the first"?

From *The Unfinished War: Vietnam and the American Conscience* by Walter H. Capps. Copyright © 1982 by Walter H. Capps. Reprinted by permission of Beacon Press.

The Vietnam War was fought in many places, on many fields, on many planes, all at the same time. The formal military activity was restricted to Indochina, but the war was also fought on television. Furthermore, it was waged on college and university campuses. One recalls the uprisings in Berkeley, the National Guard at Kent State, and the burning of the Bank of America building in Santa Barbara. On every campus, in every city square, and in virtually every living room a complex and multidimensional battle took place.

The conflict was enacted in less obvious ways too—not only in direct conflict, argumentation, protest marches, sit-ins, and rallies, but in changes in styles of art, music, and literature, and in shifts in modes of dress and manners. One could tell on which side of the issues people stood by the clothes they wore, the vocabulary they used, the literature they cited, the music they listened to, and of course the length and style they wore their hair.

Some said that the fundamental quarrel was not about the potential threat of communism in Vietnam, but about what it is to be an American, and indeed, what the future course of humankind ought to be.

Contrasting Cultures

As the events both at home and abroad, overt and subjective, worked their way, it became apparent that two contrasting American cultures had come into being. The differences in the ways each looked and thought became sharper than ethnic, racial, or economic distinctions. Two kinds of value systems had been spawned, with fissures deeper than those between Protestants and Catholics. Families were split, less by natural generational differences than by divergent attitudes, sensitivities, temperaments, and fundamental allegiances. The Biblical prophecy that when the great day comes, brothers will be turned against brothers, fathers against children, and children against parents seemed to have been fulfilled in the existing tensions. Each side complained that the other didn't understand what was happening. The other side responded that it couldn't understand because it couldn't hear.

Fundamentally, the Vietnam War was a contest between two views of human priorities [the Armageddon mentality and the Eden mentality]. . . .

The world of Armageddon is shaped by conflict. The forces that prevail in life are the ones that win, that defeat their foes and demonstrate their superiority on the battlefield. Confrontations make allegiances firm, choices irreconcilable, and fidelities absolute. Events are always decisive, and the colossal drama toward which all things point is final. In Armageddon, the destiny of the world is enacted in struggles to the finish between diametrically opposed power centers.

Eden resonates differently. Whatever boundaries pertain only differentiate Eden from all else; they have no internal bearing. Everything in Eden belongs; all inhabitants are citizens, and all are entitled to the resources of Eden, without exception. There are no hierarchies, no polarization, no stratification, no class struggle. There are no decisive choices, either; the goal is simply to maintain Eden. Eden is garden instead of battleground, it is harmony rather than conflict. It is warm, fecund, full of vegetation, beautiful, alluring, original, and all-encompassing. But Eden lacks precision.

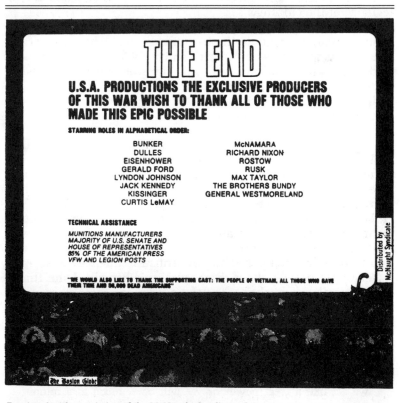

Reprinted with permission of the McNaught Syndicate, Inc.

The radical differences between the expectations of Armageddon and the impulses of Eden provide the framework for much of what has happened within the United States, and throughout the world, in the post-World War II era. Some of the time, for some of the people, motivation has come from Armageddon, while for others the compulsions have been those of

Eden. The one encourages a readiness to confront the adversary; its temper is tough, resolute, defensive, self-protective. The other exhibits an interest in enunciating the underlying harmony; it speaks of maintaining the essential components of the living environment while proclaiming the blessings of global harmony. . . .

Unresolved Quarrel

For most of the post-World War II era, the inhabitants of Eden and the advocates of Armageddon have been at such severe odds that it has been as if there were two United States of America, competing with each other for supremacy and the allegiance of the citizenry. . . .

The trauma of Vietnam was a product of the projection of this fundamental quarrel onto the battlefield; what became most visible during the war was America in conflict with America—the dark night within the nation's soul. The war remains unfinished because the quarrel has not been resolved.

How did it happen this way? What forces gave the drama such orientation?

Dean Acheson, secretary of state under President Truman, offered some reminiscences that illuminate these questions. Writing in a book appropriately titled *Present at the Creation,* Acheson stated that it took some while for Americans to recognize that "the whole world structure and order that we had inherited from the nineteenth century was gone" after World War II. What replaced it, Acheson observed, was a struggle "directed from two bitterly opposed and ideologically irreconcilable power centers"—the world's great superpowers, whose rivalry had a pervasive influence upon all significant subsequent events.

Nearly thirty years later, Richard Nixon described the fundamental challenge in almost the same language that Acheson had used:

> The old colonial empires are gone. The new Soviet imperialism requires a new counterforce to keep it in check. The United States cannot provide this alone, but without strong and effective leadership from the United States, it cannot be provided at all. We cannot afford to waffle and waver. Either we act like a great power or we will be reduced to a minor power, and thus reduced we will not survive—nor will freedom or Western values survive.

The United States certainly wished to have it both ways: to retain some semblance of the world structure that it inherited from the nineteenth century (enough, that is to say, to support strong alliances between former colonial powers, the majority of which continued to identify themselves as allies within the "free world"), and at the same time, to make certain that the contest with the Soviet Union would be played out in its favor.

As it happened, the beginning of strong United States involvement in Vietnam coincides exactly with the beginning of the construction of this postwar U.S. foreign policy. Similarly, the period in which the United States' presence was felt in Vietnam—from September 2, 1945, to May 1, 1975—coincides exactly with the period in which these foreign-policy objectives were being enunciated. Thus it was to be expected that American policy toward Vietnam would reflect the tension between these two competing principles. . . .

Altruism *and* Competition

Ostensibly, America had not become active in Vietnam to promote selfish ambitions, to advance its own desires, or even to protect its vested interests. All that it attempted could be justified on the basis of the cardinal principle—the need to maintain a stable and benevolent world order.

Leader of the World

Inexorably, the decisions [about Vietnam] reflected America's idea of its global role—a view that the United States could not recoil from world leadership.

Stanley Karnow, *Vietnam: A History,* 1983.

Unfortunately, this professed altruistic motive became hopelessly entangled with the discordant twin objective of winning the competition with the rival power center. Before long, it became inevitable that the second objective would be taken as the means to insure the realization of the first. An expectation grew that stable world order could be achieved if the United States could win the contest with the Soviet Union, now simply referred to as the adversary. Logically speaking, the two principles were interdependent from the very moment following the end of the Second World War when foreign policy was being reformulated. . . .

Accordingly, when crucial choices were placed before American decision-makers, the outcome was inevitable. Certainly most U.S. Presidents wished to have it both ways—to keep the two objectives in harmony and balance. When they couldn't, however—when the twin ambitions became manifestly incompatible and contradictory—the leaders found most support in advancing the American cause against its primary competition. No American President could afford politically to be soft on communism, so each felt obliged to push the get-tough policy to prominence. In doing so, each allowed the ideological struggle to assume critical and strategic dominance, and whenever this occurred, the "patriotic temper" (promoting "the politics of national assertion") gained mastery over the inward-looking politics of compassionate reform. The same temper won out in the leaders' attitude toward the nation's involvement in Vietnam: Vietnam was the testing ground not simply for the free-enterprise system, but for the conflict in American will and resolve, manifested for the entire world, including the American citizenry.

Polarization

If the United States had not invested the situation in Vietnam with rivalry with Communist powers, the tragedy might have been avoided. If it had perceived the conflict as a civil war, it would have had no good reason to become involved. If it had seen the situation simply as a clash between colonialists and nationalists, it might not have entered military engagement. But because it viewed the war as part of the fundamental conflict between the world's two great superpowers, the United States eventually felt a responsibility to commit its forces. The quality and intensity of that commitment was nurtured by the religious sanctions of the patriotic temper and the Manichaean mythology by which the rivalry was expressed. In this rendition, America was placed on the side of good, in opposition to evil. Light was pitted against darkness, freedom against bondage, America against anti-America—yes, even God against the Devil.

Within a relatively brief span of time, therefore, the postwar world became sharply polarized, exhibiting all of the characteristic invitations for takeover by an Armageddon mentality. By the time of the Gulf of Tonkin Resolution in 1964, the way had been cleared by Korea in 1950, the Berlin blockade in 1961, and the Cuban missile crisis in 1963. All of these challenges had been met successfully, to America's advantage. Vietnam was simply next in the series. The nation could be confident that the problem would be solved in a relatively short time. But by now the equations were inexact.

To be sure, Ho Chi Minh espoused the Communist philosophy and had strong loyalties to both China and the Soviet Union. He had been trained in the teachings of Marx and Lenin and was thoroughly committed to Marxist thought and the Communist social and political program. Yet the plot the Americans envisioned bore only generalized application to the actual drama in Vietnam. U.S. leadership tried to direct the scenes with little or no knowledge of local circumstances and incentives. It tried to erect in South Vietnam a government which the people clearly resisted. It wished to promote certain Western forms of democratic decision-making among a people who had had no preparation and had shown no strong inclinations for them. It possessed only slight acquaintance with the indigenous sociocultural matrix, based on a combination of Confucian, Taoist, Buddhist, and native religious influences and organized according to ancient Chinese mandarinic systems. . . .

Fear of Losing Face

Thus the primary consideration soon became not the importance of a noncommunist South Vietnam in itself but the repercussions to be expected from reneging on this commitment. As concerns the impact internationally, the fear was of disillusionment with the worth of the alliances contracted by the U.S. and the encouragement of other Communist-led "wars of national liberation" which might follow a retreat from Southeast Asia. With regard to the domestic scene, the steadfast defense of South Vietnam was to preempt the charge of being soft on communism, an accusation to which Democratic presidents, mindful of Yalta and the "loss of China," were particularly sensitive.

Guenter Lewy, *America in Vietnam*, 1978.

Stanley Hoffmann, a Harvard specialist in international government, describes American military and political hubris in Vietnam this way:

The central problem of American policy—of any policy—is the relevance of its ends to specific cases: the more ambitious or ideological a policy, the more indispensable it is to analyze the realities of each case with critical rigor before applying to it one's concepts or preconceptions, for otherwise the statesmen will trip into the pitfalls of irrelevance, "adventurism," or unreality.

He continues:

Our own policy was of necessity ambitious because of our very role as a superpower; and it has, if not an ideology, at least a set of principles and dogmas such as resistance to aggression, attachment to self-determination, opposition to forceful communist takeovers, etc. . . .

The tragedy of our course in Vietnam lies in our refusal to come to grips with those realities in South Vietnam that happened to be decisive from the viewpoint of politics.

Understandably, all such ventures are doomed to failure because they embody the expectation that the structure and order of the world can be established and maintained if the United States achieves success in its contest with its chief rival.

Beguiled and misshaped by the full weight of the mythological anticipation—that it was a righteous cause and that righteousness should prevail—the military venture was confutable from the first.

65

"The decision makers made one crucial mistake: . . . they 'underestimated the resistance and the determination of the North Vietnamese.'"

Underestimating the Enemy Caused Defeat

John Mueller

John Mueller is a professor of political science at the University of Rochester in New York. He specializes in international politics and foreign and defense policies. Mueller has conducted extensive research and published numerous papers on the Vietnam War. In the following viewpoint, he contends that U.S. involvement in Vietnam was well thought out but U.S. leaders underestimated the determination and fanaticism of the North Vietnamese.

As you read, consider the following questions:

1. Why does the author argue there was a special urgency to Vietnam's position in 1965 that contributed to America's intervention there?
2. What does Mueller mean when he discusses "the extraordinary fanaticism of the enemy"?

In her best-selling book, *The March of Folly,* Barbara W. Tuchman assesses several historical instances in which, as she sees it, "folly" was committed: Decision makers acted contrary "to the way reason points and enlightened self-interest suggests." Her most extensively discussed example is the American decision to "betray herself in Vietnam." Successive administrations should have known their policy was doomed to failure, she argues, and had the "moral courage" to reverse course.

With the blessings of hindsight—something Mrs. Tuchman sternly eschews early in her book—we now know that U.S. policy in Vietnam was a tragic mistake. But a decision should not be judged for reasonableness simply according to its success or failure, but according to the process by which it was made. All important decisions contain an irreducible amount of uncertainty and guesswork, and nobody succeeds all the time. What we can sensibly demand of decision makers, whether they be presidents or stock market analysts, is that they carefully assess their values, examine alternatives and pursue the strategy with the best probability of success.

Carefully Considered Action

By these standards, the American intervention into the war in Vietnam was far from a case of folly; it may well have been one of the most fully considered, carefully reasoned actions in our history. And thus the gloomy lesson is that failure could have been prevented only by dumb luck, not by more enlightened decision making.

Pivotal, of course, was the decision in 1965 to send vast numbers of American troops to take over the war effort and to prevent what seemed to be an imminent collapse of the South Vietnamese military. This decision process went on for months, and extensive documentation on it is available. The evidence suggests that the leaders did all the right things: They evaluated fundamental values and premises, they assessed possible alternatives and they came up with a strategy with reasonable promise of success.

In 1965 there was a broad consensus, both within the government and without, that Vietnam was, in reporter David Halberstam's assessment at the time, "a strategic country in a key area . . .—one of only five or six nations in the world that is truly vital to U.S. interests." As Mrs. Tuchman observes, this was an extension of the policy of containing international communism that had guided American policy in the postwar era (and still does, for the most part). What she fails to appreciate is that there was a special urgency to Vietnam's position in 1965: Communist China to the north was crowing belligerently about aiding and encouraging other Vietnams around the globe, while the huge island republic of Indonesia to the south was gradually locking itself into a semi-alliance with China. (Within a year or two, after masses of American troops were committed to Vietnam, these conditions were to change radically: There was a violent anti-Communist coup in Indonesia; and China, its foreign policy an almost universal failure, was to turn northward to dispute with the Soviet Union, as well as inward to embark on that bizarre, self-destructive ritual of purification known as the Cultural Revolution. But U.S. decision makers could hardly have known in 1965 that this was going to happen.)

Mysterious Enemy

I am more convinced than before that the United States could never have won a conflict in this alien land, where the enemy was tenacious, dedicated—and everywhere. . . .

In short, the Vietnam conflict was waged in an environment too complex and mysterious for Americans to comprehend.

Stanley Karnow, *Minneapolis Tribune*, May 11, 1981.

What is impressive about the decision making of 1965 is not that the containment consensus prevailed, but that those holding this view were so willing to entertain fundamental challenges to their position. In a tightly reasoned argument, Undersecretary of State George Ball attacked the application of the containment policy to Vietnam and urged judicious withdrawal. Moreover, Mr. Ball's position, which was far more radical than almost anything heard at the time outside the government, was not stifled at low levels but allowed to percolate to the top; as Mrs. Tuchman observes, Mr. Ball went through the argument point by point with the man ultimately responsible, President Lyndon Johnson.

Mr. Ball's argument was rejected not out of whim or myopia, but because the others decided, after careful reflection, that Vietnam really was a vital interest and that, though risky, the infusion of American troops was the best policy. As part of this consideration, thoughtful assessments were made of the probable U.S. casualty rates over the next couple of years—estimates that proved to be quite accurate. It is doubtful that American decision making upon entering World War II showed such careful, fully rounded consideration of essential values and probable costs.

In all this, the decision makers made one crucial mistake: As Secretary of State Dean Rusk observed in 1971, they "underestimated the resistance and the determination of the North Vietnamese." Mrs. Tuchman ascribes this mistake to "wooden-headedness," but the lessons of the past suggest the misestimation was highly reasonable: The willingness of the Communists to accept punishment in Vietnam was virtually unprecedented in the history of modern warfare.

An Extreme Case

If one takes the hundreds of participating countries in international and colonial wars since 1816 and calculates for each the battle death rate as a percentage of the pre-war population, it quickly becomes apparent that Vietnam was an extreme case. Even discounting heavily for exaggerations in the "body count," the Communist side was willing to accept battle death rates that were twice as high as those accepted by the fanatical, often suicidal Japanese in World War II. Indeed, the few combatants who took losses as high as the Vietnamese Communists were mainly those such as the Germans and Soviets in World War II who were fighting to the death—for their national existence—not merely for expansion like North Vietnam.

The failure of American decision makers to appreciate the extraordinary fanaticism of the enemy is hardly evidence of "wooden-headedness." Mrs. Tuchman suggests the U.S. should have taken the warnings of various French leaders on this issue. But French military history in the last century or so, fraught with inept leadership, precipitous collapse and mutiny, hardly made the advice seem very credible. Anyway, even the French had been able to control the area for decades against local resistance, and in 1954 they had been able to get the Communists in Indochina to accept a peaceful partition, a reasonable halfloaf, after inflicting casualties vastly lower than those delivered by the Americans a decade later. Moreover there were many relevant instances of successful wars against Communist insurgencies: In Malaya in 1960, in the Philippines in 1954, in Greece in 1949, dedicated Communist forces gave up or faded away after being substantially battered; why would one necessarily expect the Vietnamese Communists to be different?

Mistake—But Not Folly

Thus the war can be condemned as a mistake, but not a "folly." Decision makers knew what they were doing, often reassessed their premises, compared possible policy alternatives and tried their best to predict the outcome. If there was "folly," it was in Hanoi, where the leadership (made "paranoid" by U.S. bombing, explains Mrs. Tuchman) relentlessly sent its youth to the south to be ground up by the American war machine without, it appears, a serious evaluation of the relationship between potential gain and inevitable cost, or of alternative, less costly strategies.

VIEWPOINT

4

"At the center . . . was a failure to decide clearly whether the problem was primarily an internal insurgency or an aggression."

Poorly Planned Strategy Caused Defeat

Norman Hannah

In the following viewpoint, Norman Hannah states that U.S. leaders were unable to decide the nature of the war in Vietnam. This led to confused and ineffective strategies, he writes. Hannah is a retired foreign service officer who served in various capacities connected to Southeast Asia from 1947 to 1970.

As you read, consider the following questions:

1. What central decision about Vietnam did U.S. leaders fail to make, in Hannah's view?
2. Why did neutralization fail, according to Hannah?
3. Why does the author believe time was a crucial factor in U.S. failure in Vietnam?

Norman Hannah, "Vietnam Deception—Not Conspiracy, But Indecision," *The Washington Times*, September 30, 1982, © *The Washington Times*, 1982. Reprinted with permission.

At the center of . . . [U.S. failure] was a failure to decide clearly whether the problem was primarily an internal insurgency or an aggression. President Kennedy himself talked sometimes of aggression and sometimes of civil war. Which did he believe? Roger Hilsman, former assistant secretary of state for the Far East under Kennedy, writes that, "The president preferred to treat the problem of Vietnam as something other than war." But what? Hilsman doesn't say. But this reflects a dangerous ambivalence. Splitting the difference between opposites is often possible in politics but when the stage of possible war has been reached the gray shading must give way to definite choice. Unfortunately, the by-word of the day was, "Keep your options open."

The ambivalence of the president spread throughout the government. As late as 1965, when we were already committing U.S. ground forces, President Johnson and Secretaries Dean Rusk and Robert S. McNamara were publicly wrestling with the dilemma. The chairman of the Joint Chiefs of Staff, Gen. John Wheeler, thought, "the essence of the problem is military." Averell Harriman, Hilsman and White House aide Michael Forrestal saw the problem, in Hilsman's words, "as one of civil war rather than external aggression." Walt Rostow saw a major threat in Hanoi's infiltration through Laos. But, according to Hilsman, Kennedy regarded the infiltration trails through Laos as a political trap, "a built-in excuse for failure" (rather than a built-in cause of failure.)

Gen. Maxwell Taylor supported counter-insurgency doctrine and recommended more advisers and helicopters but, ambivalently, along with these he recommended deployment of some 8,000 U.S. troops in the autumn of 1961. Equally ambivalently, President Kennedy approved the advisers and helicopters but, in a familiar Washington political gambit, reserved judgement on the troops while allowing the planning for deployment to go ahead.

Vulnerable President

The confusion started in the aftermath of the Bay of Pigs when President Kennedy adopted separate strategies toward Laos and Vietnam. After the Cuban disaster he felt too vulnerable at home to undertake commitments in distant, landlocked Laos where North Vietnamese forces, with Soviet support, were taking advantage of a boiling internal struggle.

But at the same time he felt too vulnerable to appear supine and hence needed to act vigorously in South Vietnam which offered greater possibilities and seemingly less risk. To accomplish this straddle, he decided to accept Averell Harriman's judgement and negotiate with the USSR toward the neutralization of

Laos while embarking on a vigorous internal support campaign in South Vietnam in accordance with the new "counter-insurgency" doctrine then being hammered out.

Military Confusion

It was the job of military professionals to judge the true nature of the Vietnam War, to communicate the facts to our civilian decision makers, and to recommend appropriate strategies. . . . It is indicative of our strategic failure in Vietnam that so many years after our involvement the true nature of the Vietnam War is still in question. . . .

To have understood the true nature of the Vietnam War not only required a strict definition of the enemy, it also required a knowledge of the nature of war itself. Our understanding was clouded by confusion over preparation for war and the conduct of war, by fears of nuclear war, by fears of Chinese intervention, and by the misconception that we were being challenged by a whole new kind of "revolutionary" war that could be countered only by the "strategy" of counterinsurgency.

Harry G. Summers Jr., *Society*, November/December 1983.

Neutralization was the link between the different strategies in Laos and South Vietnam. If neutralization worked, that would cut Hanoi's logistical link to South Vietnam which could then be handled as an internal problem. And the administration need not risk the backlash of the Bay of Pigs.

As a short term tactic to gain time this had merit but we had no longer-range strategy and we became frozen in the rigid pattern of the hollow facade of neutralization. The agreements on Laos failed the day they were signed because Laos became Hanoi's invasion route to South Vietnam. We became frozen in a strategy which:

1. Prevented using U.S. forces to stop the aggression through Laos;

2. Required pouring more and more men and arms into South Vietnam to pacify its countryside against invaders who continued to stream in through Laos.

So we were involved in an internal pacification where we shouldn't have been and we were not deployed to stop the aggression where it occurred which is the only place we should have been in military force. Small wonder there was confusion and disagreement over what we were doing and whom we were fighting.

We never developed a front line in Vietnam because we never decided to confront the enemy in his primary role as aggressor (in Laos) but waited until he had assumed his spurious "insurgent" role in South Vietnam. A front line concentrated both sides in a narrow area which simplified the obtaining and interpreting of intelligence. The Vietnam war was a war of statistics. Lacking a front line to measure progress or loss, our only measure was by the continuous digestion and regurgitation of statistics.

In this way, the amorphous nature of our strategy contributed to the quarrel over intelligence estimates. . . . It is not necessary to postulate a conspiracy. In fact, to do so detracts from the real question which is—did we know and agree on what we were trying to do *and how* we were trying to do it? The answer is clearly, "No!" Naturally, different sides will report and emphasize those statistics which prove their respective points of view. And they did.

Was it more important to suppress the enemy already in South Vietnam or to close the route by which reinforcements were coming? If one emphasizes the internal war already in existence, then the enemy within must be suppressed first, such as the village para-military which Adams and Allen of the CIA [Central Intelligence Agency] wanted to include and Gen. William Westmoreland wanted to exclude.

But, if one emphasizes the external aggression, then it was more important to close the external reinforcement route by which up to 20,000 or 25,000 North Vietnamese forces were arriving every one of the autumn months of 1967 leading up to the Tet Offensive of January 1968.

But there is a critical linkage between the two propositions. The longer we wait to deal with the external route of reinforcement, the more severe becomes the internal problem, thereby making it even more difficult to get away from the pressing internal threat. And this is what happened to us—we waited and waited and then it was too late.

Time Ran Out

Gen. Westmoreland said . . . that he had told President Johnson in March 1967 that, "the war could go on indefinitely if the U.S. did not cut the infiltration trails through Laos." In his book *A Soldier Reports*, he says he had prepared plans for cutting the trails, a project which he says both Ambassadors Henry Cabot Lodge Jr. and Ellsworth Bunker favored. But, he went on to say, the operation would require three divisions and, "I would be unable for a long time to spare that many troops from the critical fight *within* South Vietnam."

In effect, he was giving the internal suppression priority over closure of the external route of aggression without taking account of the fact that by so doing he was allowing time to work

73

against him. He confirmed this later when he told us that after the Tet Offensive the enemy was depleted but, unfortunately, by then time had run out on the president back in Washington and he could not act.

Unclear Objectives

In his analysis of the Vietnam War (*The War Managers*, University Press of New England), Brigadier General Douglas Kinnard found that "almost seventy percent of the Army generals who managed the war were uncertain of its objectives.". . .

Former Secretary of Defense Clark Clifford testified that when he took over in 1968, no one could tell him what constituted "victory," no one could tell him our plan to end the war. This was a fatal deficiency, for as Karl von Clausewitz had warned,

> No one starts a war—or rather, no one in his senses ought to do so—without first being clear in his mind what he intends to achieve by that war and how he intends to conduct it.

Harry G. Summers Jr., *The New Republic*, July 12, 1982.

I recall a Honolulu conference in 1966 at Pacific Command headquarters, when the subject was how to increase our rate of attrition of infiltration. Afterward, I asked Gen. Westmoreland what he would do if the enemy would simply increase his *input* of infiltration at the top end of the Laos trails enough to offset the attrition that we inflicted so that the *output* in South Vietnam did not fall or even increased.

"We'll just continue to grind them up as we are doing," he replied, grimly. The figure of speech was apt. Our strategy was often described as a "meatgrinder." The question was: Who would tire first, he who feeds the machine or he who grinds? The test was settled at the Tet Offensive. We, the grinders, tired first.

> *"For the first time in modern history, the outcome of a war was determined not on the battlefield but on the printed page."*

U.S. Journalists Caused Defeat

Robert Elegant

Robert Elegant was a foreign correspondent and commentator and, in his words, "a participant as well as an observer in the Viet Nam imbroglio from 1955 to 1975." He covered the war for *Newsweek* and the *Los Angeles Times/The Washington Post* News Service. Until 1965 he opposed U.S. military intervention in Vietnam. He then changed his mind because he believed the U.S. had to contain China's aggressive and expansionist foreign policy. In the following viewpoint, he contends that the defeat of South Vietnam can be largely blamed on the biased and inaccurate reporting of his fellow journalists.

As you read, consider the following questions:

1. In the author's opinion, for whom did reporters covering the Vietnam War write?
2. What role does the author contend television played in Vietnam?
3. Why does Elegant maintain that Western journalists deceived themselves about the nature of the liberation of Indochina?

Robert Elegant, "How to Lose a War: Reflections of a Foreign Correspondent," *Encounter*, August 1981. Reprinted with permission.

In the early 1960s, when the Viet Nam War became a big story, most foreign correspondents assigned to cover the story wrote primarily to win the approbation of the crowd, above all their own crowd. As a result, in my view, the self-proving system of reporting they created became ever further detached from political and military realities because it instinctively concentrated on its own self-justification. The American press, naturally dominant in an "American war," somehow felt obliged to be less objective than partisan, to take sides, for it was inspired by the *engagé* "investigative" reporting that burgeoned in the United States in these impassioned years. The press was instinctively "agin the government"—and, at least reflexively, for Saigon's enemies.

During the latter half of the fifteen-year American involvement in Viet Nam, the media became the primary battlefield. Illusory events reported *by* the press as well as real events *within* the press corps were more decisive than the clash of arms or the contention of ideologies. For the first time in modern history, the outcome of a war was determined not on the battlefield but on the printed page and, above all, on the television screen. Looking back coolly, I believe it can be said (surprising as it may still sound) that South Vietnamese and American forces actually won the limited military struggle. They virtually crushed the Viet Cong in the South, the "native" guerrillas who were directed, reinforced, and equipped from Hanoi; and thereafter they threw back the invasion by regular North Vietnamese divisions. Nonetheless, the war was finally lost to the invaders *after* the U.S. disengagement because the political pressures built up by the media had made it quite impossible for Washington to maintain even the minimal material and moral support that would have enabled the Saigon regime to continue effective resistance. . . .

The Brotherhood

In my own personal experience most correspondents *wanted* to talk chiefly to other correspondents to confirm their own *mythical* vision of the war. Even newcomers were precommitted, as the American jargon has it, to the collective position most of their colleagues had already taken. What I can only call surrealistic reporting constantly fed on itself, and did not diminish thereby, but swelled into ever more grotesque shapes. I found the process equally reprehensible for being in no small part unwitting. . . .

Most correspondents were isolated from the Vietnamese by ignorance of their language and culture, as well as by a measure of race estrangement. Most were isolated from the quixotic American Army establishment, itself often as confused as they themselves were, by their moralistic attitudes and their political prejudices. It was inevitable, in the circumstances, that they came to write, in the first instance, for each other. . . .

Maximum Reportage

Because there was no declared war, maximum freedom of reportage was permitted from the battlefield. (At one point, there were some 500 American newsmen and TV operators in Vietnam, each striving for the type of sensational story that would yield a by-line or several minutes on the tube.) War as suppertime entertainment entered its mature phase. . . .

Not only did reporters generally lack experience and an in-depth understanding of the complexities of Asian politics, they also did what came naturally—sought the most sensational angle. And there was no small amount of political bias, fortified by their being able to see all the corruption, inefficiency, and divisions of the "ins," but not being able to assess the shortcomings of the "outs."

Robert A. Scalapino, *Society*, November/December 1983.

After each other, correspondents wrote to win the approbation of their editors, who controlled their professional lives and who were closely linked with the intellectual community at home. The consensus of that third circle, the domestic intelligentsia, derived largely from correspondents' reports and in turn served to determine the nature of those reports. If dispatches did not accord with that consensus, approbation was withheld. Only in the last instance did correspondents address themselves to the general public, the mass of lay readers and viewers. . . .

Not surprisingly, one found that most reporting veered farther and farther from the fundamental political, economic, and military realities of the war, for these were usually *not* spectacular. Reporting Viet Nam became a closed, self-generating system sustained largely by the acclaim the participants lavished on each other in almost equal measure to the opprobrium they heaped on "the Establishment," a fashionable and very vulnerable target.

The Cloud of Unknowing

For some journalists, perhaps most, a moment of truth through self-examination was never to come. The farther they were from the real conflict, the more smugly self-approving they now remain as commentators who led the public to expect a brave new world when the North Vietnamese finally "liberated" South Viet Nam. Even those correspondents who today gingerly confess to some errors or distortions usually insist that

77

the true fault was not theirs at all, but Washington's. The enormity of having helped in one way or another to bring tens of millions under grinding totalitarian rule—and having tilted the global balance of power—appears too great to acknowledge. It is easier to absolve one's self by blaming exclusively Lyndon Johnson, Richard Nixon, and Henry Kissinger.

I found few American correspondents to be as tough-minded as one Briton I knew who was very close to the action for many years in the employ of an American wire-news service. "I'm ashamed of most of what I wrote in Viet Nam," he told me. "But I was a new boy, and I took my lead from the Americans, who were afire with the crusading spirit of '60s journalism—the involvement, man, in the good fight. When I look at what's happened now, I'm ashamed of my ignorance—and what I helped to do to the Vietnamese.". . .

Journalistic institutions are, of course, rarely afflicted by false modesty. They have not disclaimed credit for the outcome of the war, and their representatives have taken public bows for their successful intervention. The multitude of professional prizes bestowed upon the "bi-story" coverage of Viet Nam certainly implied approval of the general effort.

Media's Key Role

However, the media have been rather coy; they have not declared that they played a *key* role in the conflict. They have not proudly trumpeted Hanoi's repeated expressions of gratitude to the mass media of the non-Communist world, although Hanoi has indeed affirmed that it could not have won "without the Western press." The Western press appears either unaware of the direct connection between cause (its reporting) and effect (the Western defeat in Viet Nam), or strangely reluctant to proclaim that the pen and the camera proved decisively mightier than the bayonet and ultra-modern weapons.

Nor have the media dwelt upon the glaring inconsistency between the expectation they raised of peaceful, prosperous development after Saigon's collapse and the present post-war circumstances in Indochina. . . .

Blaming the U.S.

Any searching analysis of fundamental premises has remained as unthinkable to "the critics" as it was during the fighting. They have remained committed to the proposition that the American role in Indochina was totally reprehensible and inexcusable, while the North Vietnamese role—and, by extension, the roles of the Khmer Rouge in Cambodia and the Pathet Lao in Laos—was righteous, magnanimous, and just. Even the growing number who finally deplored the repressive consequences of the totalitarian victory could not bring themselves to reexamine the premises that led them to contribute so decisively to those victories. Thus William Shawcross, before his sententious book, *Sideshow*, wrote of the Communists' reshaping of Cambodian society: "The process is atrociously brutal." Although "the Khmer people are suffering horribly under their new rules," this is how Shawcross unhesitatingly assigned the ultimate blame:

> They have suffered every day of the last six years—ever since the beginning of one of the most destructive foreign policies the United States has ever pursued: the "Nixon-Kissinger doctrine" in its purest form. . . .

Most correspondents on the scene were not quite as vehement. But they were moved by the same conviction of American guilt, which was so fixed that it resisted all the evidence pointing to a much more complex reality. Employed in the service of that crusading fervor was, for the first time, the most emotionally moving medium of all.

The Tet Offensive

A single event brought to a halt the steady deepening of American involvement in the Vietnam War. A concerted, nationwide Communist assault—the Tet Offensive—caught the United States and South Vietnam off-guard and shocked the American people. Our forces quickly crushed the enemy. It turned out to be a major military defeat for the Communists in South Vietnam, but grotesquely inaccurate news-media reporting turned it into a major political and psychological victory for them in the United States. . . .

Although it was an overwhelming victory for South Vietnam and the United States, the almost universal theme of media coverage was that we had suffered a disastrous defeat. This was true not only in the first chaotic hours of the offensive but also weeks later after the fog of war had lifted. One network reporter flatly said we were "losing" the war. Another stated that it was increasingly clear that "the only rational way" out of the war "will be to negotiate, not as victors, but as an honorable people." The steady drumbeat of inaccurate stories convinced millions of Americans that we had lost a major battle.

Richard Nixon, *No More Vietnams*, 1985.

Television, its thrusting and simplistic character shaping its message, was most shocking because it was most immediate. The Viet Nam War was a presence in homes throughout the world. Who could seriously doubt the veracity of so plausible and so moving a witness in one's own living room?

At any given moment, a million images were available to the

camera's lens in Saigon alone—and hundreds of millions throughout Indochina. But TV crews naturally preferred the most dramatic. That, after all, was their business—show business. It was not news to film farmers peacefully tilling their rice fields, though it might have been argued that nothing happening was news when the American public had been led to believe that almost every Vietnamese farmer was regularly threatened by the Viet Cong, constantly imperiled by battle, and rarely safe from indiscriminate U.S. bombing.

A few hard, documented instances. A burning village was news, even though it was a deserted village used in a Marine training exercise—even though the television correspondent had handed his Zippo lighter to a non-commissioned officer with the suggestion that he set fire to an abandoned house. American soldiers cutting ears off a Viet Cong corpse was news—even if the cameraman had offered the soldiers his knife and "dared" them to take those grisly souvenirs. . . .

The Reasons Why

The main question persists. Why was the press—whether in favor of official policy at the beginning or vehemently against the war at the end—so superficial and so biased?

Chief among many reasons was, I believe, the politicization of correspondents by the constantly intensifying clamor over Viet Nam in Europe and America. Amateur (and professional) propagandists served both sides of the question, but the champions of Hanoi were spectacularly more effective. They created an atmosphere of high pressure that made it exceedingly difficult to be objective. . . .

A Naive Expectation

Many newcomers were shocked to find that American and Vietnamese briefing officers did not always tell them the truth even about a minor tactical situation. Despite their pose of professional skepticism, in their naivete they expected those officers to tell not merely the truth but the *whole* truth. Far from feeling the deep mistrust of officialdom they affected, the newcomers were dismayed by the briefing officers' inability (or unwillingness) to confide in them unreservedly. Older correspondents did not expect candor from briefing officers. They had learned several wars earlier that the interests of the press and the interests of the military did not normally coincide. They also knew that the briefing officers were themselves often uninformed—concerned, perhaps sometimes excessively, for military secrecy—and resentful of correspondents' badgering. . . .

Official deceit was thus exacerbated by incompetent journalism. While complaining about the press, many U.S. officials, who knew they were fighting "a media war," sought to manipulate—rather than inform—correspondents. But they were not skilled at manipulation. While complaining about the government's duplicity, many editors assigned correspondents who were not qualified to fill a normal foreign post, much less to thread the labyrinthine complexities of the Indochina War. Some editors told their correspondents what they wanted, while many correspondents had made up their own minds before they arrived "in country." . . .

Beyond the pressures exerted upon them, most correspondents—serving six-month to two-year tours—were woefully ignorant of the setting of the conflict. Some strove diligently to remedy that crippling deficiency by reading widely and interviewing avidly. Many lacked the time or the inclination to do so—or any real awareness of how crippling their ignorance was to them professionally. . . .

Despite their own numerous and grave faults, the South Vietnamese were, first and last, decisively defeated in Washington, New York, London, and Paris. Those media defeats made inevitable their subsequent defeat on the battlefield. Indochina was not perhaps the first major conflict to be won by psychological warfare. But it was probably the first to be lost by psychological warfare conducted at such great physical distance from the actual fields of battle—and so far from the peoples whose fate was determined by the outcome of the conflict.

"What alienated the American public . . . was not news coverage but casualties."

U.S. Journalists Did Not Cause Defeat

William M. Hammond

William M. Hammond has written numerous books and articles on Vietnam, and has taught history and political science at Trinity College in Washington, D.C. In the following viewpoint, he argues that U.S. journalists were generally supportive of the U.S. war effort in Vietnam. He concludes that faulty strategy, not the U.S. media, caused defeat.

As you read, consider the following questions:

1. What in the author's opinion were the fundamental flaws of Lyndon Johnson's Vietnam strategy?
2. How did the press respond to government and military public relations campaigns about the Vietnam War, according to the author?
3. According to Hammond, what are the limits of public relations?

Reprinted from William M. Hammond, *Public Affairs: The Military and the Media, 1962-1968.* Washington, DC: Center of Military History, United States Army, 1988.

Most of the public affairs problems that confronted the United States in South Vietnam stemmed from the contradictions implicit in Lyndon Johnson's strategy for the war. The president was convinced that the conflict was necessary but believed that the American public and Congress lacked the will, without very careful handling, to carry it to a successful conclusion. Accordingly, he sought to move the country toward an acceptance of war, but in so doing to alienate as few Americans as possible. A policy of gradually increasing pressures against North Vietnam seemed the best approach. Besides minimizing public relations problems and preserving as much leeway as possible for his domestic agenda, it would reduce the chance of a major confrontation with North Vietnam's allies, the Soviet Union and Communist China, and might persuade Hanoi to abandon its aggression against South Vietnam before all-out war erupted. At the very least, it would introduce the American public and Congress to the war by degrees while buying time for the military to prepare a proper base of action in South Vietnam. Doing just enough to placate scattered but vocal pro-war elements in Congress and the news media, it would also preserve options for the president that might disappear if the so-called hawks gained ascendancy.

Johnson had his way, but at the cost of his own credibility. By postponing some unpopular decisions while making others only after weighing how the press and public might react, he indeed hardened the American people and Congress to the necessity for military action, enabled the armed services to build up strength in South Vietnam, and kept the hawks largely at bay. Yet in the process he also peppered the public record with so many inconsistencies and circumlocutions that he prompted one commentator to observe that the record of his administration's "concealments and misleading denials . . . is almost as long as its impressive list of achievements."

Strategic Flaws

Once the United States had become fully committed to the war, major flaws in the administration's strategy created more public relations problems. Given the restrictions and limited goals Johnson had adopted—no extension of the ground war to North Vietnam, no invasion of Laos or Cambodia, no action that would induce Communist China to enter the war—the practical initiative rested with the enemy. He could choose when or where to fight. If American or South Vietnamese forces delivered a serious blow, he could withdraw into his sanctuaries to mend and regroup. All the while, his adherents could hide among the South Vietnamese, subverting the military and civilian bureaucracies and preparing for the day when the United

States would tire and withdraw. Under the circumstances, the only viable option open to the United States was to convince the enemy that there was no hope for the Communist cause. To do that, however, the administration had first to convince the American people that South Vietnam was either worth a prolonged war of attrition or that U.S. forces could win in the end without a major sacrifice of lives and treasure.

Elusive Benefits

The reason for the loss of public support for the Vietnam War was that the United States never had a very convincing case for intervention in the first place; and whatever moral and strategic reasons it did have for intervention were far outweighed by the costs of the war. So it is a gross oversimplification to say that American public opinion turned against the Vietnam War simply because they could watch it, unlike earlier wars, on television. Public opinion turned against the war because the costs of the war were in plain sight while the benefits to be gained by continuing the war were quite elusive.

Ernest Evans, *Wars Without Splendor,* 1987.

Neither alternative was possible. For many reasons—political immaturity brought on by years of French misrule; a corrupt, entrenched bureaucracy; a lack of initiative aggravated by the "can do" impatience of the U.S. military; a basic American failure to understand the oriental mentality—the South Vietnamese were unreceptive to the sort of reforms that might have made their cause attractive to the American public. As for the enemy, with the Soviet Union and Communist China replenishing his materiel losses and with the number of young men coming of age every year in North Vietnam outpacing his battlefield casualties, he could lose every battle and still win. He had only to endure until the cost of the war for the United States increased to levels intolerable over the long term. Although there were moments of insight—General William C. Westmoreland's reflections on the "political attrition" the Johnson administration was inflicting upon itself and the military, Ward Just's article on the marines' programs in the I Corps Tactical Zone—neither the administration nor the press appears to have recognized the implications and potential consequences of the president's strategy.

As the war progressed, the frustrations endemic to the conflict nevertheless found their way into the press with disconcerting regularity. While capable of victories, reporters claimed, the South Vietnamese Army was all too ready to surrender the burden of the fighting to the United States. In the same way, they noted, American forces won on the battlefield but made little progress toward a satisfactory settlement of the war. Meanwhile, corruption remained rampant within the South Vietnamese bureaucracy, and the pacification program appeared either to make little headway or, as at Ben Suc, to be counterproductive.

Public Relations Campaigns

The Johnson administration responded with public relations campaigns to demonstrate that the South Vietnamese were indeed effective, that pacification was working, and that American forces were making progress. The press dutifully repeated every one of the president's assertions. Yet as the Saigon correspondents continually demonstrated, each official statement of optimism about the war seemed to have a pessimistic counterpart and each statistic showing progress an equally persuasive opposite. When General Westmoreland commented at the National Press Club in November 1967 that the enemy could no longer conduct large-unit operations near South Vietnam's cities, his statement received wide, mostly straightforward coverage in the press. Then, only two months later, the Tet offensive established that Communist forces retained the ability to attack the cities and to confound even the most astute advertising claims.

As the war progressed, information officers found themselves caught between the president's efforts to bolster support and their own judgment that the military should remain above politics. Beginning with General Earle G. Wheeler's decision to disregard the advice of the Honolulu information conference that the Military Assistance Command should leave justification of the war to elected officials in Washington, they found themselves drawn progressively into politics, to the point that by late 1967 they had become as involved in selling the war to the American public as the political appointees they served.

Blaming the Press

Complicating the situation further was a conflict in Saigon between the American press and the military. With censorship politically impossible, the military had to make do with a system of voluntary guidelines that largely eliminated security problems but left reporters free to comment on the inconsistencies that plagued the U.S. effort. Believing that the press had in most cases supported official policies in earlier American wars, especially World War II, many members of the military expected similar support in Vietnam. When the contradictions engendered by President Johnson's strategy of limited war led instead to a more critical attitude, the military tended increasingly to blame the press for the credibility problems they experienced, accusing television news in particular of turning the American public against the war.

In so doing, critics of the press within the military paid great attention to the mistakes of the news media but little to the work of the majority of reporters, who attempted conscientiously to tell all sides of the story. They also misassessed the nature of television coverage, which, despite isolated instances to the contrary—the burning of Cam Ne, General Loan's execution of the Viet Cong officer—was most often banal and stylized. What alienated the American public, in both the Korean and Vietnam Wars, was not news coverage but casualties. Public support for each war dropped inexorably by 15 percentage points whenever total U.S. casualties increased by a factor of ten.

Don Wright, *Miami News*. Reprinted with permission.

The news media, for their part, responded in kind. Citing the clandestine bombing of Laos, the slowness with which information from the field reached Saigon, and instances of perceived dissembling, reporters accused the military of attempting to mislead the American public. Yet even as they leveled this charge, they yielded far too readily to the pressures of their profession. Competing with one another for every scrap of news, under the compulsion of deadlines at home, sacrificing depth and analysis to color, they created news where none existed—Peter Arnett's story about the use of tear gas, Don Webster's report on the severing of an enemy's ear, a whole string of stories on the dire position of the marines at Khe Sanh—while failing to make the most of what legitimate news did exist. The good and bad points of the South Vietnamese Army and government, the wars in Laos and Cambodia, the policies and objectives of

Hanoi and the National Liberation Front, the pacification program—all received less coverage in the press, positive or negative, than they probably should and could have. It is undeniable, however, that press reports were still often more accurate than the public statements of the administration in portraying the situation in Vietnam.

In the end, President Johnson and his advisers put too much faith in public relations. Masters of the well-placed leak, adept at manipulating the electorate, they forgot at least two commonsense rules of effective propaganda: that the truth has greater ultimate power than the most pleasing of bromides and that no amount of massaging will heal a broken limb or a fundamentally flawed strategy. Even if . . . [they] had managed to create the sort of objectivity they sought in the press, they would have failed in their larger purpose. For as long as the president's strategy prevailed, the enemy would hold the initiative and casualties would continue, inexorably, to rise.

"With our laziness and narcissism feeding each other, we marched off to impose our will on the Vietnamese people by bloodshed."

U.S. Policy Failed Because It Was Immoral

M. Scott Peck

M. Scott Peck is a practicing psychiatrist and author who is best known for his book *The Road Less Traveled*. He served in the Army Medical Corps during the Vietnam war years of 1963 to 1972. The following viewpoint, excerpted from his book *People of the Lie: The Hope for Healing Human Evil*, states that U.S. policies failed in Vietnam in part because they were fundamentally evil. Basing his conclusions on his study of evil in the field of psychiatry and his experiences in the Army, Peck contends America is likely to repeat the mistake unless it recognizes and eradicates the twin causes of evil—laziness and narcissism.

As you read, consider the following questions:

1. Why does the author think America's involvement in Vietnam was based on an unrealistic idea?
2. What does Peck mean when he argues the real reasons for America's involvement in Vietnam were laziness and narcissism?
3. Do you agree with Peck's contention that American citizens were ultimately responsible for American evil in Vietnam? Why or why not?

From *People of the Lie*. Copyright © 1983 by M. Scott Peck, M.D. Reprinted by permission of SIMON & SCHUSTER, Inc.

Basically, we fought the war because of a combination of three attitudes: (1) communism was a monolithic evil force hostile to human freedom in general and American freedom in particular; (2) it was America's duty as the world's most economically powerful nation to lead the opposition against communism; and (3) communism should be opposed wherever it arose by whatever means necessary.

This combination of attitudes comprising the American posture in international relations had its origins in the late 1940s and early 1950s. Immediately following the end of World War II, the Communist USSR, with extraordinary speed and aggressiveness, imposed its political domination over almost the entirety of eastern Europe: Finland, Poland, Lithuania, Latvia, Estonia, East Germany, Czechoslovakia, Hungary, Bulgaria, Albania, and presumably Yugoslavia. Seemingly only by American money and American arms and leadership was the rest of Europe prevented from falling into the clutches of communism. Then just as we were bolstering the defense against communism's western flank, it exploded in the East, with the whole of China falling under Communist domination in 1950 almost overnight. And already the forces of communism were clearly threatening to expand through Vietnam and Malaya. The line had to be drawn. Given the explosive expansion of communism on all sides of the USSR, it is no wonder that we perceived it in 1954 as an evil monolithic force, so dangerously threatening to the entire world that we needed to become engaged against it in a life-and-death struggle that left little room for moral scruples.

Communism Not Monolithic Nor Evil

The problem, however, is that by a scant dozen years later there was a wealth of evidence to indicate that communism was not (if, in fact, it had ever been) a force that was either monolithic or necessarily evil. Yugoslavia was clearly independent of the USSR, and Albania was becoming so. China and the USSR were no longer allies but potential enemies. As for Vietnam, any slightly discerning examination of its history revealed it to be a traditional enemy of China. The impelling force behind the Vietnamese Communists at that point in their history was not the expansion of communism but nationalism and resistance to colonial domination. Moreover, it had also become clear that despite the constraints on their civil liberties, the people in Communist societies were generally faring better than they had under their pre-Communist forms of government. It was also clear that the people in many non-Communist societies, with whose governments we had allied ourselves, were suffering violations of human rights that matched those of the USSR and China.

Our military involvement in Vietnam began in the period between 1954 and 1956, when the idea of a monolithic Communist menace seemed realistic. A dozen years later it was no longer realistic. Yet at precisely the time when it had ceased to be realistic, when we should have been readjusting our strategy and withdrawing from Vietnam, we began to seriously escalate our military involvement there in defense of obsolescent attitudes. Why? Why, beginning around 1964, did America's behavior in Vietnam become increasingly unrealistic and inappropriate? There are two reasons: laziness and—once again—narcissism.

Squalid National Effort

Our waging of the war, not our losing of it, disgraced us in men's eyes. . . .

Our national effort was squalid in concept and execution. We tried to bend an ancient and civilized people to our will, and we failed, but not before we used our overwhelming power and technology to the full. We cratered vast stretches of Vietnam with our bombs. We destroyed villages without number and herded their inhabitants into stockades. We poisoned the wells, the forests and the farms with Agent Orange. We bulldozed millions of acres of forest and jungle.

All in all we killed over two million of them, mostly civilians. We napalmed women and children. Many of our soldiers disintegrated and did terrible things which haunt them today.

Charles Owen Rice, *The Catholic Bulletin,* January 13, 1982.

Attitudes have a kind of inertia. Once set in motion, they will keep going, even in the face of the evidence. To change an attitude requires a considerable amount of work and suffering. The process must begin either in an effortfully maintained posture of constant self-doubt and criticism or else in a painful acknowledgement that what we thought was right all along may not be right after all. Then it proceeds into a state of confusion. This state is quite uncomfortable; we no longer seem to know what is right or wrong or which way to go. But it is a state of openness and therefore of learning and growing. It is only from the quicksand of confusion that we are able to leap to the new and better vision.

Lazy and Self-Satisfied Leaders

I think we may properly regard the men who governed America at the time of My Lai—the Johnson administration—as lazy and self-satisfied. They, like most more ordinary individuals, had little taste for intellectual confusion—nor for the effort involved in maintaining a "posture of constant self-doubt and criticism." They assumed that the attitudes they had developed toward the "monolithic Communist menace" during the preceding two decades were still the right attitudes. Although the evidence was obviously mounting to throw their attitudes into question, they ignored it. To do otherwise would have placed them in the painful and difficult position of having to rethink their attitudes. They did not take up the work required. It was easier to proceed blindly, as if nothing had changed.

Thus far we have been focusing on the laziness involved in "clinging to old maps" and attitudes that have become obsolete. Let us also examine the narcissism. We are our attitudes. If someone criticizes an attitude of mine, I feel he or she is criticizing *me*. If one of my opinions is proved wrong, then *I* have been wrong. My self-image of perfection has been shattered. Individuals and nations cling to obsolete and outworn ideas not simply because it requires work to change them but also because, in their narcissism, they cannot imagine that their ideas and views could be wrong. They believe themselves to be right. Oh, we are quick to superficially disclaim our infallibility, but deep inside most of us, particularly when we have apparently been successful and powerful, we consider ourselves invariably in the right. It was this kind of narcissism, manifested in our behavior in Vietnam, that Senator William Fulbright referred to as "the arrogance of power."

Evil Policy

Ordinarily, if our noses are rubbed in the evidence, we can tolerate the painful narcissistic injury involved, admit our need for change, and correct our outlook. But as is the case with certain individuals, the narcissism of whole nations may at times exceed the normal bounds. When this happens, the nation—instead of readjusting in light of the evidence—sets about attempting to destroy the evidence. This was what America was up to in the 1960s. The situation in Vietnam presented us with evidence of the fallibility of our world view and the limits of our potency. So, rather than rethinking it, we set about to destroy the situation in Vietnam, and all of Vietnam with it if necessary.

Which was evil. Evil has already been defined most simply as the use of political power to destroy others for the purpose of defending or preserving the integrity of one's sick self. Since it had become outmoded, our monolithic view of communism was part of our national sick self—no longer adaptive and realistic. In the failure of the Diem regime, which we sponsored, in the failure of all our "advisers" and Green Berets and massive economic and military aid to counteract the expansion of the Viet Cong, the sickness or wrongness of our policies was exposed to ourselves. Rather than alter these policies, however, we launched a full-scale war to preserve them intact. Rather than admit what would have been a minor failure in 1964, we set about rapidly escalating the war to prove ourselves right at the expense of the Vietnamese people and their self-aspirations. The issue ceased to be what was right for Vietnam and became an issue of our infallibility and preserving our national "honor."

"What shall I put down as the reason for dying?"

Sanders/*The Milwaukee Journal*. Reprinted with permission.

Strangely enough, on a certain level, President Johnson and the men of his administration knew that what they were doing was evil. Otherwise, why all the lying? It was so bizarre and seemingly out of character that it is difficult for us merely to recall the extraordinary national dishonesty of those days. . . . Even the excuse President Johnson gave in order to begin bombing North Vietnam and escalate the war in 1964—the "Gulf of Tonkin Incident"—was apparently a deliberate fraud. Through this fraud he obtained from Congress the authority to wage the war without Congress ever formally declaring it (which was its constitutional responsibility). Then he set about "borrowing" the money to pay for the war—diverting funds earmarked for other programs and extorting "savings bonds" from the salaries of federal employees—so that the American public would not have to immediately pay increased taxes or feel the burden of the escalation. . . .

Responsibility of All Americans

But it would be a mistake and a potentially evil rationalization itself for us to blame the evil of those days entirely on the Johnson administration. We must ask why Johnson was successful in defrauding us. Why did we allow ourselves to be defrauded for so long? Not everyone was. A very small minority was quick to recognize that the wool was being pulled over our eyes, that "something rather dark and bloody" was being perpetrated by the nation. But why were most of us not aroused to ire or suspicion or even significant concern about the nature of the war?

Once again we are confronted with our all-too-human laziness and narcissism. Basically, it was just too much trouble. We all had our lives to lead—doing our day-to-day jobs, buying new cars, painting our houses, sending our kids to college. As the majority of members of any group are content to let the leadership be exercised by the few, so as a citizenry we were content to let the government "do its thing." It was Johnson's job to lead, ours to follow. The citizenry was simply too lethargic to become aroused. Besides, we shared with Johnson his enormous large-as-Texas narcissism. . . .

By allowing ourselves to be easily and blatantly defrauded, we as a whole people participated in the evil of the Johnson administration. The evil—the years of lying and manipulation—of the Johnson administration was directly conducive to the whole atmosphere of lying and manipulation and evil that pervaded our presence in Vietnam during those years. . . .

Americans as the Villains

I am convinced it will be the judgment of history—that America was the aggressor in that war during those years. Ours were the choices that were most morally reprehensible. We were the villains.

But how could we—we Americans—be villains? The Germans and the Japanese in 1941, certainly. The Russians, yes. But the Americans? Surely we are not a villainous people. If we were villains, we must have been unwitting ones. This I concede; we were largely unwitting. But how does it come about that a per-

93

son or a group or an entire nation is an unwitting villain? . . .

The term "unwitting villain" is particularly appropriate because our villainy lay in our unwittingness. We became villains precisely because we did not have our wits about us. The word "wit" in this regard refers to knowledge. We were villains out of ignorance. Just as what went on at My Lai was covered up for a year primarily because the troops of Task Force Barker did not know they had done something radically wrong, so America waged the war because it did not know that what it was doing was villainous.

I used to ask the troops on their way to battle in Vietnam what they knew about the war and its relationship to Vietnamese history. The enlisted men knew nothing. Ninety percent of the junior officers knew nothing. What little the senior officers and few junior officers did know was generally solely what they had been taught in the highly biased programs of their military schools. It was astounding. At least 95 percent of the men going off to risk their very lives did not even have the slightest knowledge of what the war was about. I also talked to Department of Defense civilians who directed the war and discovered a similarly atrocious ignorance of Vietnamese history. The fact of the matter is that as a nation we did not even know why we were waging the war.

A Nation of Villains

How could this have been? How could a whole people have gone to war not knowing why? The answer is simple. As a people we were too lazy to learn and too arrogant to think we needed to learn. We felt that whatever way we happened to perceive things was the right way without any further study. And that whatever we did was the right thing to do without reflection. We were so wrong because we never seriously considered that we might not be right. With our laziness and narcissism feeding each other, we marched off to impose our will on the Vietnamese people by bloodshed with practically no idea of what was involved. Only when we—the mightiest nation on earth—consistently suffered defeat at the hands of the Vietnamese did we in significant numbers begin to take the trouble to learn what we had done.

So it is that our "Christian" nation became a nation of villains. So it has been with other nations in the past, and so it will be with other nations—including our own once again—in the future. As a nation and as a race, we shall not be immune to war until such a time as we have made much further progress toward eradicating from our human nature the twin progenitors of evil: laziness and narcissism.

"The thrust of the policy of containment and protection . . . is . . . something for Americans to be proud of."

U.S. Policy Was Not Immoral

Bui Diem with David Chanoff

Bui Diem was the South Vietnamese ambassador to the United States from 1967 to 1972. He now lives in Washington, D.C., and is president of the National Congress of Vietnamese in America. In the following viewpoint, he argues that America's fundamental goal of protecting South Vietnam from communism was morally sound. The U.S. should be criticized for how it implemented its Vietnam policies, not for the policies themselves, Bui writes. This viewpoint was excerpted from Bui's book *In the Jaws of History*, cowritten with David Chanoff. Chanoff has coauthored several other books with Vietnamese authors, including *The Vietnamese Gulag* and *Portrait of the Enemy*.

As you read, consider the following questions:

1. Who does Bui maintain is ultimately responsible for the defeat of South Vietnam?
2. What international circumstances does the author describe which, in his opinion, made America's intervention in Vietnam seem reasonable at the time?
3. What basic belief of U.S. antiwar protesters turned out to be false, according to Bui?

From IN THE JAWS OF HISTORY by Bui Diem with David Chanoff. Copyright © 1987 by Bui Diem. Reprinted by permission of Houghton Mifflin Company.

Vietnamese of my generation came of age in the early forties with the hope that after almost a century as second-class citizens in their own country, they would have a chance to recover their dignity and achieve their independence from France. They dreamed also of peace and a decent life for themselves and their children. It was their misfortune that instead of independence, peace, and a decent life, they saw only revolution, war, and destruction. For three decades they existed in the maelstrom. And even now, when Vietnam no longer has to deal with foreign invaders, their misery continues. Theirs has been a tragedy of historic proportions.

In an interview with Walter Cronkite in 1963, President John Kennedy said, "In the final analysis, it's their war and they are the ones who will either win it or lose it." Much as we might like to, there is no getting away from Kennedy's judgment. The South Vietnamese people, and especially the South Vietnamese leaders, myself among them, bear the ultimate responsibility for the fate of their nation, and to be honest, they have much to regret and much to be ashamed of. But it is also true that the war's cast of characters operated within a matrix of larger forces that stood outside the common human inadequacies and failings. And it was these forces that shaped the landscape on which we all moved. . . .

American Intervention

As I look back on the external forces that shaped our lives, it is the American intervention that stands out. French colonialism, after all, is dead and gone, a subject for historians who prefer the inert remains of the past to the passions of the present. As for Vietnamese communism, no one but the fervid or the blind any longer argues the merits of a system that has brought in its wake only war and deprivation and mass flight. (Not that having been right comforts us as we house our refugees and send what sustenance we can back to our families.) But American intervention is a living issue. In the train of failure in Vietnam, and in the face of hard choices elsewhere, the questions of its correctness and its morality still inform American foreign policy debates. Americans still seek to learn the lessons of intervention, and so do America's smaller allies, who cannot help but see in the fate of Vietnam intimations of their own possible futures.

For critics of the Vietnam War, the original decision to intervene was wrong, a result, as one of them put it, of a "steady string of misjudgments." It was wrong because American policymakers in the sixties failed to assess correctly the vital interests of the United States, because they exaggerated the geopolitical importance of Vietnam, and because they had an inflated con-

96

cept of American capabilities.

Although it is neither my business nor within my competence to pass judgment on how the United States defined its interests at that time, it is my impression that such arguments are made on a distinctly *a posteriority* basis. I remember vividly the political atmosphere in the United States in the summer of 1964, the summer of the Tonkin resolution and Barry Goldwater's nomination, when I first visited this country. At that time the Johnson administration and practically the entire Congress were in favor of the commitment to defend Vietnam (the resolution passed in the Senate, 98 to 2, and in the House, 416 to 0). And so, *mirabile dictu*, were the national news media.

Vietnam Was No Different

The assertion that the Vietnam War was an immoral war was heard more and more often as the years dragged on. This said less about the war than about the construction that critics were putting on the idea of morality. Like all wars, Vietnam was brutal, ugly, dangerous, painful, and sometimes inhumane. This was driven home to those who stayed home perhaps more forcefully than ever before because the war lasted so long and because they saw so much of it on television in living, and dying, color.

Many who were seeing war for the first time were so shocked at what they saw that they said *this* war was *immoral* when they really meant that *all* war was *terrible.* They were right in saying that peace was better than war. But they were wrong in failing to ask themselves whether what was happening in Vietnam was substantively different from what had happened in other wars. Their horror at the fact of war prevented them from considering whether the facts of the war in Vietnam added up to a cause that was worth fighting for. Instead, many of these naïve, well-meaning, instinctual opponents of the war raised their voices in protest.

Richard Nixon, *No More Vietnams*, 1985.

Moreover, the context of international affairs in that period provided good reasons for this nearly unanimous opinion, reasons that went beyond the specific perception of North Vietnamese aggressiveness. It was then the aftermath of the Communist attack in Korea, and China's Communist leaders were broadcasting the most belligerent and expansionistic views, even as they attempted to establish a Peking-Jakarta axis with Indonesia's pro-Communist President Sukarno. For the fragile governments of Southeast Asia the situation seemed serious indeed. Although twenty-five years later it became fashionable among some Americans to belittle Communist threats to the region's stability, among the responsible governments at the time there was deep anxiety.

Even for those South Vietnamese who thought they saw the inherent dangers in American intervention, there was still nothing illogical about it. The American interest in Vietnam, even its land intervention, seemed a natural extension of U.S. policies in Europe (the Marshall Plan, the Berlin airlift, Greece) and Asia (Korea) aimed at preventing the expansion of combined Soviet and Chinese power (at least until the early 1960s, no one could imagine that the two Communist giants would become antagonists). And for the Europeans who were able to rebuild their countries and save their democratic institutions, for the Germans in Berlin, for the Greeks, and for the South Koreans, those policies were not wrong. Nor were they based on misjudgments of geopolitical realities. In Vietnam the policy failed. But that is not to say that it was wrong there either. The disastrous mistakes that were made were mistakes in implementation rather than intention. But the thrust of the policy of containment and protection, that I do not think can be faulted. It is, on the contrary, something for Americans to be proud of.

A Moral War

The more vocal critics of the war in the sixties and seventies characterized the intervention, not just as wrong, but also as immoral. Their charge was based primarily on the theory that the war in Vietnam was a civil war, and that consequently American intervention was an act of aggression against people who were fighting to free themselves from an oppressive regime and unify their country in accord with the aspirations of the great majority of decent-minded Vietnamese.

It is my own belief that this theory held the field for so long primarily because it was a powerful attraction to the many Americans who were angry at their own government and society and were looking for issues to hang their anger on. Certainly, the facts that refuted it were readily available. From early on, both Saigon and Washington knew beyond a doubt that the National Liberation Front—the Vietcong—was a creation of the Communist party, and that without North Vietnamese organization, leadership, supplies, and, starting in 1964, without the North Vietnamese regular army, there would have been no revolution to speak of and no war. It was one of my greatest frustrations that our firm knowledge of this—both from widespread and incontrovertible evidence and also from personal experience among many of us of Communist "front" techniques—made no impact on popular understanding in the West. Regardless of what was there to be seen, people saw only what they wished.

98

After the war, when propaganda no longer mattered, the party dropped its pretense. "Our Party," said Le Duan in his 1975 victory speech, "is the unique and single leader that organized, controlled, and governed the entire struggle of the Vietnamese people from the first day of the revolution." During the war, the North Vietnamese never openly admitted they had troops in South Vietnam. (Le Duc Tho even kept up the pretense with Henry Kissinger, although Kissinger knew the situation as well as he knew his own name, and Tho, of course, knew that he knew it.) But afterward the party treated this subterfuge simply as an excellent piece of public relations and its own role as a matter of intense pride. As the North Vietnamese general Vo Ban told French television interviewers in 1983, "In May 1959 I had the privilege of being designated by the Vietnamese Communist Party to unleash a military attack on the South in order to liberate the South and reunify the fatherland."

Noble Cause

It is time we recognized that ours was, in truth, a noble cause. A small country newly free from colonial rule sought our help in establishing self-rule and the means of self-defense against a totalitarian neighbor bent on conquest. We dishonor the memory of 50,000 young Americans who died in that cause when we give way to feelings of guilt as if we were doing something shameful, and we have been shabby in our treatment of those who returned. They fought as well and as bravely as any Americans have ever fought in any war. They deserve our gratitude, our respect and our continuing concern.

Ronald Reagan, speech, 1980.

During the heyday of the antiwar movement, I marveled at the innocence of its spokesmen in believing something different from this. I wonder even now if they ever feel shame for their gullibility and for their contribution to the tragedy. But they are not heard from. It was, after all, only one chapter in their lives, as it was only a chapter in the book of American history.

Conclusion

The issue of morality, then, comes down to whether it was moral for the United States to have supported an admittedly flawed South Vietnamese regime in its attempt to survive against a totalitarian antagonist. Here, too, the answer seems to me self-evident. However unpalatable leaders like Nguyen Van Thieu might have been, South Vietnam was full of pluralistic ferment and possibilities for change and development. It was a place where good people could hope for something better to evolve, where they could even fight for it, as so many strong-minded opposition politicians, intellectuals, and writers did. None but ideologues can compare such a place with the chilling police state that destroyed it. And none, I think, can fairly question the morality of the effort to prevent its destruction.

To my mind, the lessons of American intervention in Vietnam have to do not so much with the geopolitical or moral underpinning of the war, but rather with the way the intervention was implemented. The real question was not whether to intervene, but how to intervene effectively.

a critical thinking activity

Locating Scapegoats

During World War II the Nazis in Germany systematically killed millions of Jews. The Nazis continually propagandized the outrageous lie that Jews were responsible for many of Germany's social problems. Jews became the victims of irrational leaders who glorified force, violence, and the doctrine of racial supremacy. One of the principal propaganda weapons used against the Jews by Germany's leaders was the tactic of scapegoating.

On an individual level scapegoating involves the process of transferring personal blame or anger to another individual or object. Most people, for example, have kicked their table or chair as an outlet for anger and frustration over a mistake or failure. *On a group level, scapegoating involves the placement of blame on entire groups of people or objects for social problems that they have not caused.* Scapegoats may be totally or only partially innocent, but they always receive more blame than can be rationally justified.

The cartoon on the next page illustrates an example of scapegoating. Nguyen Van Thieu, president of South Vietnam from 1967 to 1975, is scapegoating American soldiers who fought in Vietnam. He considers it entirely the fault of American soldiers that his country lost the war.

Because societies are so complex and complicated, problems are often not completely understood by any single citizen. Yet people always demand answers and there exists a human tendency to create imaginary and simplistic explanations for complex racial, social, economic, and political problems that defy easy understanding and solution. The Vietnam War falls into this category. During the war Americans could not agree on the reasons for involvement. Since the war's end, Americans cannot agree on the reasons for its dismal conclusion. Both situations provide fertile ground for scapegoating.

101

Examine the following statements. *Mark S by any statement that you believe is an example of scapegoating. Mark N by any statement you believe is not an example of scapegoating. Mark U by any statement which you are unsure is an example of scapegoating.*

> S = an example of scapegoating
> N = not an example of scapegoating
> U = unsure or undecided

1. Communists are responsible for most of the world's war and violence.
2. Biased journalists bear major responsibility for America's failure in Vietnam.
3. Capitalism is more dependent on the profit motive than is communism.
4. President Johnson was responsible for sending the most U.S. combat troops to Vietnam.
5. Antiwar demonstrators pressured American leaders to withdraw U.S. troops from Vietnam.
6. Undisciplined black soldiers were responsible for America's loss in Vietnam.
7. Corrupt Saigon allies were responsible for the fall of South Vietnam.
8. Liberals in American society and government undermined U.S. efforts in Vietnam and are responsible for the Communist victory.

Periodical Bibliography

The following articles have been selected to supplement the diverse views presented in this chapter.

Bruce Cumings	"Reckoning with the Korean War," *The Nation*, October 25, 1986.
Mark Falcoff	"Let's Be Honest About Vietnam," *The American Spectator*, December 1987.
David Halberstam	"Of Hubris and Hondas," *New Perspectives Quarterly*, Fall 1988.
Jeffrey Hart	"Vietnam Wasn't Lost to Vietcong," *Conservative Chronicle*, October 25, 1989. Available from *Conservative Chronicle*, Box 11297, Des Moines, IA 50340-1297.
H.D. Kaplan	"Remembering Vietnam," *Commentary*, December 1987.
Jeffrey P. Kimball	"The Myth of the Liberal's Lost, Limited War," *Indochina Newsletter*, January/February 1989. Available from the Asia Resource Center, 2161 Massachusetts Ave., Cambridge, MA 02128.
Lawrence W. Lichty and Edward Fouhy	"Television Reporting of the Vietnam War," *The World & I*, April 1987.
Timothy J. Lomperis	"Giap's Dream, Westmoreland's Nightmare," *Parameters*, June 1988. Available from the Superintendent of Documents, U.S. Government Printing Office, Washington, DC 20402.
R.D. Patrick Mahoney	"The Tragedy of Southeast Asia," *The New American*, February 1, 1988.
Newsweek	"The Press Didn't Lose the Vietnam War," September 11, 1989.
Douglas Pike and Benjamin Ward	"Losing and Winning Abroad," *Current*, May 1988.
Norman Podhoretz	"Vietnam: The Revised Standard Version," *Commentary*, April 1984.
Neil Sheehan	"Vietnam, and the Battle for Reality," *U.S. News & World Report*, October 24, 1988.
Ronald H. Spector	"U.S. Army Strategy in the Vietnam War," *International Security*, Spring 1987.
Harry G. Summers Jr.	"How We Lost," *The New Republic*, April 29, 1985.

CHAPTER

3

What Are the Legacies of Vietnam?

Chapter Preface

Perhaps the most significant legacy of the Vietnam War is its cost in human lives. The Vietnam Veterans Memorial in Washington, D.C., a long, black wall that lists the names of American soldiers killed in action, is a stark reminder of this legacy. The memorial includes over 58,000 names, but some people estimate that over 100,000 Americans, both soldiers and civilians, were killed over the course of the war. A 1969 Gallup Poll found that 55 percent of those surveyed personally knew someone who had been killed or wounded in Vietnam.

The Vietnamese lost even more people. Almost two million Vietnamese were killed and four million were wounded. Today there are over 350,000 disabled Vietnamese being supported by their government.

Other legacies of the Vietnam War are less tangible and more controversial. They include how the war affected the societies of the U.S. and Vietnam and what lessons were learned by both countries. These legacies are important, for if we have a better understanding of them, future suffering might be prevented by wiser policies.

"The long-term effects of the defoliation, the bombing of villages and the countryside . . . had much to do with the human rights issues that surround . . . Viet Nam, today."

Vietnam Remains Scarred by the War

Don Luce

Don Luce was a director of Clergy and Laity Concerned, a religious organization that opposed the Vietnam War. He spent thirteen years in Vietnam as a social worker and journalist, and currently directs the Asia Resource Center, a Washington, D.C. educational organization. In the following viewpoint, Luce argues that Vietnam is still recovering from the devastation and social disruption caused by the Vietnam War. He believes the U.S. should provide medical and technical aid to Vietnam.

As you read, consider the following questions:

1. What does Luce argue has been the impact of Agent Orange on Vietnam?
2. According to the author, how did the Vietnam War disrupt the Vietnamese society and economy?
3. How have people been treated in re-education camps in Vietnam, in Luce's opinion?

Don Luce, "The Devastating War: Disastrous to Indochina and to Human Rights," *Engage/Social Action*, September 1986. Reprinted with permission.

The end of the Viet Nam War in April 1975, left much of that country a wasteland. The long-term effects of the defoliation, the bombing of villages and the countryside, and the development of a consumer-oriented economy in South Viet Nam, had much to do with the human rights issues that surround Indochina, and especially Viet Nam, today. The devastation left by the war has been complicated by the US government's decision to "punish Viet Nam." Ironically, punishing Viet Nam has been disastrous to US interests as well as for the Vietnamese.

The human rights issues in Indochina today include poverty in Viet Nam, the boat people, re-education centers, persons missing-in-action and the presence of Vietnamese troops in Kampuchea. Before considering these issues, it is important to look at Viet Nam at the war's end and consider how that situation contributed to the problems of today.

Agent Orange

Some 12 percent of South Viet Nam's land was sprayed with Agent Orange and other chemical defoliants, which killed many permanent crops (rubber, fruit trees, coffee, timber). At the end of the war Viet Nam did not have the resources to start seedlings and replant the forests and plantations at once. Thus, the income from these crops has been lost to the Vietnamese.

Just as important, much of the area sprayed included forested mountainsides, and the defoliation left these areas exposed. When the monsoon rains hit, nothing remains to hold the water, which rushes down the mountainside and floods the farmland in the flat coastal areas below. In some areas, the exposed land without organic matter laterizes (or forms a six to eight inch layer of brick consistency at the surface). It will take perhaps a century or more for mosses and occasional clumps of grass to break down the laterite so the people can again use the land.

Much has been written about the effects of Agent Orange on American Viet Nam veterans, but little has been said about the Vietnamese who lived in the sprayed areas year after year. Some of the effects become visible at the Phu Sanh Gynecological Hospital in Saigon. Glass crocks line the wall of one room, floor to ceiling.

Each crock contains a still-born baby, to which women from Ben Tre province gave birth since 1980. Some babies have three arms; some have two bodies above the waist; one stillborn has a face on its abdomen; another's umbilical cord protrudes like some Cyclops' eye from the center of its forehead.

The Viet Duc Hospital in Hanoi specializes in cancer. There, row after row of cancer patients hope for a cure for their dreaded disease. Vietnamese doctors have carefully correlated the cancer incidence among the Vietnamese population to exposure to Agent Orange, but the US government (and US chemical companies) discount this, saying that the Vietnamese use crude methods and use the data for propaganda. But American medical scientists who have gone to Viet Nam and studied the evidence agree with the Vietnamese.

Hazardous Unexploded Bombs

More munitions were expended (a Pentagon term!) in the Viet Nam War than in World War II and the Korean War combined. By 1975 parts of Viet Nam looked like the surface of the moon! Malaria-causing mosquitoes and other disease-carrying insects found the water-filled craters good breeding grounds. The pressure of the bombs compacted the soil making it nearly impossible to put back into agricultural use (except for fish ponds!).

Devastation

The devastation that the United States left as its legacy has been quickly removed from consciousness here, and indeed, was little appreciated at the time. Its extent is worth recalling. In the south, 9,000 out of 15,000 hamlets were damaged or destroyed along with some 25 million acres of farmland and 12 million acres of forest: 1.5 million cattle were killed; and there are 1 million widows and some 800,000 orphans. In the north, all six industrial cities were damaged (three razed to the ground) along with 28 of 30 provincial towns (12 completely destroyed), 96 of 116 district towns, and 4,000 of some 5,800 communes; 400,000 cattle were killed and over a million acres of farmland were damaged. Much of the land is a moonscape, where people live on the edge of famine with rice rations lower than Bangladesh.

Noam Chomsky, *The Bulletin of Concerned Asian Scholars,* April/December 1989.

About 2 percent of the bombs, artillery shells and landmines, used in Viet Nam did not explode on impact. Farmers still look for the mines and unexploded shells with pointed bamboo sticks; they poke the stick into the soil every three inches to see if they hit something hard.

When American soldiers left an area in the country, they often seeded it with mines, and they kept maps of where they left these mines in case they went back. In 1977 I was told by a colonel at the Pentagon that, yes, the maps existed, but they wouldn't give them to the Vietnamese. I told the colonel that I had just seen 47 people, mostly children, in the Qui Nhon Hospital with serious wounds from the mines and shells stepped on by mistake or hit with the farmer's plow. The colonel responded: "Well the - - - Vietnamese should have thought of that before they started the war."

US and South Vietnamese military strategists believed that by moving the rural population into "protected population centers" the National Liberation Front (NLF) and North Vietnamese would have no source of recruits, food, intelligence information or places to melt into the population. At first they called these Agrivilles, the Strategic Hamlets; then New Life Hamlets; then New, New Life Hamlets; and finally, Refugee Camps. Based on Mao Tse Tung's theory of guerrilla warfare—the people are the sea; the guerrillas are the fish—the government moved more than half of South Viet Nam's population off the farms to dry up the NLF/North Vietnamese sea.

These people could only find service area jobs: washing clothes, shining shoes, pushing drugs, working in the bars and brothels, selling trinkets and souvenirs to the soldiers, trading on the black market. The movement of families from everything they knew into the bizarre situation of South Viet Nam's cities during the war tore apart the family structure.

After the farm population moved into the cities, South Viet Nam became dependent on the United States for its survival. The rice came from Texas and South Carolina; cheese, flour and cooking oil from the US Food for Peace program was passed out to hungry refugees (or sold by corrupt officials).

Successful operators in prostitution, drugs, or the black market made a lot of money. Inflation became a problem. Soon enormous quantities of luxury goods appeared in the market to keep the new-rich happy and to soak up the piasters, Hondas, Johnny Walker whiskey, air conditioners, hair spray, refrigerators and other luxuries. Many people became addicted to these goods. When the war ended, however, gas for the Hondas disappeared, electricity for the air conditioners vanished, the flow of other luxuries ended and worse, even the rice supply became short.

The Right to Food

The most basic right of all people is to have enough to eat. At the end of the war Viet Nam had very little food. US imports of about seven hundred million pounds of rice a year plus all the other food stopped immediately. Former farmers were reluctant to return to fields where landmines and other explosives waited in the weeds for a child flying a kite or running in the grass to trip a wire or the farmer's plow to explode an artillery shell.

The Vietnamese government established policies to assure equal distribution of the limited food. The government also set up New Economic Zones and sent nearly everyone in the cities out on work-camps. Some persons, particularly ethnic Chinese, had a choice of going to a New Economic Zone or leaving the country. The New Economic Zones meant a harsh, pioneer life, but the alternative would have meant even less food.

These refugees have been: (A) South Vietnamized.
(B) NorthVietnamized. (C) Victimized. (D) All of the above

Paul Conrad, © 1972, *Los Angeles Times*. Reprinted with permission.

No bloodbath, as predicted by most US government officials, occurred. But thousands of people were sent off to what the US press and government called "re-education" and what the Vietnamese government called "work/study." People who worked for Americans as well as South Vietnamese government and military officials all went. For some it became a relatively easy short period of lecture and discussions. For persons like drug addicts and former prostitutes, it meant health care and development of job skills. However, for others it has been a long, cruel ordeal. . . .

Many people (some estimates go as high as 10,000) are still in re-education, particularly South Vietnamese military intelligence personnel. But sometimes other individuals get caught in Viet Nam's cumbersome bureaucracy. For example, one man who worked on an American-sponsored shoeshine-boy project remains in re-education after 10 years. He has now gotten on the ODP (Orderly Departure Program) list, but that involves both Vietnamese and US bureaucracy.

Because of an attempt to organize an armed insurgency (supported and led by right-wing Vietnamese in the United States), the Vietnamese government is reluctant to release people from re-education who they think will join this insurgency. . . .

Recommendations

Life is difficult for the people of Viet Nam. While some persons will argue that most of the problems have happened in any war—for instance, consider the World War II destruction—there is a major difference. After World War II, the United States helped our former enemies to rebuild—and we're proud of it! We also know that by helping to rebuild Germany and Japan, we helped our own economy as well. Similarly, the United States could do much to ease the problems many Vietnamese have, to resolve the MIA (missing-in-action) question and to generally lower tensions in Southeast Asia. The United States could act to:

• *Normalize relations with Viet Nam.* This would allow trade. Many factories, especially in South Viet Nam, need spare parts to operate. The United States has the best offshore drilling capacity to help the Vietnamese exploit their offshore oil. This action would also facilitate our countries' talking to each other—a good beginning in solving problems.

• *Allow and encourage assistance to Viet Nam.* Presently, groups like Church World Service, Oxfam America, the Mennonite Central Committee and the American Friends Service Committee must apply for licenses to send aid. Often they're turned down, even for such innocuous things as primary school kits or knitting yarn. . . .

• *Offer the Vietnamese and Laotians the technology and equipment to clear the various munitions from their fields and forests.* Presently, the Quakers and Mennonites are helping in Laos to clear out explosives. . . .

• A final recommendation for all of us—simply that we seek to be friends with each other. New schemes to "punish Viet Nam" will only increase the pain for all.

"The Vietnam War now seems much less important in Asia, where it was fought, than it does back in the United States."

Vietnam Has Recovered from the War

James Fallows

James Fallows is Washington editor of *The Atlantic Monthly*, and author of *More Like Us*, a book on American society. From 1986 to 1989 he lived in Japan and Malaysia. Fallows wrote the following viewpoint after a trip to Vietnam in 1988. He argues that the Vietnamese people have put the Vietnam War behind them, and that the war has had a greater and more lasting impact on the U.S. than on Vietnam.

As you read, consider the following questions:

1. What physical legacies of the war did Fallows observe in Vietnam?
2. How did most Vietnamese feel about the war, according to the author?
3. What did Fallows find interesting about his conversations with people in Vietnam and surrounding countries?

James Fallows, "No Hard Feelings?" *The Atlantic Monthly*, December 1988. Reprinted with permission.

In 1988 my wife and I traveled through two of the most miserable parts of Asia—Burma and Vietnam. We were in Burma just as the antigovernment protests were beginning, and what we saw made the subsequent upheaval there completely unsurprising. But what we saw in Vietnam made the lasting bitterness and contention over what America did in Vietnam seem, if not surprising, way out of proportion. The Vietnam War now seems much less important in Asia, where it was fought, than it does back in the United States. In most of Asia, including Indochina, America's role in the war is part of the dead and uninteresting past, as the Korean War was to most Americans a few years after it ended. America is the only place where the Vietnam War is still going on.

The Group Tour

I went to Vietnam as part of a group tour, to my chagrin. . . . Joining a tour wounded my vanity as a reporter and offended my sense of individualism, which is sharpened each time I run into a group of Japanese tourists massed behind a leader holding a flag. Also, Vietnam Tourism pushes its monopoly advantage to the hilt, charging about $100 a day for food and lodging whose open-market value must be about $15.

But as it turned out, the group-travel approach had its advantages. For one thing, the group was small—only nine people besides my wife and me, just enough to be crammed uncomfortably into the rickety Russian-made mini-bus on which we spent most of the nine days of our trip. Also, every member of it had some ulterior motive for taking what was not exactly a relaxing journey. One traveler was a German priest, thoroughly disguised behind a slapstick comedian's manner, who would sneak into Catholic churches at each stop and try to make contact with the local clergy. A mild-mannered banker turned out to have been stationed near the DMZ [Demilitarized Zone] as a Marine in 1968. A novelist from England had just finished a book set in Vietnam during the war. She wanted to visit Vietnam before the book came out, so that on her publicity tour she could tell people that of course she'd seen all the places she had written about. A chaplain from the Belgian Army seemed to have memorized the history and after-action intelligence assessment of every combat engagement in Indochina since the late 1940s. And so on.

The group tour also forced us to see a lot of territory in a short time. We flew first from Bangkok to Hanoi, and then two days later to Da Nang, halfway down the county. There we switched to the Russian bus and drove north to Hué forty miles south of the old DMZ. Then, over the next four days, we drove down the length of what had been South Vietnam, to Saigon, following

Highway 1, the famous "Street Without Joy." The road was rough, the bus leaked when it was rainy and was stifling the rest of the time, the hotels had rats and spiders in the rooms and, in Dalat, bats flapping outside the window. The journey combined, in short, the good and the bad of driving across the United States in a beat-up car, stopping briefly at fleabag motels. It was similar in the time it required and in the resulting grubbiness and fatigue but also in the satisfaction of seeing how the topography and cultures fit together. . . .

Few Signs of America

The fundamental surprise was how few signs there are of America's presence. If you didn't know that the United States had put so much time, money, hope, and despair into Vietnam, you'd never guess it from the looks of the country today.

Lack of Bitterness

Given the devastation visited upon this country by American armies over a period of twenty years, I would have thought that quite a few people might express, or at least retain, a feeling of bitterness. Apparently not. The Vietnamese whom I encounter in the markets, on ferries, in hotel elevators and restaurants laugh at my long nose and make a point of saying that they're happy to know I'm an American. They try their musical variations of English (recently learned or long remembered) and tell me that they have friends, yes, or relatives, you see, in California, New York, and Louisiana. The children wear baseball caps marked with the insignia of American corporations and T-shirts promoting Madonna and Coca-Cola.

Lewis H.Lapham, *Harper's Magazine,* May 1989.

The Philippines announces the long-term presence of the United States in a million ways: street names, people's names, styles of architecture, clothes. In Vietnam most traces of "the American war"—as they call it, to distinguish it from "the French war"—are gone. Language is one illustration. You wouldn't expect to find English-speakers in the North, where Americans never were, but even in the South they are rare. In the North and the South alike French is more useful than English. The oldest French-speakers are the best, having gone to colonial schools—but English-speaking among the stratum of people now in their thirties and forties, who would have learned from the Americans, is not there. . . .

Language is part of a much larger truth about the relative impact of the French and the Americans. Countless places in the country tell you unmistakably that the French were here—with place names, the Catholic churches, and the layout of the resort town of Dalat and the old colonial capital in Hanoi. The American barracks and aircraft shelters are usually crumbling and deserted.

Little Physical Evidence

There is much less physical evidence of the war than I had expected. Now, I may have been missing something, because I had never seen Vietnam before and had no before-and-after perspective. For instance, as the bus jounced along one particularly craggy stretch of Highway 1, I assumed that it was just another bad road, like so many in Burma. The Belgian expert quickly pointed out that the road had been damaged by artillery during an engagement between the French and the Viet Minh, thirty-five years earlier, and had never been repaired. Also, we did not see any of the highland or forest areas that were subjected to the heaviest defoliation and reportedly are still wastelands. But we saw many areas that had been battlegrounds, and the relics of battle were few. The walls of the famous Citadel, in Hué, are pocked with bullet marks—but from ten yards away they look merely weatherbeaten. On the long drive down the coast from Da Nang to Nha Trang there is a boxcar-shaped trailer resting on a cliff, with US ARMY and a big white star on the side, but it was the only large piece of leftover materiel I saw. On street corners in Saigon children sometimes wash themselves using old American helmets turned upside down as basins. The courtyard of the Military Museum in Hanoi contains the crumpled wreckage of an American B-52 (plus that of a Chinese fighter plane, shot down in the border war in 1979). Some of the trucks lumbering along the roads say Dodge or even DeSoto on the front, but the great majority are Russian. In the famous Cu Chi district, outside Saigon, there are dozens of bomb craters, most of which have filled with water and become small round ponds. But this was one of the most heavily bombed parts of the entire country. In most other places, notably including Hanoi, there is no damage that immediately calls attention to itself. I'm sure that in reality there is damage. But if you weren't constantly thinking, *Wait a minute, this is Vietnam!* the surroundings would not remind you that Americans had ever thought this was an important place.

The Vietnamese seem less interested in chewing over the meaning of the war than Americans do. Indeed, when guides, museum officials, shopkeepers, or passers-by said "the war," they seemed to mean something that started in the late 1940s and ran through the early 1980s, involving fighting against the French, Americans, South Vietnamese, Chinese, and Cambodians, successively. At the major military exhibits I did not detect any tone of contempt in the descriptions of American (or

115

French) combat efforts. For instance, in Cu Chi the Viet Cong had built more than a hundred miles' worth of tunnels in an elaborate network that reached right under a major American base. A slight, intense-looking woman, who said that she had lived in the tunnels for almost ten years, explained that the tunnels had been designed to endure saturation bombing by B-52s and assaults by the fearless American "tunnel rats." "The Americans trained Hispanic soldiers and others of short stature to fight in the tunnels," she said, through a translator. "But through skillful use of booby traps their efforts were repelled." The emphasis was on how stoic and ingenious the Vietnamese had been to overcome all that firepower, not on the failure of the Americans. I got the strong feeling from most of the guides (we dealt with five in all) that they were much less fascinated by this ancient history than the visiting Americans were. One guide seemed totally bewildered when we asked to go to Cu Chi instead of the attraction usually chosen by Vietnam Tourism: as I remember, it was listed in the brochure as a "relatively prosperous rug-making cooperative."

Views of Other Asians

The main explanation for the Vietnamese attitude is probably that they won the war, so they don't have to keep brooding about the hows and whys of what they did. But when I noticed their relative indifference to events that are twenty years past, it connected with a clear impression I'd developed in the preceding two years in Southeast Asia.

An American Obsession

A Vietnamese gentleman seated at the bar . . . identifies himself as "import-export" and remarks on the suppleness with which his countrymen adjust to historical circumstance. The Vietnamese, he says, have assigned the "American war" to the past—to the archive of wars that they have been fighting for 2,000 years, against the Mongols and the Chinese as well as the Japanese and the French. . . .

Maybe it is only the Americans who still harry themselves with the memory of the war.

Lewis H. Lapham, *Harper's Magazine,* May 1989.

In my conversations with officials in a number of the "domino" countries—Thailand, Malaysia, Singapore, Indonesia— and others in what Americans think of as Vietnam's general neighborhood, like the Philippines and Korea and even Japan, I've realized that something has been missing. Nobody has ever brought up America's years in Vietnam—how terrible it was that we lost the war, how it changed the Asian balance of power for America to pull out, how wrong it was for America to get involved in the first place, or anything else of the sort. Vietnam, as a country, is a huge factor in Asian politics. It is important because it has occupied Cambodia for so long (and implicitly threatened Thailand), because it has allowed the Russians to encamp at Cam Ranh Bay (threatening everybody), and because it keeps emitting so many refugees. But the Vietnam War, as we think of it, is not important.

Let me elaborate on this, since it may sound incredible to Americans. In Malaysia, which spent most of the 1950s defeating a Communist insurgency, and in Thailand, which spent most of the late 1970s doing the same thing, people have not shown any interest in America's Vietnam War. Once I had dinner with the director of Malaysia's military-intelligence bureau. The only thing he wanted to talk about was whether the Japanese would re-arm. In Japan and Korea, where people are obsessed with the decline of American power, and in the Philippines, where America's power seems like God's, no one has asked me how America could have let itself lose in Vietnam, or argued that America should have toughed it out to win, or mentioned the subject at all. In some of his speeches Lee Kuan Yew has said that America's withdrawal from Vietnam has been destabilizing, but I take him as the exception that proves the rule. Most of the time when Lee talks about a historic shift of power away from the United States, he is talking about a shift in trade balance and debt, something that happened under President Reagan, not under the long-gone Johnson and Nixon. . . .

The Vietnamese obviously care more about their war than their neighbors do, but what I saw reinforced the conclusion I had reached in the neighboring countries: the Vietnam War will be important in history only for what it did internally to the United States. What it did internally is immense, but the effects may be easier to deal with if we recognize that we are talking about something Americans did to one another, not an event that changed world history.

Cambodia

By fighting the war but not winning it, the United States probably changed Asian history in one important and grievous way. If it had either stayed out of the war or hung on indefinitely, perhaps the Khmer Rouge holocaust in Cambodia would never have taken place. But the overall balance of power in Indochina now is probably about the same as it would have been if the United States had never become involved. The Cambodian and Laotian sanctuaries were maddening to the American military, because tongues of those countries' territory lap into Vietnam. For the same reason, they would probably have seemed intol-

117

erable to the Vietnamese. "Really, it is *force majeure* for our army to be there," said the one non-propagandistic guide we encountered. "Because of the geography, our borders could never be secure with a hostile Cambodia. Maybe without the United States, Pol Pot would never have come to power—but it seems a stretch of logic to hold America responsible for his becoming a homicidal maniac.

A Bad Place to Fight a War

Of course, the United States might have preserved both Cambodia and South Vietnam from the North if it had won the war. But without rehashing twenty years' worth of arguments let me say that a short visit to modern Vietnam made this seem an even bigger "if" than I had thought it before. I will never, never understand how an American politician, strategist, or general could have seen this place and thought that a Western army could outlast the locals in an extended ground war. The Vietnamese seem *fierce*. There's a sweetness or gentleness or fecklessness at the core of most of the surrounding cultures— Filipino, Malay, Burmese, Thai. These Vietnamese did not seem sweet or gentle to me: they seemed ferocious and tough, even in peacetime, even when they were smiling and trying to please us as visitors. The nearby countries that did vanquish their Communist guerrillas relied on nationalistic and ethnic tools that were turned against the French and the Americans in Vietnam. In Malaya, for example, the Communists were overwhelmingly ethnic Chinese, which greatly simplified the job of isolating them in a mainly Malay population. The same factor worked against Americans in Vietnam. And of course there is the notorious Vietnamese terrain. I am not exactly making a fresh point, but the staleness *is* the point. Even though I've heard for twenty years that this was a bad place for Americans to fight a war, I found myself walking around saying, "My God! How could anybody think this could be done?"

If we exclude the possibility of outright, conclusive victory, then the difference America made in Vietnam was to delay everything for ten years—"everything" consisting of the North's conquest of the South and the advent of communism. Conceivably, that might have been worth it, although it's hard to see how. Asian countries are over the Vietnam War because they've recognized how little difference it made.

3 VIEWPOINT

"Vietnam not only invalidated the U.S. strategy of containment but destroyed any consensus about what sorts of military operations are legitimate."

The War Weakened U.S. Military Power

Alvin H. Bernstein

Alvin H. Bernstein is chairman of the Strategy Department of the Naval War College in Newport, Rhode Island. In the following viewpoint, he argues that the Vietnam War has left U.S. political and military leaders reluctant to use military force in other countries. As a result, Bernstein maintains, the U.S. has lost international influence and has been helpless in the face of international terrorism.

As you read, consider the following questions:

1. Why does the author believe it is harmful for the U.S. to refuse the option of military intervention in other counties?
2. According to Bernstein, what central dilemma does the U.S. face?
3. Why does the U.S. need a global strategy, according to Bernstein?

Alvin H. Bernstein, "U.S. Has No Strategy for Intervention," *The Wall Street Journal,* November 10, 1986. Reprinted with permission of The Wall Street Journal © 1986 Dow Jones & Company, Inc. All rights reserved.

The most enduring legacy of the Vietnam conflict is the vacuum it has left in the U.S. military's operational kit bag. The experience in Southeast Asia, the abolition of the draft and the creation of the all-volunteer force have diminished—almost to the point of invisibility—the chances of the U.S. ever again committing troops to combat in the Third World for more than a brief action or for a limited purpose—precisely the conditions that applied when the U.S. intervened in Grenada.

Vietnam not only invalidated the U.S. strategy of containment but destroyed any consensus about what sorts of military operations are legitimate, aside from a conventional defense against a Soviet invasion of Europe or possibly Japan.

The U.S. continues to grope for a coherent approach to conflicts that in any way resemble the Vietnam War. There is no clear policy for dealing with insurgencies (such as the one in the Philippines) or invasions directed against Third World friends by the Third World enemies of the U.S. (such as could happen in the Persian Gulf or on the Thai-Cambodian border). The U.S. is ambivalent when it comes to supporting counterinsurgencies waged by more or less friendly rebels (as in Cambodia, Afghanistan and Nicaragua). In fact, as events in the Middle East make obvious, the U.S. has dithered over what to do about any sort of systematic but unconventional violence designed to diminish America's international influence.

The Weinberger Doctrine

The public, Congress, the media and most senior U.S. military leaders take the attitude that the Vietnam experience must be avoided at all costs. Most Americans have not yet faced and would prefer not to contemplate the fact that the U.S. might someday have to intervene somewhere, as we did in Grenada.

Although nonintervention in any given case may be politically permissible and even wise, an accumulation of such decisions might damage U.S. interests. Those who would not want to intervene abroad can argue convincingly on behalf of their view because of the nature of the tactics being used against the U.S. today.

Low-intensity warfare achieves its goals incrementally. It uses violence to humiliate, to intimidate, to curtail our influence and remove U.S. influence abroad, to diminish U.S. credibility in the eyes of those who might rely someday on the U.S. for protection. At the same time it stirs up divisive debates at home and creates serious tensions between the U.S. and its formal allies. All this it achieves with a level of violence that allows Americans to convince themselves that the country can absorb the punishment without responding. After all, such low-intensity conflict never immediately threatens the survival of the

U.S. The situation it creates may annoy, even temporarily enrage, but does not really frighten.

The most articulate and convincing formulation of the noninterventionist position comes from [former] Secretary of Defense Caspar Weinberger. His argument, expressed in what has come to be known as the Weinberger Doctrine, illustrates the Pentagon's isolationist mood. It is a product partly of the Vietnam War and partly of the October 1983 bombing of the Marine barracks in Lebanon. In brief, Secretary Weinberger insists that if we commit troops again we must do so wholeheartedly, with clear political objectives, with the intention of winning, with the support of the American people, and only as a last resort. A great many officers share this view, and it is one of the greatest single inhibitions to any future limited U.S. use of force, though experience has shown it is not absolute.

American Withdrawal

I think there is a very definite legacy from Vietnam. It really changed what had been an attitude of confident realism that we had now learned to use measured force in pursuit of our national objectives, and that we could deal in a sophisticated way with the problems of the world. Our first reaction after Vietnam was to withdraw and in a sense be the way we had been for the first hundred and fifty years of our existence. There was a difference, though. We used to withdraw because we thought we were too good for the world. After Vietnam we said, "No, we're not good enough. We've failed. We supported a corrupt regime."

We've come partly out of that, but the overhang still invests discussions about issues that have very little relevance to Vietnam.

Brent Scowcroft, *The Bad War*, 1986.

Our military's attitude of "let's go all the way or let's not go at all" is easy to sympathize with. It stems from the deep resentment many of our senior officers still feel about the treatment they received from civilian leaders and noisy segments of American society when they returned from Vietnam, leaving 55,000 of their fellows dead on the battlefield.

They know in their hearts that they lost in Vietnam, not because they performed poorly, but because they were kept on a leash by civilian authority, rendered impotent by a political, no-win strategy, and never allowed to do what they believe they had the military capacity to do—destroy the enemy's forces. Their determination not ever again to endure the sort of pointless loss and humiliation that Vietnam represented is a powerful force to be reckoned with, especially since the military leadership has managed to convince many of its civilian overseers that it is right.

Lebanon gave them an extremely unpleasant sense of deja vu. That experience only confirmed their conviction that civilian authority understands little or nothing of military operations and will continue to send the armed forces on extremely difficult, messy missions—not only keeping the peace in anarchic Lebanon but freeing the Mayaguez or rescuing hostages in Iran—only to turn around and excoriate them for their incompetence when the inevitable recurs. This distrust among the senior officer corps grows stronger, of course, when reform-minded, self-styled experts and journalists, who have never seen combat themselves, drone on about the armed forces not getting anything right since Korea, and when respected members of Congress, who ought to know better, lend their support and prestige to such demoralizing accusations.

A Global Strategy

The country, then, faces a dilemma. If the public finally agrees that the Weinberger Doctrine is right and ought to be adopted, it has to acknowledge that the U.S. will cease being a military power in the way that it used to be. The U.S. cannot rule out military intervention in small, ambiguous wars and yet maintain the credibility of our commitments abroad. Nor can we protect our citizens from terrorist attacks if we are reluctant to devise and execute limited military responses in order to deter future attacks.

If the country decides to reject the Weinberger Doctrine and its implications, however, U.S. leaders have to start thinking seriously about things that were missed as the country became involved in the war in Vietnam. We need a global strategy that establishes geopolitical priorities and develops alternatives to the discredited policy of universal containment. This involves making choices. In order to decide where the U.S. should commit troops, it must have a firm idea of the relative importance to our national security of such countries as the Philippines, Pakistan, Peru, Tunisia, Nicaragua, Iran and Thailand. Where do these countries fit into our strategic requirements?

Military leaders must have some sense of where the crucial strategic areas are that we must control in order to deter or defend against a Soviet attack. If they cannot provide this the country runs two unacceptable risks. It might either stumble into another Vietnam where resources are expended to no real purpose or it might stand idly by while the U.S. loses influence in some part of the Third World that is essential to the defense of the West.

U.S. troops have been killed in Lebanon, have invaded

Grenada and bombed Libya, yet there is no doctrine, no systematic framework, not even the beginnings of a consensus, for where and how to use limited force in unconventional missions. Instead, U.S. forces remain reactive, forced into action either by political pressure combined with our own threatening rhetoric, as in Libya, or by conditions that simply could no longer be ignored, as in Grenada. Only a global strategy will prevent us from swinging unpredictably and perilously between ad hoc reactive containment and de facto noninterventionism.

New Forms of Response Needed

What, then, should be done? As Secretary Weinberger said, the U.S. should use force only when there are clearly defined political and military objectives. For this the U.S. needs not only a set of geopolitical priorities but a wide range of operational choices that would cost no more and take no longer than our democracy will bear. To develop the ability to execute such options does not mean a return to containment and military intervention.

The terrorism being conducted against the U.S. is too threatening to our national interests and too unorthodox in its techniques to allow us to plan only for conventional warfare in Europe. New forms of limited, unconventional response must be developed if Americans are to cope with the conflicts we are almost certain to face in the future. Otherwise U.S. forces become like those helpless and bewildered Redcoats during the Revolutionary War, or the tragically anachronistic British cavalry at the start of World War I, both clinging to outmoded forms of combat, easy prey to the new tactics of enemies and not quite certain why the old, tried and proven methods are no longer working.

"Might does not make right; might makes enemies."

The War Showed the U.S. the Limits of Military Power

Thomas C. Fox

Following the Vietnam War, some commentators argued that the U.S. was suffering from a "Vietnam syndrome." They stated that the U.S. experience in Vietnam made political leaders afraid to intervene in other countries. In the following viewpoint, Thomas C. Fox argues that those who complain about the Vietnam Syndrome miss the fundamental lessons from the Vietnam War: that military power is limited in its ability to reshape other countries to meet U.S. goals, and that the U.S. has no right to try. Fox is editor of the *National Catholic Reporter*.

As you read, consider the following questions:

1. What are the three lessons Fox sees in Vietnam?
2. Why does the author believe racism was a part of American involvement in the Vietnam War?
3. According to Fox, why are those who want to revise the lessons of Vietnam wrong?

Thomas C. Fox, "Vietnam 'Revised'—American Arrogance Lesson Never Learned," *National Catholic Reporter*, March 11, 1983. Reprinted with permission.

The Vietnam war has crept back into the public forum. The Vietnam veterans finally got a memorial which reminds us that young men die in wars. . . .

But the most interesting—and disturbing—aspect of this renaissance of interest is the effort being made, allegedly with a distance and dispassion now finally possible, to "revise" the lessons of the Vietnam war. The first major "revisionist" account appeared in 1982 in book form entitled *Why We Were in Vietnam*, a work of Norman Podhoretz, who argued that a better understanding of the Vietnam experience could lead us to a stronger national commitment to the defense of freedom.

Podhoretz argued that U.S. intentions in Vietnam were selfless, if misdirected, and that it is now time we recognized the effort marked one of the high points, not low points, in U.S. history.

Since then, others with predilections similar to Podhoretz's have tuned in, and we are even beginning to read, as in *The New York Times Magazine*, that the United States "was probably in a stronger position in Vietnam in 1972, just before the Paris peace accords, than at any previous point in the war." The implication, of course, was that we should have held out for better terms or even possibly continued the war which was beginning to go our way.

Personally, I am pleased when people show interest in Vietnam. I lived in Vietnam for nearly five years during the heaviest U.S. military involvement. I learned to speak the language and got to know the people. I feel fairly certain most Americans have not learned the lessons of the war. Some of these lessons are applicable today, especially in the midst of loose talk about reasserting American will around the world.

Before we march into some new conflict or get even more embroiled in El Salvador or Honduras, it might be worth taking a quick look at three lessons to come out of the war.

Failure to Understand Other Cultures

1. We fail miserably to understand the people, cultures and histories of other nations.

In the case of Vietnam, millions of lives would have been saved, for example, had we learned Vietnamese history and literature. The word "Viet Nam," for example, means "Southern People." The Vietnamese define themselves as those people south of China who fought for 1,000 years to win their independence from their giant northern enemy. The sense of Vietnamese nationalism grew out of this conflict. Vietnam's national heroes have always been those who led the resistance against outside invaders. Some 100 years of French colonial rule reinforced the notion, and by the time the western powers allowed France back into Vietnam following World War II, the

Communists and nationalists were one and the same force.

Eventually, they drove out the French in 1954, the year the United States decided to take their place.

Seen in this light, the American effort to set up a South Vietnamese government in 1954 was a precarious endeavor at best. And the American involvement was fatally doomed by 1965 when U.S. ground troops entered Vietnam on a large scale. Every U.S. soldier who set foot on Vietnamese soil reinforced the righteousness of the nationalist resistance.

Anti-Communism Not Enough

2. An anti-Communist ideology is insufficient as a base for building a popular government. And if that ideology is an implant by the United States, the puppets eventually get to pull the strings.

The U.S. government formed and supported the South Vietnamese government from its inception, taking anti-Communist Catholics out of northern Vietnam and making them the nucleus of the new regime, although Catholics represented only 10 percent of the Vietnamese population. The Saigon government never really "won" the support of most Vietnamese. It was widely viewed as corrupt and dominated by the military, whom the Vietnamese do not respect. The government offered an anti-Communist structure built with a massive U.S. propaganda organization which preached the fear of a Communist take-over.

Maturity Needed

The real lesson of Vietnam cannot be that America will prevail anywhere if only we try hard enough—or at the other extreme, that we are doomed to defeat, whatever the place, time, or circumstance. The real lesson is that a great power must be mature enough to adopt practical and proportionate policies. We've got to be tough-minded, not simple-minded.

The New Republic, May 16, 1983.

Government leader after government leader recognized he owed his position to U.S. policy, but also knew the Americans needed him to fulfill their own mission. So who was in control? The Americans were never in a position to insist on true reforms, the end to the hated corruption—however self-defeating. Astute Saigonese, perhaps recognizing the futility of the U.S. actions, developed a "take the money and run" attitude through much of the war. The entire U.S. effort was built on sand.

3. Might does not make right; might makes enemies.

Everything the Americans brought to Vietnam reeked of perceived superiority. The Vietnamese felt this condescension im-

126

mediately and resented it. Few of the millions of Americans who came to Vietnam ever lived among the Vietnamese. All U.S. officials—those who needed to know most—lived in "little Americas," villas or compounds fenced in with barbed wire and defense posts.

The most blatant forms of racism were spawned in a "them against us" attitude shared by nearly every American. Little or no respect was ever shown by the foreigners to Vietnamese customs, traditions, religious beliefs or values. Everything the Americans had to offer, they assumed, was superior. "If only the gooks could learn to live like us—but, of course, gooks can't."

America brought its firepower, too. I once heard it suggested that 5,000 U.S. bullets were fired against each enemy shot. The notion sounds preposterous unless you were there.

The destruction was almost always one-sided: we had the helicopter gunships, the B-52s, the gatlin guns on the C-47s. Young American soldiers hunted, yes *hunted,* men, women and even children from helicopter gunships flying over "free-fire zones." What kind of government would allow a foreign force to establish a "free-fire zone" in one's own nation?

U.S. artillery outposts, secure behind claymore mines and sandbags, were assigned quotas. Night after night they fired into the darkness every few minutes, sending random terror into the countryside.

The means of warfare, always appalling, grew less discriminating with each passing month. Until by the early 1970s the U.S. sent daily B-52 missions from Guam, carpeting central Vietnam and the Mekong delta with millions of tons of bombs. The Christmas bombing of Hanoi in 1972 was only the most visible manifestation of this arrogance of power.

Other Destruction

U.S. might showed up in other destructive ways: nearly one-third of the South Vietnamese population was eventually homeless and forced into refugee camps or squatters' huts near the cities. Young women were viewed as only a potential means of sexual gratification. The elderly, traditionally the source of wisdom in Vietnam, were ridiculed and stripped of authority. The Americans looked to the military leaders for Vietnam's new national leadership.

The payoffs for going along with the Americans were immediate material gains. Imported fans, refrigerators, Japanese Hondas, televisions, portable radios, tape decks, cigarettes and wines were all paraded before the Vietnamese in an effort to teach consumerism to the country. Unfortunately western individualism helped tear apart eastern collective, family-based values. Those Vietnamese who went along became not only misfits in a nation seeking an identity, but victims in their own land.

U.S. might literally pillaged Vietnamese society, a task made easier by blinding American arrogance. But this same blindness assured a U.S. defeat—and continues today in U.S. foreign policy.

Faulty Revisions

Those asking that we "revise" the lessons of the war never learned those lessons in the first place. They now refer to Vietnam syndrome, characterized by timidity in asserting U.S. military power. We need to stand up to defend freedom worldwide, they tell us. We need to be proud of our valiant efforts in Vietnam, they would have us believe.

But they are wrong. For precisely the blind national will, false national pride and an unending belief in U.S. military power—that they wish to rekindle—led us into war and again could slip us into a senseless conflict.

Whenever I hear the call to stand up and march on behalf of freedom, I pause, remember Vietnam and ask, "for whom?"

"Perhaps this is the last tragedy from the war in Vietnam—the way in which it has crippled the idealism of an entire generation."

The War Destroyed American Idealism

William Greider

The group of Americans probably most affected by the Vietnam War is the baby-boom generation—the seventy-five million Americans who were born between 1946 and 1964. Many of this group either fought in the Vietnam War or protested against it. In the following viewpoint, William Greider examines the results of a survey of this generation. Greider writes that the Vietnam War destroyed youthful idealism and patriotism, and left these people without national heroes. Greider is national editor of *Rolling Stone*.

As you read, consider the following questions:

1. What lessons have Americans learned from Vietnam, in Greider's view?
2. Why does Greider label the Americans surveyed isolationist?
3. What is one reason the U.S. has not become militarily involved in another war after Vietnam, according to the author?

William Greider, "The *Rolling Stone* Survey" and "Hell, No, We Won't Go!" *Rolling Stone*, April 7, 1988. Copyright © 1988 by William Greider. Reprinted by permission of the author.

129

In 1986 the editors of *Rolling Stone* decided to commission a group portrait of the young Americans who are now the nation's largest bloc of voters. They include the so-called baby boomers, born during the years of prosperity after World War II and now parents themselves. They are the first generation to experience life, from infancy to adulthood, in the glowing presence of television. At least potentially they are the generation that will set the tone of the national experience for the next twenty years or so.

But who exactly is this group? And what do they believe? What do they really want? The members of this generation have been constantly labeled and relabeled in various ways. During the turbulent political and social upheavals of the Sixties and early Seventies, they were loosely depicted by the media as rebellious and idealistic. Then they became the Me Generation of the Seventies and the yuppies of the Eighties. In each era the labels caught a glint of the truth but grossly distorted the larger picture.

To capture this more complicated reality, *Rolling Stone* commissioned Peter D. Hart Research Associates to conduct a wide-ranging survey of Americans aged eighteen to forty-four, covering aspects of their lives, from political preferences to private morality, from economic anxieties to social ideals. For years, Peter Hart has been recognized as one of the most influential pollsters in American politics. The survey he conducted for the magazine was intended to provide a more thorough analysis of this generation than anything done previously.

The *Rolling Stone* Survey does not attempt to predict which presidential candidate will win the hearts and minds of this pivotal generation. But the survey does answer more profound questions: What does this generation want to hear from its leaders? What does this generation yearn for in the public arena as well as the private sector? . . .

The Heroes

Their heroes are dead. Yet their heroes live on in memory as giants of idealism. Their heroes were men of courage who challenged the established order, who espoused love and peace and attacked prejudice and inequality. And their heroes were both murdered in their prime.

It is impossible, of course, to know an entire generation by a single fact, yet the responses of young Americans to a question about their heroes was perhaps the most revealing result of the survey. When asked to select or volunteer two people they most admired who had been active in public life at some time in the last twenty years, they did not choose a great president or a titan of business and finance or name a celebrity from the world of sports or entertainment. They turned instead to the past, when the idealism of many of them was a powerful force at work in American society.

The public figure whom they still revere above all others is a black Baptist preacher from Georgia who was murdered in 1968: Dr. Martin Luther King Jr. Their second most admired hero is a controversial young senator from New York who was also assassinated in 1968: Robert F. Kennedy. Thirty-eight percent selected King as the public figure they most admired; 25 percent selected Kennedy.

No Explanation

Prior to the defeat in Vietnam, most Americans had been content to think of themselves as honorable people, unerringly drawn to the side of what was true and noble and right—not the kind of people to push women and children away from the last helicopter out of town. If the war proved them wrong in this judgment, it was because the war was never honestly declared and because, at the end of it, nobody, certainly none of its official sponsors, could say why 58,000 American soldiers were dead and another 300,000 wounded. What could be said was that America had lost not only a war but also the belief in its virtue.

Lewis H. Lapham, *Harper's Magazine*, May 1989.

King and Kennedy both stood for the values that, according to the survey, this generation still believes in. Peace and justice, tolerance and equality. Both men, in different ways, were raw and eloquent leaders who confronted America's smug sense of complacency, who agitated for change, who spoke out for dissenters and the dispossessed. It is a gloomy commentary on American public life that in the last twenty years, no one else has come along to match King and Kennedy in the memories of younger Americans. And that both of these heroes were killed, their dreams of peace and justice still unrealized. That single fact could serve as a powerful symbol for the generation itself. Blighted legacy is a theme that surfaces throughout the survey.

The Sixties

The turbulence of the Sixties was the formative experience for this generation, even for those who were babies when King and Kennedy were killed and only learned about the civil-rights movement and antiwar protests later, from the media or at school or from older brothers and sisters. The Sixties experience, especially the civil-rights movements, is the source of their enduring idealism—a sense of open-mindedness. Asked which aspects and events of the Sixties especially influenced them, respondents cited the civil-rights movement more than any other. Asked to describe ways in which they had a different outlook from their parents' generation, they viewed themselves as more tolerant and less prejudiced, more willing to try new things, more committed to equality for women, more liberal, more optimistic, less religious.

Yet they must be surprised—even a little disappointed—by their own adult attitudes. They are more conservative than they expected themselves to be, more career oriented and a great deal less politically active than they would have predicted. Forty-six percent regard politics as not important in their lives. Fifty-one percent vote regularly—a smaller percentage than other groups of Americans. Only a tiny fraction of them are personally active on public issues, even on positions they support overwhelmingly, such as opposition to foreign wars and nuclear armaments.

Vietnam

The survey suggests this reluctance also stems from the Sixties experience—the twin tragedies of King and Kennedy, but more profoundly the bitter disillusionment resulting from the war in Vietnam. Nearly half the members of this generation have personal knowledge of the human losses suffered in Indochina—48 percent knew someone, friend or relative or acquaintance, who was killed or wounded there. Among those in their late thirties, the figure goes up to 70 percent. Twenty-nine percent call the war the most compelling event in their lives over the last twenty years.

The lesson still resonates powerfully in their attitudes—a distrust of public life that is reflected in their spontaneous responses. What did they learn from Vietnam? Their answers are totally negative: A senseless war in which Americans died for no reason. Too many casualties, too many deaths. Either fight to win or don't fight at all. The war destroyed faith in government. Americans were not heroes, fighting for a just cause. Stay out of other countries' problems.

No more Vietnams . . . no more heroes. The legacy is a kind of wounded idealism—a sense of retreat from the original promise offered by this generation, a generation that would reshape the nation with its different, more generous values. Instead, on the whole, this generation has retreated into itself.

This wounded sense of history helps explain why Ronald Reagan became spectacularly popular, especially among the younger members of the generation, who had no personal experience with the Vietnam War but heard about it endlessly from their elders and the news media. For them, Ronald Reagan looked like the first good thing that had happened in some time to American politics—a confident, optimistic leader who dwelled on America's strength and virtue, not its disgrace and failures. Reagan scored well on the list of most admired public figures but also drew heavy negative responses. Twenty-five percent said he was the public figure they respected most, but 10 percent said they respected him the least, leaving him with an overall rating of 15 percent. As his image has been tarnished by scandal, the president has become yet another source of disillusionment.

How much would you say you have been affected by the Vietnam War?

	A Great Deal	Quite a Bit	Only Some	Not Much	Not at All
All Respondents *Total Affected: 55%*	12%	17%	26%	24%	19%
Ages 18-24 *Total Affected: 35%*	4%	9%	22%	32%	29%
Ages 25-29 *Total Affected: 46%*	9%	14%	23%	29%	22%
Ages 30-34 *Total Affected: 60%*	13%	21%	26%	28%	11%
Ages 35-39 *Total Affected: 81%*	23%	26%	32%	10%	8%
Ages 40-44 *Total Affected: 61%*	18%	18%	25%	15%	21%

William Greider, *Rolling Stone*, April 7, 1988.

More to the point, there has always been a profound contradiction in the youthful enthusiasm that bubbled up for Reagan—because he and his admirers wanted very different things. The Reagan doctrine reinvigorated the cold-war imperative in American foreign policy, the willingness to confront the Soviets, at least through surrogates, on many foreign fronts. That is absolutely the opposite of what this generation wants in foreign policy.

Isolationism

This generation is isolationist—in a world that is increasingly interdependent. The gut question in anyone's world view is this: Under what circumstances would one be willing to serve in the armed forces and go to war? The answers in the *Rolling Stone* Survey are stunning: 40 percent of this generation, including 27 percent of the men, could not identify any circumstance under which they would go fight for the country. Only 33 percent of the men would willingly fight alongside our allies to defend

Western Europe. Only 19 percent of the men would be willing to serve in a war to keep a third-world nation from falling to the communists. Only 22 percent would enlist to defend our sources of oil in the Persian Gulf.

In fact, they said the only war worth fighting would be one that directly threatened our own borders—if a conflict broke out in Mexico or Canada. Even then, 27 percent of the men said they would still not be willing to go. Rambo's popularity notwithstanding, the patriotic ethos that has governed American life since World War II has faded—pushed aside by a generation that does not trust its government to wage only just wars.

For better or for worse, this generation embodies a profound shift in political attitudes—unlike anything that has existed since the isolationist climate preceding World War II. As a new axis of public opinion, it can keep America from plunging into senseless wars. But it might also inhibit America from addressing the new global economic realities.

To appreciate how different this outlook is, compare this generation with the one just before it—the young people whose public values were formed by World War II. The victory of World War II was not only a glorious triumph for the nation, but it taught deeper lessons about what one could expect in life. The United States could stand up for just causes, and if everyone pulled together, it could win. Both the mobilization and the immediate postwar era demonstrated that the nation's energies could be focused in extraordinarily productive ways. World War II schooled an entire generation of new leaders—and it also taught everyone else how to follow them.

A Loss of Credibility

The Sixties experience taught the opposite. A generation found itself outside the system and indeed opposed to the official leadership, whether it was the grass-roots rebellion for civil rights or the popular opposition to the war. Instead of building a creative structure for the energies of the members of the generation, this dynamic exhausted their energies in conflict with the government and with one another. It taught them that the structure itself was corrupt, that individuals must follow their own moral compass and that they could not expect much moral leadership from above. The nation's framework, the sense of larger purpose and possibilities inherited from their parents' era, collapsed for this generation. It no longer seemed believable. And nothing has happened since to restore it.

Perhaps this is the last tragedy from the war in Vietnam—the way in which it has crippled the idealism of an entire generation. . . .

If future historians try to explain why the United States did *not* invade Nicaragua in the 1980s or go to war against other hostile regimes in third-world countries, the answer might be found in the foreign-policy attitudes of the young men who would have been called upon to fight.

They won't go. They do not want any part of another confusing war in a foreign land. They are not willing to enlist in the armed services for almost any kind of conflict—short of a war in Mexico or Canada that threatens our own borders. Asked to select situations under which they would enlist, 27 percent of the men surveyed could not identify any situation that would lead them to enlist: 22 percent said they would enlist if America's strategic interests were threatened; 19 percent said they would enlist to keep a third-world nation from falling to communists; 33 percent would enlist if our close European allies were attacked; and 73 percent would enlist if war broke out on the North American continent. . . .

This is a stunning political fact—one that foreign-policy planners in the government must learn to live with, whether they like it or not. The patriotic consensus that supported the cold war for several decades, as well as Americans' engaging directly in battle against communist forces, has vanished, at least among the young.

Skepticism

Its place has been taken by an inward-looking caution about all foreign entanglements—a skepticism that resembles the public's isolationism in the days before Pearl Harbor. What should the United States do if faced with another conflict like Vietnam? Only 24 percent think the country should fight, this time using more force. Fifty-five percent favor staying out. Another 15 percent say it depends. . . .

The explanation, of course, is the collective memory of the humiliating American struggle in Vietnam. There is not much argument about whether American involvement in Vietnam was right or wrong—only 16 percent think the United States was right to fight that war. Only 25 percent of those who are Republicans think so. They are more divided on what went wrong. Asked to select which one of four factors they thought best explained why the United States lost the war in Vietnam, 36 percent said they felt the United States failed to make a great enough military effort. Twenty percent cited the antiwar protests and the lack of support in the United States for the war. Another 20 percent felt it was because of the lack of adequate military and civilian support from our South Vietnamese allies, and 8 percent said it was because of the strength and numbers of the opposing communist forces.

The bottom line, however, is stark: before the government engages itself again in a foreign conflict, it had better have a very convincing purpose if it expects the young to rally round the flag.

6

VIEWPOINT

> *"Among all the baby-boom splits, none may be felt more intensely than the one caused by Vietnam."*

The War's Impact on Public Attitudes Is Difficult to Measure

Paul C. Light

Many observers have tried to examine how the Vietnam War affected Americans, especially members of the large baby-boom generation born between 1946 and 1964. In the following viewpoint, Paul C. Light argues that the baby-boom generation cannot be analyzed as a group because it contains many internal divisions. One of the key divisions, he states, is between those who fought in Vietnam and those who protested against it. He contends that these two groups have very different attitudes toward the war. Light is the associate dean and professor of political science at the Hubert H. Humphrey Institute of Public Affairs at the University of Minnesota in Minneapolis.

As you read, consider the following questions:

1. What does the author cite as enduring political beliefs of Vietnam War protesters?
2. According to the author, why are Vietnam Veterans hard to classify politically?
3. Why does Light predict that Vietnam Veterans may yet forge an alliance with war protesters?

Excerpted, with permission, from *Baby Boomers* by Paul C. Light, © 1988 by Paul C. Light.

All baby boomers were not born identical. Some were born male, others female. Some were born black, others white. Some were born rich, some poor, but most were born in the middle. These divisions have yet to surface as intragenerational conflicts, but they exist nonetheless. . . .

The problem for anyone trying to tap the baby boom as a generation is that there is no such thing as a standard-issue baby boomer. The generation—like other generations—appears to be divided most by age, gender, education, economic class. One division important and particular to the baby boom is service in Vietnam. Vietnam vets are different from Vietnam protestors. . . .

A Divided Generation

Among all the baby-boom splits, none may be felt more intensely than the one caused by Vietnam. On one side are the baby boomers who served in the armed forces between the formation of the American Military Assistance Command on February 6, 1962, and the departure of the last American troops on March 29, 1973. On the other side are the baby boomers who served in the protests to stop the war. Years after the fall of Saigon, the two remain far apart politically. As former Secretary of the Navy, and Vietnam veteran James Webb, suggests, "the real problem began in the 1960s with the debates about the war itself and continues because of our inability as a nation to assimilate that divisive experience."

Protestors

Those who protested the war still retain some of their sharp liberalism from the 1960s. Protest involved far more than showing up for a rally. Along with the blue jeans and tie-dyed shirts, protest involved a distinctive lifestyle and outlook. From legalization of marijuana to equal rights for women and minorities, from opposition to the war in Vietnam to support for the war on poverty, the protest movement involved a package of ideas; one did not join for a day. As political scientists M. Kent Jennings and Richard Niemi argue, protestors have kept active politically, suggesting an "enduring cleavage organized around a set of unique historical experiences," even if some of their issues have been blunted by their passage through the life cycle.

Trace elements of the 1960s and early 1970s appear on a number of attitudes, including support for the rights of the accused, help for minorities, and government intervention in the economy. The protestors have softened with time, but remain relatively liberal. The only issue on which there has been no retreat by the protestors is women's rights. In 1973, 91 percent of the Vietnam protestors supported equality for women. In 1982, the number was essentially unchanged, offering solid evidence of what Jennings calls "absolute continuity." In fact, if anyone changed on women's rights during the 1970s, it was the non-protestors. They became more liberal over time, moving from 77 percent in support of equality for woman in 1973 to 84 percent in 1982, finally catching up to their once radical peers.

Veterans

In contrast, Vietnam veterans have been more difficult to place on the political spectrum. "Vietnam was a swirling, ever-changing place that in itself defies a simple common shared experience," Myra MacPherson writes. "Veterans who saw heavy combat and those who saw little do not speak the same language. Nor do those who went in 1964, when the country was moving through the long twilight of cold war containment, have much of a bond with the reluctant draftee who went to a hot and futile war in 1970."

Jennings and Niemi's findings support this conclusion. Even though vets moved through history at the same time as the protestors, they were not marked in "politically distinguishable ways or with different outcomes that would set them apart from other members of their generation," Jennings and Niemi concluded in 1981. "By contrast, the protestors responded to the political-historical environment in a singular fashion," one that once carried a great potential for mobilization.

Feelings about U.S. Involvement in Vietnam, by Veteran Status

	Supported	Confused	Opposed	N
Vietnam veteran	46	10	45	(227)
Vietnam era veteran	32	19	49	(260)
Nonveteran	19	14	67	(472)

Ellen Frey-Wouters and Robert S. Laufer, *Legacy of a War.* Reprinted by permission of M.E. Sharpe, Inc., Armonk, New York, 10504.

However, veterans may eventually come together as a voting block as they find it now acceptable to both acknowledge their service in Vietnam and to talk about their personal reactions. Both were once taboo. As vets find that others shared their experiences, they may find some common ground. They may find, for example, that no matter where they served, they shared a bizarre experience.

"What would be the worst set of social, economic, and political, and psychological conditions you could create for the returnee?" Vietnam vet John Wilson asked in congressional testimony in 1980. His answer deserves full reading:

> First, you would send a young man fresh out of high school to an unpopular, controversial guerrilla war far away from home. Expose him to intensely stressful events, some so horrible that it would be impossible to really talk about them later to anyone else except fellow "survivors." To ensure maximal stress, you would create a one-year tour of duty during which the combatant flies to and from the war zone singly, without a cohesive, intact, and emotionally supportive unit with high morale. You would also create the one-year rotation to instill a "survivor mentality" which would undercut the process of ideological commitment to winning the war and seeing it as a noble cause. Then at DEROS [Date of Expected Return from Overseas Service] you would rapidly remove the combatant and singly return him to his front porch without an opportunity to sort out the meaning of the experiences with the men in his unit. No homecoming welcome or victory parades. Ah, but yet, since you are demonic enough, you make sure that the veteran is stigmatized and portrayed to the public as a "drug-crazed psychopathic killer." By virtue of clever selection by the Selective Service system, the veteran would be unable to easily reenter the mainstream of society because he is undereducated and lacks marketable job skills. Further, since the war itself was difficult, you would want to make sure that there were no supportive systems in society for him, especially among health professionals at VA [Veterans Administration] hospitals, who would find his nightmares and residual war-related anxieties unintelligible. Finally, you would want to establish a GI Bill [of post-service education and housing benefits] with inadequate benefits to pay for education and job training, coupled with an economy of high inflation and unemployment. Last, but not least, you would want him to feel isolated, stigmatized, unappreciated, and exploited for volunteering to serve his country. Tragically, of course, this scenario is not fictitious: it was the homecoming for most Vietnam veterans.

This shared experience may create common vet problems long into the future, which in turn might mobilize vets politically. If a report in the *New England Journal of Medicine* is correct, Vietnam vets may face statistically higher odds of drug and alcohol dependency, depression, and marital stress than their peers. Vets may also face statistically higher odds of suicide and death from motor vehicle accidents. The most likely explanation, according to the authors of the study, "is that military service during the Vietnam War caused an increase in subsequent deaths," whether because of post-traumatic stress disorder—that is, the delayed effects of having served in heavy combat—or some other unknown factor.

According to the statistics, the higher suicide and accident rates are not restricted just to those who actually served; men born from 1950 to 1952 who were merely eligible for the draft through unlucky lottery numbers had a 13 percent higher probability of suicide over the 1974-83 period. According to the authors of the statistical analysis, the data hold a clear message for future presidents: "before sending young men to war, especially one in which they may have experiences similar to those of Vietnam veterans, those who make the decision should weigh all the costs. The casualties of forced military service may not be limited to those that are counted on the battlefield.". . .

America Remains Divided

The debate over Vietnam has changed surprisingly little from the early '70s. Great division still exists over whether we should have been involved in that war. A majority of Americans remains sharply critical of the way the war was conducted.

The Washington Post and ABC News asked a national sample of adults whether, in hindsight, the United States should have avoided sending troops to Vietnam, or should have sent troops but "gone all out to win the war."

About half—54 percent—said the United States should not have sent troops. Another 36 percent said the United States was right to have entered the war and should have "gone all out to win." The rest were undecided.

The Washington Post National Weekly Edition, April 29-May 6, 1990.

In dealing with the huge Veterans Administration bureaucracy, the Vietnam vets are starting to sound much like the protestors once did. They are less trusting of the VA than older vets and more frustrated with the red tape and the lack of openness. Like the protestors, they do not trust any big organization. Like the protestors, they are becoming more aggressive in demanding change. Now that the vets have finally been welcomed home, some may yet forge an alliance with the protestors.

a critical thinking activity

Distinguishing Between Fact and Opinion

This activity is designed to help develop the basic reading and thinking skill of distinguishing between fact and opinion. Consider the following statement: "The United States military was involved in Vietnam in 1965." This is a fact which no historian or diplomat would deny. But the statement "The Vietnam War was a noble cause for the U.S." is an opinion. Many anti-war protesters who called the Vietnam War immoral would disagree with that statement.

When investigating controversial issues it is important that one be able to distinguish between statements of fact and statements of opinion. It is also important to recognize that not all statements of fact are true. They may appear to be true, but some are based on inaccurate or false information. For this activity, however, we are concerned with understanding the difference between those statements which appear to be factual and those which appear to be based primarily on opinion.

Most of the following statements are taken from the viewpoints in this chapter. Consider each statement carefully. *Mark O for any statement you believe is an opinion or interpretation of facts. Mark F for any statement you believe is a fact. Mark I for any statement you believe is impossible to judge.*

If you are doing this activity as a member of a class or group, compare your answers with those of other class or group members. Be able to defend your answers. You may discover that others come to different conclusions than you do. Listening to the reasons others present for their answers may give you valuable insights in distinguishing between fact and opinion.

> O = *opinion*
> F = *fact*
> I = *impossible to judge*

141

1. We should be ashamed of our efforts in Vietnam.

2. The courtyard of the Military Museum in Hanoi contains the wreckage of an American B-52.

3. Young Americans today are not willing to fight in countries like Vietnam.

4. Vietnam veterans face statistically higher odds of depression and drug addiction than their peers who did not fight in the war.

5. American troops officially left Vietnam on March 29, 1973.

6. Surveys have shown that Vietnam veterans and Vietnam protesters remain sharply divided in their political beliefs today.

7. About 12 percent of the land area in South Vietnam was sprayed with Agent Orange and other chemical defoliants.

8. The United States should provide economic assistance to Vietnam.

9. Since its defeat in Vietnam, the U.S. has unfortunately been unwilling to use military force when its national interests have been threatened.

10. The Vietnam War is much less important in Asia than in the United States.

11. The baby-boomers surveyed by *Rolling Stone* listed Robert F. Kennedy and Martin Luther King Jr. as their heroes.

12. Vietnamese people today are often friendly to American visitors.

13. The Vietnam War destroyed people's faith in government.

14. The U.S. invasion of Grenada, unlike the Vietnam War, was completed in a short period of time.

15. The Vietnam War disrupted the Vietnamese economy and society.

16. Americans failed to understand the culture of the Vietnamese.

17. The Vietnamese drove the French out of Vietnam in 1954.

18. During the Vietnam War nearly one-third of the South Vietnamese population became homeless.

19. Thousands of Vietnamese people were sent to work camps after the Vietnam War.

20. The U.S. military leadership has yet to learn the lessons of Vietnam.

Periodical Bibliography

The following articles have been selected to supplement the diverse views presented in this chapter.

William Adams	"Screen Wars," *Dissent*, Winter 1990.
Noam Chomsky	"The United States and Indochina: Far from an Aberration," *The Bulletin of Concerned Asian Scholars*, April/December 1989. Available from *The Bulletin of Concerned Asian Scholars*, 3239 9th St., Boulder, CO 80304-2112.
Nancy Cooper	"'Go Back to Your Country,'" *Newsweek*, March 14, 1988.
John Gregory Dunne	"The War That Won't Go Away," *The New York Review of Books*, September 25, 1986.
Michael T. Klare	"A Blueprint for Endless Interventions," *The Nation*, July 30-August 6, 1988.
Colin Leinster	"Vietnam Revisited: Turn to the Right?" *Fortune*, August 1, 1988.
William S. Lind	"An Operational Doctrine for Intervention," *Parameters*, December 1987.
Michael Massing	"Conventional Warfare," *The Atlantic Monthly*, January 1990.
Richard Morin	"Fifteen Years Later, the War Within Continues over Vietnam," *The Washington Post National Weekly Edition*, April 30-May 6, 1990.
Nguyen Van Canh	"Since the Fall of Saigon," *The World & I*, April 1987.
Keith B. Richburg	"Remember the War, Hanoi Implores— Because the U.S. Owes Us," *The Washington Post National Weekly Edition*, August 10, 1987.
Al Santoli	"Asylum and Assimilation in America," *The World & I*, May 1989.
Jonathan Schell	"Speak Loudly, Carry a Small Stick," *Harper's Magazine*, March 1989.
Larry Voeller	"The Vietnam Era Blues," *Newsweek*, September 5, 1988.
Paul A. Witteman	"Vietnam Fifteen Years Later," *Time*, April 30, 1990.

CHAPTER 4

How Has the Vietnam War Affected Veterans?

THE
VIETNAM
WAR

Chapter Preface

One of the most discussed Vietnam War topics has been the fate of the 2.8 million men and 10,500 women who served the U.S. in Vietnam. When these veterans returned home, many found that the American public did not welcome them back as it had welcomed the veterans of World War II. Vietnam veterans found themselves stereotyped as baby-killers, drug abusers, and psychopaths. Some veterans found the readjustment to civilian life difficult, and faced problems of divorce, unemployment, and substance abuse.

A widely recognized turning point in society's view of Vietnam veterans was the dedication of the Vietnam Veterans Memorial in Washington, D.C. in 1982. Since then, public recognition and respect for Vietnam veterans has grown. The medical community has also recognized the lasting severity of the physical and emotional traumas suffered by many Vietnam veterans, and has developed treatment and therapy programs. But people still debate the extent of the problems Vietnam veterans face and what society owes them today. The viewpoints in the following chapter examine these issues.

"About 470,000 of the approximately 3.14 million men who served in Vietnam 'are current cases of PTSD' [post-traumatic stress disorder]."

Vietnam Veterans Suffer from Psychological Problems

David Gelman

Many Vietnam veterans have blamed ongoing psychological problems, such as nightmares, guilt, and alcoholism, on their wartime experiences. The term post-traumatic stress disorder (PTSD) has been used to describe their condition. In the following viewpoint, David Gelman argues that many Vietnam veterans are affected by the disorder because of the traumatic experiences they had in Vietnam, and because of the mistreatment they suffered when they returned to the U.S. Gelman is a senior writer for *Newsweek*.

As you read, consider the following questions:

1. What important differences exist between Vietnam veterans and veterans of World War II, according to the author?
2. What are some of the symptoms of post-traumatic stress disorder that Gelman describes?

Sometimes you run across individuals who are really still in Vietnam, and you have to walk back to Vietnam with them and walk them back out. I must've been involved with 450 people over three years, and it gets to you.

More times than he cares to remember now, Frank Delfi has taken that walk to Vietnam and back again with stressed-out veterans of the war, trying to help them get their bearings. It was only a few years ago that he himself was grappling with "horrendous" headaches and sleeplessness, symptoms of the post-traumatic stress disorder (PTSD) that had plagued him since his own discharge from the Army in 1968. He had been practically living on aspirin and hoping he could get through a night without the "little dreams" that took him right back to the terrifying chaos of the 1968 Tet offensive. Now, at 41, Delfi is director of placement for the Vietnam Veterans Leadership Program in New York, a privately sponsored therapy and job-counseling program that helped him get his life under control.

To Delfi, the continued anguish of many Vietnam vets is a fact of his daily working life, although he thinks the media sometimes exaggerate the problem. There are those, nevertheless, who have remained sharply skeptical about the authenticity of these psychic casualties of the war. . . .

A Growing Number of PTSD Cases

In July 1988, however, the authors of a comprehensive five-year study by the Research Triangle Institute reported to Congress that 15 percent, or about 470,000, of the approximately 3.14 million men who served in Vietnam "are current cases of PTSD." (Around 7,000 women, mostly nurses, were also victims, the study said.) That figure was strikingly higher than the 66,000 total reported a few months earlier by the Centers for Disease Control. The two studies used somewhat different methods, and the discrepancy seemed bound to add tinder to an argument almost as politicized as the debate over the war itself. But the RTI researchers say their own survey, funded by the Veterans Administration, is the "most representative" yet. One difference, they note, is that the CDC asked veterans only about symptoms experienced in the month prior to the interviews. In fact, some health officials are convinced the incidence of PTSD is actually growing. . . .

Through the 1970s, psychiatrists themselves remained divided over the true extent of the problem. But in 1980, after years of astringent controversy, it was finally given a name and included a in the diagnostic manual of the American Psychiatric Association (DSM-III). The RTI report indicates there have been major advances in diagnosing PTSD since then. Doctors, nevertheless, are still not sure why some soldiers were hit by the disorder while the majority apparently came through unscathed. What we need to find out now, says Terence Keane, research coordinator of the RTI study, "is who does and who doesn't develop traumatic response."

PTSD is in the direct line of evolution from "shell shock" and "battle fatigue," names it carried in earlier wars. But those conditions were often short-lived. Doctors have been trying to understand what was different about Vietnam—why so many young survivors of the war seemed unable to reconnect with normal life, some plunging into drugs, alcohol and violence, others hunkering down and withdrawing—living "in a psychic Vietnam," as Dr. Harvey Schwartz, editor of the 1984 volume, "Psychotherapy of the Combat Veteran," characterized a vet he was treating.

Nightmares and Flashbacks

Danny Roth stared into the moonlit kill zone at the edge of the jungle and watched death crawl toward his platoon. The Viet Cong were moving into position for an assault. Roth eased the safety off his M-16 as his heart hammered against his chest. He gently squeezed the trigger and angry red tracers lit up the night as hundreds of guns on both sides exploded into action, muffling the screams of dying men.

That's when Roth (not his real name) snaps awake, forced back to reality by the sound of his own scream. The nightmare is an endless replay of combat he experienced in 1971 as an Army infantryman in Vietnam. "The hell of it is that the nightmare comes even during the day," said the southern Indiana veteran. "Something just triggers it, and there I am—a 20-year-old kid in a firefight."

The American Legion Magazine, May 1989.

One difference was the absence of a warm welcome for returning veterans. Most Vietnam GI's went to the war alone and came home alone, unlike their fathers in World War II who went and returned on troopships, in an aura of heroism, often with bands saluting them at dockside. Another was the age of the soldiers. It has often been said that this was a war fought mainly by the poor, but it was also perhaps our first war fought by adolescents. The average age of the Vietnam fighting man was 19.2 years, compared with 26 in World War II—"the youngest group we have fielded as a nation since the Civil War," according to Walter Penk, director of psychology for the department of mental health in Massachusetts. These were soldiers still in their formative years, a cohort particularly susceptible to

148

the traumatic, terror-filled "imprinting" many of them were later to have undergone.

For a time, it was thought that a victim had to be predisposed to it by childhood traumas or an unstable family background. But as the current, revised version of DSM-III defines it, it is the result of "an event that is outside the range of usual human experience and that would be markedly distressing to almost anyone." The definition is meant to cover not only war trauma but almost every sort of shock, from auto accidents to airplane hijackings. The hallmarks include recurring nightmares, involuntary memories, "hypervigilance"—the feeling of imminent danger—and "flashbacks," a vivid re-experiencing of the event. For some there may also be a long period of numbness in the wake of the trauma, one reason for the delayed reaction often associated with the syndrome.

Doctors have been trying to fight the image of returned veterans as "walking time bombs," waiting to explode at any provocation—a notion promoted in part by press accounts and television shows that never seem to tire of stories about berserk veterans. In truth, though there are no definitive statistics, rates of crime, suicide and drug and alcohol abuse among veterans are known to be high. According to a report released by the House Committee on Veterans Affairs in 1979, more than 400,000 vets were in prison, on probation or parole or awaiting trial. (No later estimates are available.) But while those numbers are disturbing, the average PTSD victim apparently leads a life of quieter desperation.

Moral Confusion

The Vietnam War was not only America's first losing war but probably its most unpopular. By early 1968, when the Tet offensive was perceived as a disastrous setback for the U.S. effort, the war was coming under furious attack at home. Many soldiers who started their service then began under a cloud of moral confusion. There was also the very nature of the fighting—sinister guerrilla warfare in which soldiers were often unsure who the enemy was. It was, especially, a war fought without boundaries, spilling over among a civilian population of women and children and constantly tumbling into transgressions. Beyond seeing close "buddies" killed—a shattering loss for adolescents—many GI's took part in atrocities or witnessed them. (One veteran tells of seeing his buddies detonate a grenade in a woman's vagina. Another was ordered to throw an old woman down a well, then drop a grenade on her.)

There are indications that in many cases of PTSD, some sort of social pathology was already at work. The RTI study, for instance, found the highest rates of PTSD among blacks (19 percent) and Hispanics (27 percent), many from troubled, unstable families. Schwartz recounts the case of "Patient B," a 33-year-old white man who came to a VA clinic for treatment. In the 13 years since his discharge he had been suffering from recurrent nightmares, outbursts of anger, headaches and mental lapses. One of nine children, he had grown up in terror of his brutal father, next to whom he felt small and inadequate. "With excitement and admiration he would describe in detail the power and grandeur of his father's 'tools'," notes Schwartz.

Reprinted by permission of NEA, Inc.

In Vietnam, besides losing many of his buddies, Patient B had one culminating experience: one day he saw a "frail old man" walking along a dike "just carrying a tool" and killed him with a single shot. "No one said anything," he recalled. On the contrary, his lieutenant, who had seen the shooting, promptly claimed it as his own kill, adding to his body count.

For some young soldiers, the treacherous, undefined Vietnam battlefields thus became a kind of free-fire zone of the mind. Under conditions that seemed to suspend the limits of permissible behavior, some GI's played out unconscious and murderous aggressions. They were different from ordinary psychiatric patients, says Schwartz, "because they didn't just fantasize killing a father or mother, they *did* it." Indeed, some of the combat stories doctors have had to listen to are so disturbing that the therapist's ability to hear them out without feeling revulsion for the patient has become an issue in the psychiatric literature about Vietnam veterans. Says Schwartz: "You have to be able to tolerate massive amounts of horrible effect."

Soldiers still of tender years looked to their officers as figures of parental authority who would put the stamp of approval or disapproval on their conduct. But that didn't always happen. Like Patient B's lieutenant, some officers tacitly or even explicitly approved the killing. Then the soldiers came home to a civilian world that sometimes openly reviled them or, in any event, failed to offer them the blessing that returning warriors traditionally have received from their elders. "It was a profound insult, a breaking of the covenant between a nation and its soldiers," says Erwin Parson, a consulting psychologist with the Vietnam Veterans Leadership Program.

Ultimately the soldiers were left with a burden of guilt they couldn't handle. Most therapists agree that unconscious guilt is "central" in the etiology of stress disorder. Buried guilt, fanned by a hostile reception at home, flares into rage; flight from guilt leads to withdrawal, or to the driving restlessness that impels many veterans to jump from job to job. . . .

Solid Proof

By now, according to staff psychiatrist Art Blank, the VA has treated more than half a million veterans and 150,000 family members. Scientifically, at least, there is little controversy left about the validity of the stress disorder. "It's as solid as anything," says psychiatrist Bessel van der Kolk of the Massachusetts Mental Health Center. "There is a very good animal model of inescapable response. Tortured animals show hyperactivity, hyperarousal, and they continue to react even to minor stimuli as if they were being re-exposed to the same shock."

Health officials now believe that given sufficient stress, anyone can fall victim to PTSD, regardless of family background. Although the disorder tended to strike most heavily at the blacks and Hispanics who largely fought the war, VA centers are beginning to see officers and other veterans from middle-class backgrounds. By no means have all PTSD sufferers come in out of the cold. Uncounted thousands more, among them World War II and Korean War vets, are believed to be still out there, wrestling with their demons. Doctors hope that with help now available, victims will no longer have to carry on their struggle alone. The Vietnam veterans are finally getting the recognition they sought, even if it had to be in illness rather than the triumph of homecoming.

"I've met hundreds of Viet vets over the years, and I've yet to encounter one who fits the prevailing stereotypes."

The Psychological Problems of Vietnam Veterans Are Exaggerated

William K. Lane Jr.

William K. Lane Jr. is a speech writer and Vietnam veteran. In the following viewpoint, he argues that the media and movies portray Vietnam veterans as losers or mentally ill. Lane maintains that these images are stereotypes, and that most Vietnam veterans have successfully readjusted to civilian life.

As you read, consider the following questions:

1. What does Lane find objectionable about movies such as *Platoon*?
2. How much effect does Lane believe Vietnam had on his life?
3. How does the author describe the Vietnam veterans he knew?

Movies about Vietnam are the latest phase in Hollywood's nonstop assault on the American spirit. The films are often accompanied, in the print media and on TV, by advice from Vietnam veterans groups, "outreach" organizations, and the like, that we who fought in that conflict should see these movies only with a "support group." One organization advised us not to see "Platoon" alone; another cautioned us to spend time "decompressing with friends after it." We've been told about the danger of "nightmares" and warned of the ultimate horror: "flashbacks." Jane Fonda, our dart-board version of World War II's Betty Grable, claims she and a group of veterans "wept" in a theater lobby after seeing the movie.

Excuse me while I barf.

This ludicrous blubbering and psychobabble has puzzled me for 17 years. Every unveiling of a Vietnam memorial on TV news seems to star the same two central-casting vets wearing fatigues—both bearded, one with pony tail—hugging each other and sobbing. It's embarrassing.

The other image is created by the cultural termites in Hollywood: the American soldier in Vietnam as racist, neurotic, drug-crazed, feral, a hopeless pawn of a rotten society sent to fight an unjust war. Even the cartoonish Rambo character is a societal misfit, a mumbling killer exorcising his demons in a revenge ritual.

The vast majority of men who fought in that war—people like me—simply do not fit any of those images. Many of us are embarrassed by them, especially in the presence of veterans of Iwo Jima and Midway and Pork Chop Hill—most of whom saw much more horror than Vietnam soldiers ever did and managed to continue their lives without whining, acting nutty, or looking for a free ride.

This is not to say that Nam was not a searing experience. Indulge me as I present some images I dredged up in an attempt to stimulate a few "flashbacks."

I arrived in Vietnam in early 1968, as green as the beret I wore, and was assigned to the Special Forces "A" team that had the dubious distinction, two weeks later, of being one of the first attacked during the Tet offensive. My memories of that battle are of the incredible roar and chaos that occurs when two rifle companies open up on each other; of a day and a night pinned down behind tombstones in a Buddhist cemetery; of picking up a terrible sweet smell for the first time and knowing instinctively that it was death.

I remember an old French priest who insisted I follow him during a lull in the battle because he wanted me to see a bullet in his church. The bullet turned out to be a howitzer shell that had come through an open window and embedded itself in the steps of the altar without exploding. We got the "bullet" out for him when things calmed down a week or so later, but I do remember genuflecting as I left the church in awe, and then going back to the grim work.

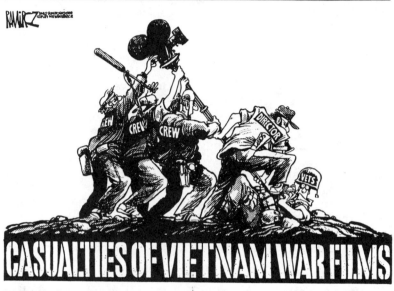

Ramirez/Copley News Service. Reprinted with permission.

I can still see the terror in the eyes of the North Vietnamese prisoners brought before me. I was the first American they had ever seen, tall and blond (then), and undoubtedly going to kill them. They nearly collapsed in relief when I handed each of them a few of my Luckies and told them, "No sweat."

I remember the exhilaration brought about by extreme fatigue and our victory over the North Vietnamese regiment that had invaded our area. And I recall the curses, the hatred we felt when the *New York Times* clips arrived claiming the Vietnamese and American victory in the Tet offensive was actually a defeat.

There were other vignettes that haven't faded: a boy in a nearby village with a twisted foot caused by a badly-healed break. We begged his mother for months to let us take him into Nha Trang and have it fixed. Finally she relented, tearfully, not quite trusting us. Our medic sneaked the boy into an American hospital under care of a doctor who was part of our conspiracy. We gave him back to his mother, in a cast, with a leg as good as new. The whole village got drunk with us.

We got drunk on Thanksgiving day as well, after the giggling Vietnamese told us the "deer" we had eaten with them for

154

Thanksgiving dinner was actually a dog.

I remember trying to cram a year of good times into a week of R&R in Singapore, and then landing back in Vietnam at the air base, hung over and depressed, only to be mortared in the terminal.

But many of the starkest of memories are the bad ones. A newly married lieutenant dead after less than a week in the country, a sergeant killed in a firefight when another American shot him accidentally, piles of dead North Vietnamese, dead South Vietnamese, dead Montagnards, a dead old man in his bed in a house wrecked by battle; heat, fear, concussion, the frenzy of fighting out of an ambush.

Bad things, but no worse than many other bad things in life: car wrecks, the death of loved ones. Being fired probably can be as traumatic as being fired upon. And besides, Nam was a long time ago.

I still know where a few of my teammates are. I get a few cards at Christmas. Sometimes I see one or two and hear about others. Some did a few more tours in Nam after I left. A couple are still in the Army. Some have done better than others, but I'll bet you this: None of them would need a "support group" to go see a movie. None of them would indulge in prattle about "post-traumatic-stress disorder" and how it caused them to beat up their wives or wet their beds. None of them would be a party to the Agent Orange hustle.

And none of them would go to an Army-Navy surplus store and buy jungle fatigues and put them on and hug each other and cry for the cameras because no one gave them a parade.

The men I knew in Vietnam didn't hate each other because of race. We weren't on drugs. We didn't murder civilians. We didn't hate the Army or LBJ [Lyndon Baines Johnson] or our country. We didn't feel America owed us a free ride because we spent time defending it. We were our own "support group" over there. We don't need one here.

I've met hundreds of Viet vets over the years, and I've yet to encounter one who fits the prevailing stereotypes. There are veterans from all our wars who are sick or depressed or drug-addicted, and by all means they deserve our help and comfort. Those who were legitimately disabled deserve a special, revered status in our society. But can't we stop the fictional stereotyping that simply doesn't fit the majority of Vietnam veterans?

Some of the bravest and best men that ever wore an American uniform fought in that war. They deserve better than to be caricatured by Hollywood and represented in the media as a legion of losers.

"Untold numbers of veterans . . . may be potential casualties of the herbicide."

Agent Orange Harmed Vietnam Veterans

The American Legion Magazine

The herbicide Agent Orange was used extensively by the U.S. military during the Vietnam War. Many soldiers who were exposed to Agent Orange later claimed to have suffered from health problems, including cancer and liver damage, and having children with birth defects. In 1988 Columbia University in New York and The American Legion, a national organization of military veterans, completed a five-year study on Vietnam veterans. The following viewpoint summarizes the study's findings on Agent Orange, and argues that a significant number of Vietnam veterans are at risk for ill health because of exposure to the chemical.

As you read, consider the following questions:

1. Why do the authors criticize U.S. government research on Agent Orange?
2. What are the three main conclusions of The American Legion/ Columbia University study regarding Agent Orange?
3. How should the federal government respond to the Agent Orange problem, according to the authors?

"Agent Orange: The Final Battle," *The American Legion Magazine*, March 1989. Reprinted by permission, *The American Legion Magazine*, © 1989.

As an Army rifleman in Cambodia in 1970, Andy Grimes of Trenton, Tenn., dodged Viet Cong snipers and ambushes, and edged his way through booby-trapped terrain where one wrong step could guarantee a ticket home in a body bag. Like other "grunts," Grimes welcomed the sight of barren land where jungle once stood because it robbed the enemy of a place to hide. The defoliant Agent Orange worked well.

A Rare Disease

Grimes returned from Southeast Asia believing the war was behind him. But in 1986, he was fighting for his life in another war: doctors diagnosed him as having a rare lymphoma type of cancer in the lower abdomen. Grimes sought disability benefits from the Veterans Administration, citing his personal physician's prognosis and copies of records showing that he had served in areas where Agent Orange was used extensively. His claim was denied.

Andy Grimes did not survive his latest war. He died Dec. 5, 1988, leaving behind his wife, Virginia, and daughter, Roxanne. Also left behind was the nagging question of whether his cancer was directly related to Agent Orange exposure.

"You won't find Andy Grimes' name carved on the Vietnam Veterans Memorial, but he probably was a casualty of that war, too," said Nat'l Cmdr. H.F. "Sparky" Gierke. "The tragedy is compounded by the untold numbers of veterans who also may be potential casualties of the herbicide."

Calls for Studies

Since 1978, The American Legion has demanded that the government determine if exposure to Agent Orange can be directly linked to consistent and often unique health problems reported by veterans. Some veterans, such as Grimes, have developed rare types of cancers; others have suffered liver damage, severe chloracne, chronic pain, numbness in extremities and benign fatty tumors. In addition, many veterans who served in areas where the defoliant was used have fathered children with serious birth defects.

The VA was charged by law with researching the Agent Orange connection, but made little progress. The Legion wanted the study in the hands of an independent agency. The VA finally conceded and turned the matter over to the Centers for Disease Control in 1983. After more than four years of study and spending millions of taxpayers' dollars, the CDC concluded there was not enough information to conduct a valid study.

Meanwhile, the Legion, fed up with the dead-end government efforts, began its own probe. Headed by Drs. Jeanne and Steven Stellman, The American Legion and Columbia University Study of Vietnam Veterans was launched to examine problems faced by Vietnam veterans, including Agent Orange exposure.

The study's findings were revealed in November 1988 and published in the scientific journal, *Environmental Research*, after undergoing peer review. The results discredited the government's claim that there were not enough American troops sufficiently exposed to the herbicide to carry out a study. The Stellmans examined the record of spray missions in Vietnam, and conducted a detailed survey of 6,810 randomly selected Legionnaires who served during the Vietnam era, 2,858 of whom were stationed in Southeast Asia. Study participants were classified into groups representing low, medium and high levels of Agent Orange exposure, and 102 of the men who actually handled the herbicide were placed in a separate category.

Dioxin Is Toxic

Sometimes it seems that the Department of Veterans Affairs refuses to consider data from any circumstance other than those absolutely comparable to the Vietnam situation—as if veterans are not humans, like other humans, and the dioxin in Agent Orange is not dioxin, like other dioxin. . . .

We understand to a limited extent why chemicals such as lead and dioxin have so many manifestations in human toxicity. This complexity does not prevent us from recognizing that they are toxic. It should not present an obstacle to the fair and expeditious compensation of those who accepted the responsibility of military service in the expectation of being fairly dealt with by their country.

Ellen K. Silbergeld, *American Legion Magazine*, December 1989.

Here's what the study concluded on Agent Orange exposure and the health effects on Vietnam veterans:

• Agent Orange exposure was related to conditions such as benign fatty tumors, acne occurring during adult years, skin rash with blisters and an increased sensitivity of eyes to light. These symptoms were notably pronounced among herbicide handlers.

• Exposure also was related to an increased risk of miscarriages among the Vietnam veterans' wives.

• The number of complaints of skin problems, fatigue, feeling faint, and general aches and colds were significantly higher among men who served in Vietnam than those who didn't. Veterans exposed to Agent Orange experienced increased incidence of those symptoms.

The study, however, did not examine the link between Agent Orange and cancer. "Our study specifically was designed not to determine whether a relationship exists between herbicides and cancer, because our study population was too small to answer the cancer question," said Dr. Jeanne Stellman.

Nevertheless, researchers and other medical experts long ago established that dioxin agents are carcinogenic, or cancer-causing. Agent Orange contains dioxin.

Rain of Terror

Between 1962 and 1971, 11.8 million gallons of Agent Orange were dumped throughout Vietnam, Cambodia and Laos to strip away jungle vegetation and deprive North Vietnamese forces of concealed sanctuaries and staging areas for ambushes.

During that nine-year period, Air Force C-123 cargo planes flew spraying missions in what was known as "Operation Ranch Hand." In addition, other missions were carried out via helicopters, boats, trucks, jeeps, personnel carriers and by troops in the field, who carried the defoliant in backpacks.

In conducting the Legion study, the Stellmans examined the records of the National Academy of Sciences' HERBS tape, which documents 9,495 spray missions, including the dates, chemical agents, amounts, locations and purpose of the missions. The researchers also examined the U.S. Army and Joint Services Environmental Support group's records of spray missions. Armed with that data and the responses of those who participated in the study, the Stellmans concluded that exposure to Agent Orange can be adequately matched by comparing troop movements with spray missions. That finding contradicted CDC's claim that Agent Orange exposure cannot be adequately documented. In an editorial preceding the report of the Legion study in the December 1988 issue of *Environmental Research*, researcher Dr. Michael Gochfeld wrote: "Such a position (CDC) is unduly narrow. If accessibility of high-quality exposure data were the gold standard, virtually no occupational epidemiology would ever be performed. . . . Previous studies that have calculated morbidity, reproductive and mortality outcomes for Vietnam veterans as a group are subject to misinterpretation. The present paper (Legion-Columbia study) explains how to avoid the pitfalls. . . ."

In 1976, Maude DeVictor, a VA caseworker in Chicago, noticed a pattern of recurring health problems among veterans who reported having been exposed to a great deal of chemical defoliants during their tours in Vietnam. After extensive research, the trail led to Agent Orange and its deadly dioxin contaminants.

The discovery resulted in a media blitz about the mysterious defoliant and its possible effects on exposed veterans. Researchers were forced to reexamine their earlier conclusions.

In 1978, the VA, which had not recognized herbicide-related illnesses and health problems, reluctantly began to give veterans

Agent Orange examinations. Since 1986, the VA also has been responsible for providing treatment for those who can prove their health problems are attributable to exposure, a requirement that many veterans, including Andy Grimes, have found is almost impossible to prove.

Dan Wasserman, © 1987, Los Angeles Times Syndicate. Reprinted with permission.

"Andy felt as if nobody in the government cared about him," said Annette Grimes, a relative. "He felt his cancer was related to Agent Orange and he died without ever having that answer.". . .

"Our study clearly documents that men classified as having been exposed to Agent Orange, especially those who directly handled the chemicals, have statistically higher levels of health complaints," Dr. Jeanne Stellman said. "The pattern of those complaints is consistent with health effects seen in laboratory animals exposed to Agent Orange."

"One important finding of the study is that there is a definite need for further research," Gierke said. "To date, the federal government has not carried out its responsibility to Vietnam veterans and their families in conducting such studies. The Legion will never back off of this issue until it is resolved."

For Andy Grimes and numerous other Vietnam veterans, there remains another unanswered question: Do their names also belong on the "Wall"?

"No definitive link has been found between exposure to the herbicide and the veterans' health problems."

Agent Orange May Not Have Harmed Vietnam Veterans

Gary Taubes

Gary Taubes is a contributing editor of *Discover*, a monthly science magazine. In the following viewpoint, he questions assertions that many Vietnam veterans were harmed by Agent Orange. Government studies, Taubes argues, have shown that only a small percentage of veterans were significantly exposed to Agent Orange. Furthermore, Taubes believes that studies have not shown a link between exposure and health problems.

As you read, consider the following questions:

1. What in Taubes' opinion is the prevailing myth about Agent Orange?
2. According to the author, why is it hard to prove that dioxin harms human beings?
3. Why did the Centers for Disease Control conclude that a study of the effects of Agent Orange was unnecessary, according to Taubes?

Gary Taubes, "Unmasking Agent Orange," *Discover*, April 1988, © 1988 Discover Publications. Reprinted with permission.

Agent Orange first became notorious around the time Paul Reutershan was dying. The two events were related. A helicopter crew chief in Vietnam, Reutershan had flown hundreds of supply missions into combat zones and survived. In 1978, eight years after his tour of duty came to an end, he was brought down by a cancer so virulent that his doctors could no longer identify the organ tissue from which it had erupted. He was 28 years old.

Before he died, Reutershan sued Dow Chemical, Monsanto, and Diamond Shamrock, all of which had produced Agent Orange, the chemical defoliant used by the military in Vietnam. The case was later extended to eight other chemical companies and was joined by a total of 250,000 veterans and their kin. These were young men suffering from cancer or the relatives of men who had already died of cancer; they were men who had fathered children with birth defects; men who had simply never felt well since their years in the war; men who were anguished, pained, sick. They were men for whom no legal or scientific argument could change the fact that they were dying or the belief that they soon would be.

In 1984 the case was settled out of court. The settlement fund, whose distribution has been held up by ongoing legal disputes, is now worth $270 million—which sounds like a lot until you consider that a quarter-million people have claims on the fund. In any event, no amount of money would be likely to relieve the veterans' anxiety. And yet, as Judge Jack B. Weinstein of the federal district court in Brooklyn suggested at the time of the settlement, the veterans had not succeeded in justifying that anxiety, understandable as it was, with scientific evidence.

No Scientific Evidence

The scientific side of the Agent Orange story is this: in spite of years of effort by dozens of researchers who have spent tens of millions of dollars, no definitive link has been found between exposure to the herbicide and the veterans' health problems.

What's more, a study by the Centers for Disease Control in Atlanta suggests that such a link may never be established for the vast majority of veterans. CDC researchers had been charged by Congress with determining once and for all what effects exposure to Agent Orange had had on ground soldiers in Vietnam. In August 1987 the researchers reported that they had failed—for the simple reason that they could not find enough veterans who had been exposed to the herbicide. According to the CDC, even veterans who attributed their health problems to Agent Orange showed no more signs of contamination than the average man on the street.

Such findings could not fail to be controversial. They contradicted a prevailing myth: that most of the more than 2.5 million men who served in Vietnam, on top of having to fight an ill-conceived and unpopular war, on top of coming home to indifference and even scorn, had actually been poisoned by their own government and by careless and greedy chemical manufacturers. The CDC study has not shaken that perception among spokesmen for the veterans. If the CDC couldn't find many vets contaminated by Agent Orange, these critics suggest, it was because the CDC didn't look hard enough. Or it simply didn't want to find them.

A Reassurance

The CDC, for its part, has tried to give the results a more positive meaning. After all, if only a very small percentage of Vietnam ground troops were exposed to Agent Orange, as the study suggests, then most veterans don't have to worry about the potential health effects of exposure. "We have been trying to play it square with the veterans," says Robert Worth, head of the CDC study. "On one side you have this tremendous perceptual problem, unquestionably attributing tragedy to Agent Orange exposure. It has been internalized by thousands and thousands of vets. Many feel great but are worried about the future. The message we're putting out, I hope, should be comforting."

No Abnormal Health Problems

No scientific evidence had ever been produced to support the charges that Agent Orange exposure in Vietnam had caused everything from multiple sclerosis to cancer in the veterans and birth defects in their children. Comprehensive physical exams of the men who had done the spraying of Agent Orange and had the heaviest exposure to it were undertaken by the Air Force annually, beginning in 1982. These revealed no abnormal health problems in either the veterans or their offspring. Several other studies had come up with similar results, but none of these findings laid the controversy to rest.

One reason was that our news media gave great publicity to the touching tales of veterans who claimed that their health had been irreparably damaged by Agent Orange and little or no publicity to the scientific evidence that no causal link could be established.

Reed Irvine, *The Washington Times*, June 2, 1988.

This reassurance, if it is accepted as such, has been a long time coming. It is now nearly two decades since the government, alerted to possible dangers, put a stop in 1970 to the wholesale spraying of Agent Orange in Vietnam. By then some

11 million gallons of the stuff had been sprayed over an area as large as Connecticut. The purpose of this remarkable military strategy was not, of course, to poison American ground troops; it was to protect them from ambush by destroying the enemy's jungle cover.

Nor are the active ingredients of Agent Orange, the chemicals 2,4-D and 2,4,5-T, the main source of concern. The primary threat to the veterans' health comes from a minor contaminant in the mixture, a by-product of the manufacturing process: 2,3,7,8-tetrachlorodibenzo-p-dioxin, or simply dioxin for short. The concentration of dioxin in Agent Orange varied widely, but it is thought to have been on average about two parts per million; if so, then about 22 gallons was sprayed over Vietnam.

Dioxin is often called the most toxic synthetic chemical known to man, although that label is exactly what is in doubt. Its toxicity to animals has been proved in test after test: it kills guinea pigs, for example, in exceptionally minute doses. When administered over long periods to rats and mice, it causes birth defects and cancer.

Dioxin's Effects Unclear

But dioxin's effects on human beings are far from clear. There is no straightforward way to extrapolate toxicity measurements from animals to humans, or even from one animal to another. (For example, a dose of dioxin that would kill one hamster would kill 5,000 guinea pigs.) Nevertheless, some investigators have tried to extrapolate their findings. The resulting estimates of dioxin's cancer-causing power differ by a factor of at least 1,000. Recently the trend seems to be toward lower estimates; the Environmental Protection Agency, for one, is thinking of reducing its rating by a factor of 16—although that would still leave dioxin at the top of the agency's list of carcinogens.

The fact is that animal studies alone can never settle the issue of dioxin's danger to human beings. And since researchers cannot do laboratory experiments with humans, they must ultimately resort to epidemiology, with its painstaking methods and often ambiguous results.

An epidemiological exposure study typically has three parts. First you find a group of people who have been exposed to the suspected toxicant. Then you determine if the group has been more prone to particular diseases than the rest of the population. Finally, if there has been an excess incidence of some disease, you try to decide, by excluding all other possible factors, whether the excess is a result of exposure to the substance in question.

After all that effort you will most likely end up with an inconclusive result. If your study finds a correlation between exposure and the incidence of disease, that finding will still have to be duplicated many times before it gains general credence; it took decades, for example, to establish that cigarette smoking causes lung cancer. If your study finds nothing, it may mean there was nothing to find; or it may mean you botched the investigation.

A Money Grab

Following in the unpatriotic and greedy steps of some Revolutionary War soldiers, Coxey's Army and World War I bonus-march veterans, Vietnam vets are on the verge of enrichment from government coffers.

The money grab would yield payments for treating a variety of ailments such as chloracne or soft-tissue sarcoma on the unproven assumption that the diseases were caused by exposure to Agent Orange.

This type of fiscal extravagance would bankrupt the nation and foster irresponsibility if its rationale applied evenhandedly to all victims of misfortune.

Bruce Fein, *USA Today*, July 14, 1989.

After a number of such studies the threat posed by dioxin has stubbornly remained an on-the-one-hand-this-on-the-other-hand-that issue. On the one hand, Swedish lumberjacks exposed to dioxin-contaminated herbicides have been found to have an abnormally high rate of the rare cancers known as non-Hodgkins lymphomas; on the other hand, similar studies among Finnish forestry workers and New Zealand herbicide sprayers came up negative. A 1986 study of Kansas farmers, which is sometimes cited by veterans, found a significant excess of lymphomas, but the herbicides used by the farmers did not contain dioxin. A study of children born to Vietnam veterans in the Atlanta area revealed a slight excess of certain birth defects in children whose fathers claimed they had been exposed to Agent Orange; but studies in Arkansas, Michigan, Australia, and Hungary found no link between dioxin and birth defects. About the only thing everyone agrees on is that dioxin can cause a particularly severe form of acne.

The CDC's Agent Orange study, it had been hoped, would help cut through these contradictions. The goal was to find and examine a representative sample of Vietnam ground troops—the CDC hoped for at least 2,000—who had been highly exposed to Agent Orange.

"It was believed," says Worth, "that a fairly high proportion of men had been exposed on the ground in Vietnam. In the course of questioning, more than half the vets will say they were exposed, that they walked through defoliated areas. More than a quarter will say they were very directly exposed, in that they were present when spraying was done or did some spraying themselves. That was the perception in the minds of veterans, and that was the motivation for doing these studies."

To get a representative sample, the CDC could not rely solely on the veterans' testimony. Therefore, with the help of military officials, CDC investigators combed records of troop movements and herbicide spraying in Vietnam. . . .

This approach turned out to have serious problems. The main one was the quality of the military records: records of both spraying missions and troop locations were spotty. . . .

By the summer of 1986, the CDC had found a different and more effective approach: a blood test that could directly measure dioxin levels and thereby indirectly measure a veteran's exposure to Agent Orange. . . .

Worth and his colleagues thereupon administered blood tests to 665 ground troops identified in the aborted large-scale study. Some of the veterans, according to the hit model, had received five hits or more (the CDC workers tested as many as possible of this group); some had received between one and four hits; and some had received none. A quarter of the veterans claimed to have been directly exposed to Agent Orange, and 70 percent said they had walked through defoliated areas. As an experimental control the CDC tested the blood of 103 veterans who had also served during the late 1960s, but not in Vietnam.

The results of the tests were striking. Only two of the Vietnam veterans had blood dioxin levels higher than 20 parts per trillion, which according to the CDC is the upper limit of what can be expected normally. Moreover, veterans who had received many hits or who said they had been exposed to Agent Orange did not have higher levels of dioxin in their blood. The median level for all the exposure groups was between 3.2 and 4.3 parts per trillion—the same as for the non-Vietnam veterans and about what one would find in a typical resident of an industrialized society.

Two Conclusions

The CDC drew two main conclusions. First, as Worth says, "we have evidence for the first time that only a very small proportion of ground troops show significant exposure to Agent Orange. In essence, you can walk through a defoliated area or be around where they're spraying, and it doesn't necessarily mean that you'll get a significant dose." In other words, although ground troop veterans may be remembering their experiences with Agent Orange quite correctly, most of them were probably not contaminated.

The second conclusion followed naturally. There was no point, said the CDC, in pursuing a study of the effects of Agent Orange on a large body of exposed men because, short of spending unimaginable sums of money, no such large body could be found. In endorsing the CDC report, the Congressional Office of Technology Assessment put the matter bluntly: "There cannot be a general study of Agent Orange on ground troops.". . .

While the debate over the CDC study continues, the Air Force Ranch Hand study has cast more doubt on dioxin's toxicity. Everyone agrees the Ranch Handers were exposed to Agent Orange; they handled the stuff. (Indeed, the CDC found that some Ranch Handers still have high blood levels of dioxin, a few as high as 300 parts per trillion.)

Unnecessary Fear

The position of the majority of scientists who have examined the human health effects of dioxin is that little or no harm has been done. . . . The saga of dioxin shows that simply linking exposure and a group of diseases may provoke unnecessary and unrealistic alarm and fear. After a decade and a half of studies and debates, harm from environmental exposure to dioxin has been assessed as nondetectable.

Michael Gough, *Dioxin, Agent Orange*, 1986.

Nevertheless, according to a report released by the Air Force in October 1987, "the Ranch Hand population is faring about the same as the comparison group, with no unusual causes of death, increased frequency of death, or evidence suggesting death at younger ages." The report goes on to say that there isn't enough evidence "to implicate a causal relationship between herbicide exposure and adverse health in the Ranch Hand group."

While the CDC study suggests that only a small percentage of veterans were contaminated by Agent Orange, the Ranch Hand study suggests that so far those veterans have not suffered adverse health effects as a result. Of course, that conclusion could change. Cancers may take a long time to develop, even longer than 20 years. The issue may not be settled in a definitive scientific way for quite some time. In the meantime, Vietnam veterans who are healthy today have every reason to be cautiously optimistic.

167

"Those on both sides of the Vietnam conflict were exposed to and participated in consciousness-altering, irreversible, massive evil."

The War Made Veterans Moral Cynics

William P. Mahedy

William P. Mahedy is an Episcopal priest. He was an army chaplain during the Vietnam War, and has counseled veterans. His writings include the book *Out of the Night*. In the following viewpoint, he argues that the greatest damage the Vietnam War inflicted on veterans may have been spiritual: veterans lost their faith in God, the U.S., and humanity.

As you read, consider the following questions:

1. What American myths does the author say were destroyed by the Vietnam War?
2. Why do veterans have trouble articulating their feelings about the Vietnam War, according to Mahedy?
3. What limits does Mahedy see to both conservative and liberal views of the war?

"When I went to Vietnam, I believed in Jesus Christ and John Wayne. After Vietnam, both went down the tubes. It don't mean nothin'." Though I have heard other veterans say the same thing a thousand times in different ways, this statement made by a vet in a rap group is, for me, the most concise unmasking of American civil religion and its mythology of war. The loss of faith and meaning experienced by countless Vietnam veterans is now widely known, despite the best efforts of the religious and political right to incorporate Vietnam into the classical mythology of war. If the United States government is to rearm the country for the struggle against "godless communism"—including preparation for a protracted nuclear war—it must first encourage the remythologizing of America. Foreign policy must be consistent with our national myth: we are God's chosen people in all that we undertake. We believe America has a divine mandate to evangelize the world to its own political and economic systems. War is the sacred instrument, the great cultic activity, whereby this mission is achieved. Jesus Christ and John Wayne must again be linked after their brief separation by Vietnam.

We Cannot Admit the Truth

President Ronald Reagan has declared the Vietnam war a noble cause and the right wing has unleashed its fury against those who question the traditional mythology. The Reagan administration's attempt to dismantle the controversial Vietnam Veterans' Outreach Program shortly after taking office was consistent with this remythologizing: If the administration were to admit that the last war caused serious psychological, moral and spiritual problems, then it would be more difficult to prepare the public for a similar conflict or for a much larger conflagration. The truth about the pain, anger and disillusionment of the Vietnam veterans cannot be admitted if one espouses the traditional American civil religion. Having invested our political and cultural systems with religious characteristics, we must necessarily interpret our historical experience in terms of a sacred dimension. We must forever remain the chosen people, the "city on the hill" of our myth of origin. We cannot wage mere wars; we must fight crusades against the infidels. . . .

The Vietnam war provided no transcendent meaning by which the national purpose could be reinterpreted and transposed into a new key. War was, for the first time in American history, experienced by great numbers of its participants as sin. Psychotherapy is uneasy with the notion of sin, as are most Americans of the late 20th century. As a result, much of what the veterans have to say cannot even be articulated, much less understood. The language and the concepts they need no longer exist within the arena of public discourse.

169

REBUILDING
VIETNAM

Roy Justus, *The Star Tribune*. Reprinted with permission.

A large segment of the American religious community (which does possess the linguistic and philosophical tools necessary to deal with the moral and religious questions raised by Vietnam) chooses not to see the war as sin. In *The Unfinished War: Vietnam and the American Conscience*, Walter Capps argues that the "rise of Protestant conservatism . . . or the new religious right bears direct connection with individual and corporate wrestling over the ramifications of the Vietnam experience." Viewing the outcome of the war as a defeat of the forces of good at the heads of the powers of evil, the religious right has enshrouded itself within the American myth of origin. The Soviet Union is seen as a supernaturally evil entity which must be defeated by the United States—God's Kingdom—in an apocalyptic drama. But this false mythology, unmasked by the Vietnam experience, is certain to prove once again its utter moral and religious bankruptcy. Reflecting on Vietnam might provide some insights into the religious underpinnings which seem always to lock us into paths leading to disaster.

An Inability to Discuss Vietnam

Taylor Stevenson diagnoses the nature of the Vietnam wound as "defilement"; i.e., coming into contact with an object which "has been culturally designated as being unclean." That there is a good bit of truth in this assessment is demonstrated by the curious fact that many Vietnam veterans describe themselves as unclean. They lament the absence (or, in the case of the Washington observance, the delay) of the cleansing rituals of return, such as parades or a hero's welcome, that a society usually grants to its warriors. The almost total inability both of veterans and of the American public to discuss Vietnam for so many years is a clear indication of defilement. Stevenson sees this defilement as resulting from the breaking of two prerational taboos. These two sacred beliefs are part of American civil religion: (1) America is innocent, and (2) America is powerful. Stevenson writes:

> *America is innocent/powerful.* It is an implication of this innocency that America deserves to be peaceful and prosperous. A further implication here is that America's exercise of power is an innocent exercise of power necessary for our peace and prosperity. We were not "taught" this in any formal sense. It was not necessary to be taught this because this innocency is not a matter of idea or concept or doctrine; rather, it is a part of the texture of growing up in the United States. It is part of our story of how things *are*, how reality is structured, how life flows for us, and so on. Any violation of this asserted innocency is profoundly disturbing to our individual and social sense of structure and power. . . .
>
> What breaks this taboo and brings a sense of defilement? Any situation or event which challenges or defeats the taboo and all that the taboo protects. Did we go into Vietnam originally under the taboo "America is innocent?" The evidence is overwhelming that, for the vast majority of Americans, we did (whatever reservations some had concerning Asian land wars).

Those on both sides of the Vietnam conflict were exposed to and participated in consciousness-altering, irreversible, massive evil. Atrocity, hatred, wholesale slaughter and barbarous acts of all kinds are the stuff of war. In the name of innocent America and its god, the GIs performed their duty in the great cultic act of war. But the myth was shattered. Neither they nor their country and its god were innocent. Perhaps, had the wages of sin been victory, a belief in our innocence could have been restored; but we were defeated. The other illusion, that of power, was also shattered. The warriors, their nation and its god were shown to be powerless. The taboos had been broken. We had sinned, and the wages of sin was death. Only in this context can the pervasive loss of faith among the veterans be understood and discussed.

Innocence Destroyed

What is most clear to me now is that I knew and understood all the political issues of the time. I saw why we were there and what we were doing, and why I should do my part. And at the foundation of my understanding was trust. I trusted and believed in the essential goodness of our leaders, and in the correctness of their perceptions. There was a deeply rooted belief in me that my country was not capable of doing evil in the world. The Vietnam experience has affected us all in many ways, and the most significant has been the profound change in that belief. . . .

I came to the certain knowledge that my country was capable of doing folly, that we Americans have the capacity to do evil in the world.

James N. Kennedy, letter, *Los Angeles Times*, October 1, 1983.

If, as John Wheeler writes, "God acting about us and through us redeems the brokenness of Vietnam," then this God can only be the God revealed to us in the Hebrew and Christian Scriptures. The veteran who told me that 500 years of life would not be sufficient to atone for what he did in Vietnam is quite correct, for those he killed would still be dead. Only death will erase the emotional and spiritual scars inflicted upon the widows and orphans of his victims. The veteran who asked me, "Where was God . . . when the rounds were coming in at Khe Sanh?" asked the right question. The mystery of iniquity is too profound for the American tribal god. Religious conservatives who retreat from evil and identify religion with feeling good about Jesus, with the conversion experience and with the better life are not really prepared to grapple with the questions raised by war. Neither are the liberals who believe that personhood and human fulfillment are the end products of religion. The former construct religious and emotional defenses to insulate themselves from evil, and the latter often underestimate its power. . . .

For post-Christian vets, those whose faith was destroyed by Vietnam, I believe the most powerful single utterance in Scripture is the utterance of Jesus on the cross: "My God, my God, why have you abandoned me?" Quite clearly, they too have walked the way of the cross, and the words of the psalmist are their words too. The tragedy is that no one has pointed out this connection. Nor has anyone dealt with the next and crucial step that must be taken by those who have experienced great evil and perceived its relationship to the cross. With Jesus, one must be able to say, "Father, into your hands I commend my spirit." All that has happened to the veterans in Vietnam and since Vietnam—their broken lives, broken bodies and shattered dreams—must be placed in the hands of the Father. Experiential knowledge of the monstrous evil in the world and the recognition of humankind's utter inability to achieve any real shalom elicit the cry of agony. The next step requires the leap of faith, for the experience of evil is really the perception of God's absence from the world precisely in those situations which seem to demand a providential presence. To understand the apparent absence of God as one mode of his presence requires, first of all, the destruction of the American graven image, with its promise of innocence restored and power regained.

Rewriting History

In more than ten years of working with Vietnam veterans, I have seen many discover the true nature of their wound. Although therapy, jobs and benefits may be helpful in healing some of the hurt, the real source of the alienation and rage is gradually disclosed: it is the death of the national god. For many veterans this abyss is too deep. To survive they must rewrite the history of Vietnam in their own minds and hearts. Beating the drums of war again seems the only way to justify their own war. For others, a life of service to fellow veterans and to society is the way to overcome the evil they have experienced. The enormous dedication and selflessness shown by those in the self-help centers, in the outreach programs and in the political groups can be explained in terms of deliverance from evil. Some even articulate their ideals in religious terms: the Beatitudes and the prayer of St. Francis. . . .

The Vietnam experience has not yet been publicly connected with the dark night of the soul or with any theology of the cross. Yet I am aware of no other Christian point of reference adequate to it. Everything else "don't mean nothin'."

"What impresses me most about the vets I know is the sensibility that has emerged among them in recent years: a particular kind of moral seriousness which is unusual in America."

The War Developed Veterans' Moral Sensitivity

Peter Marin

Peter Marin is a writer and a teacher. Shortly before writing the article from which the following viewpoint is excerpted, he attended the first New York state convention of the Vietnam Veterans of America. He was greatly impressed with the sensitivity and generosity of the people he met there. In this viewpoint he describes the sense of moral complexity which the vets have developed and from which he believes the nation can learn.

As you read, consider the following questions:

1. What does the author mean by the "orphan effect"?
2. Why does Marin believe that the Vietnam war had a greater psychological impact on the participants than did earlier wars?
3. Why does Marin fear that the moral depth the veterans have developed may go to waste?

Peter Marin, "What the Vietnam Vets Can Teach Us," *The Nation*, November 27, 1982, © 1982 The Nation Company, Inc. Reprinted with permission.

What impresses me most about the vets I know is the sensibility that has emerged among them in recent years: a particular kind of moral seriousness which is unusual in America, one which is deepened and defined by the fact that it has emerged from a direct confrontation not only with the capacity of others for violence and brutality but also with their own culpability, their sense of their own capacity for error and excess. Precisely the same kinds of experiences that have produced in some vets the complex constellations of panic from which they seem unable to recover have engendered in others an awareness of moral complexity and human tragedy unlike anything one is likely to find elsewhere in America today. . . .

These are vets who have, quite literally, brought one another back from the dead, often saved one another from suicide. Their relationships are full of a tenderness and generosity that is rare among American men—at least in public. (Sometimes they themselves are blissfully unaware of it; at others, when they notice it, they seem astonished.) I cannot remember seeing anything like it save among black college students in the late 1960s or among civil rights workers and elderly blacks in the South or—oddly enough—among the members of a fraternity to which I belonged in the 1950s, who seemed, beyond all rhetoric, to be genuinely brotherly toward one another.

Seeking Justice

It is this capacity for generosity, this kind of learned concern, which colors their moral sensibility, as if there were still at work in them a moral yearning or innocence that had somehow been deepened, rather than destroyed, by the war. A few days after I came home from my stay with the vets, a friend asked me: "Well, what is it they really want?" And I said, without thinking, "Justice." That is what they want, but it is not justice for themselves—though they would like that too. They simply want justice to *exist*, for there to be justice in the world: some moral order, a moral order maintained by other men and women one can trust. Their yearning is made all the more poignant by the fact that they still do not understand that if justice is to exist, they will have to be the ones who *create* rather than receive it. They do not yet—not *yet*—see it as their own work, not because they are lazy, but simply because it is not a role they associate with themselves. Like most Americans, they do not have a sense of themselves as makers and sustainers of moral values, even though, without knowing it, that is what many of them have become. . . .

It is, paradoxically, the vets' yearning for goodness, for something to believe, which fuels their desire for justice but also makes them vulnerable to rhetoric and ritual, just as it did long ago when they went off to war.

One must remember: these were the good children. Several of them had fathers who served in World War II and passed on to them a sense of obligation and a belief in the glory of war. Many others—a surprising number, in fact—were Catholics who were inspired at an early age by John Kennedy's call to "ask what you can do for your country"; in fighting Communism (one must not forget how rigorously at the time American Catholicism was intent on confronting Communism everywhere), they would satisfy not only their parents, teachers and priests but also God and the Pope and the President—all at once. They were, in short, those whose faith in their elders, and in American myths and the American order of things, was so strong, so innocent, that war seemed beyond all doubt a good thing, a form of virtue.

Transforming Experience

No greater moral crime has been committed by the critics of the Vietnam War than to depersonalize and discredit the profound personal, transforming experience of the combat veteran. . . .

Whether the American wars of this century were a waste because politicians made them so is really irrelevant. Their meaning and significance for the surviving veteran is that when faced with the most personal, intense experience of his entire life he met the test and became part of the Brotherhood of the Brave.

Jeffrey St. John, *Conservative Digest*, December 1982.

And largely because their belief was so strong at the start—not only in the war but in all authority—their disillusionment and subsequent sense of loss were much stronger. One is tempted to call this an "orphan effect." They were cut off from any sustaining world. Church, state, parents, politicians, Army officers—all the hierarchical sources of moral truth and authority dissolved around them during the war, leaving them exposed without consolation to the stark facts of human culpability and brutality. I remember a remark I heard a vet make. He had said that he wondered if the Vietnamese people would ever forgive him for what he did. When someone asked whether he worried about God forgiving him, he answered, "*My* problem is that I haven't yet learned how to forgive *God.*"

Effects of Vietnam

When I am asked, as I often am, why the Vietnam War so much affected—and so adversely affected—these young men, I am always surprised by the question, because the answers seem to me so obvious.

In the first place, it is probable that all wars have devastating effects upon the men they use—and these were not men when they fought but adolescents, averaging just about 19 years of age. It is hard to believe that something similar to what the soldiers in Vietnam felt was not felt by the men involved in the pointless horrors of trench warfare in World War I; and I cannot help thinking about what one vet told me in Rochester about his father and World War II:

> He never talked much about it except for the usual glorious things, about service to the country and becoming a man. But every year, on New Year's Day, he would lock himself into his den and get dead drunk. He never explained why he did it, but I think now he was remembering the war and mourning. Once, just once, after I got back from Nam, he asked me what it was like, and then he began talking about his war and what he had seen and how it had felt, the killing and the death, and he didn't really feel very much different about it than I did about Nam. It was simply that he had kept it to himself.

For another thing, although what happened to many men in Vietnam did happen to other men in other wars, the cumulative psychological effects were much greater. War, to be sure, is hell, but the effects of this one were compounded by its specific characteristics, as witnessed by the fact that a higher percentage of veterans emerged from this war with psychological disturbances than, as far as we know, from any previous war. (Without question, the rate of suicide and attempted suicide is higher among Vietnam vets than among those of other wars.) Moreover, the attention paid to the damages wrought upon the veterans by this war has been much greater than in the past.

A Bad War

There are other elements that make the Vietnam War different from and even worse than other wars. Even now most Americans do not realize the extent to which it was marked by arbitrary killing and the murder of civilians—out of either official policy or the casual, recreational or simply half-mad behavior of individual men apparently subject to neither internal nor external constraint. It was a war in which innocents became fair game and in which our soldiers—who went to war convinced they were saviours and guardians of freedom—found themselves perceived by the civilian population as intruders, conquerors and even murderers. Their military leaders at several levels of command proved to be venal, dishonest or stupid, and everywhere around them flourished forms of American corruption and vice—black-marketeering, profiteering, thievery—which most of them had never seen close up before. It was a bad war fought for all the wrong reasons in all the wrong ways, and one could hardly avoid seeing that after being in it for a short while. All of the death, and all of the risk, and even all of the camaraderie and bravery that mark the lives of soldiers anywhere, even those engaged in wrong causes—all of that was rendered meaningless and unnecessary because the war itself was so obviously a bad one.

And there is, finally, one other reason for the Vietnam vets' special pain: we have, as a people, and largely without knowing it, shifted our attitudes toward war, outgrowing the ease with which we may once have accepted violence. Cultures *do* grow up; just as certain moral attitudes can atrophy, others can develop. Many Americans are no longer able to accept without question or horror the nature of war; indeed, it may well be that in future wars (save for the most obviously self-defensive) many combatants will feel, afterward, what the vets now feel about Vietnam. In short, the vets may be experiencing, as their *individual* pain, the half-conscious tensions and confusions that Americans, as a society, now bring to violence and war.

Commitment and Love

There grew up in Vietnam combat units a sense of commitment and love among the men who lived, laughed, suffered and died together. You took your turn on point, pushing into the terrible unknown of the jungle or down an exposed rice-paddy dike, you went up a hill under fire, you crawled out after the wounded —not for your country: you did it for your buddies.

William Broyles Jr., *Newsweek*, November 22, 1982.

Therefore, more than veterans of any other wars past, what these men have been forced to confront is *their own capacity for error*; they understand that whatever they experienced—the horror, the terror—has its roots and complements in their own weaknesses and mistakes. For them, all conversation about human error or evil is a conversation about themselves; they are pushed past smug ideology and the condemnation of others to an examination of the world that is an examination of self. They know there is no easy relation between one's self-image and the consequences of one's actions. They know too that whatever truths one holds at any given moment will turn out to be if not mistaken then at least incomplete, and that often one's opponents or antagonists will turn out to have been more right than one thought and probably as serious in intention as oneself. Because they cannot easily divide the world into two camps, and because they cannot easily claim virtue while ascribing evil to others, they inhabit a moral realm more complex than the one in which most others live. They know that a moral life means an acknowledgement of guilt as well as a claim to virtue, and they have learned—oh, hardest lesson of all—to judge their own actions in terms of their irrevocable consequences to others. . . .

Wasteful Isolation

But this moral depth, this seriousness, may well go to waste—that is what is most poignant about it. The vets for the most part remain so isolated, so locked into their own pain, that there are few avenues for what is within them to make its way into the larger world or be sustained and referred by the larger world. If someone somewhere would take the trouble to draw forth from the veterans what it is they feel, think and know, or to convince them to speak, all of us would be better off.

It is probably true, as Karl Jaspers pointed out almost four decades ago in talking to the German people about guilt, that people can look closely at their own moral guilt only when others around them are willing to consider *their* lives in the same way. This is precisely what the vets have been denied, and therefore their seriousness—which ought to afford them entrance into the larger world, connecting them to all those others who have thought about and suffered similar things—does not. They cannot locate men or women willing to take them as seriously as they take the questions that plague them.

That is what seems so wasteful, and there is something almost unforgivable about it. I have seen similar kinds of waste over and over in America during the past several decades: among children, whose sense of community and fair play is allowed to atrophy or is conscientiously discouraged; in universities, where the best and deepest yearnings of students go unacknowledged or untapped; even in literature, where, with very few exceptions, the capacities for generosity and concern which abound unrecognized in most men and women have gone unexamined. But for this to happen to the vets is perhaps the greatest waste of all, since, in many of them, so much understanding has so obviously emerged from their experience. . . .

Coming to Terms

The vets' difficulty in coming to terms with their own past, coupled with their refusal to put it aside, their stubbornness in clinging to its inchoate power, is not very different from the even more hidden yearnings and sorrows of many Americans about many things—yearnings for which we no longer have a usable language, and which no longer form (as they once would have) the center of our conversations about what it means to be human.

What is more, the vets' loss of the myths that ordinarily protect people from the truth has brought them face to face with several problems that beleaguer almost all those who approach value from a secular position: the difficulty of dealing with questions of good and evil in the absence of divine, absolute and binding powers or systems. We have learned by now—or we should have—that humans kill just as easily in God's absence as they do in his name, and that the secularization of values, which people believed a hundred years ago might set them free of ignorance and superstition, leads along its own paths to ignorance and superstition. To be absolutely honest, *none* of us who are secular thinkers have anything more than the tatters of past certainty to offer in regard to establishing and sustaining morality, or increasing kindness in men and women and justice in the world. These questions, which plague the vets, ought to plague every man and woman, and none of us can afford to ignore the vets' experience.

In the end, what we owe the dead (whether our own or the Vietnamese), what we owe the vets and what we owe ourselves is the same thing: the resumption of the recurrent conversation about moral values, the sources and meaning of conscience, and the roots of human generosity, solidarity and community.

The Ability to Empathize

The ability to empathize, to see life and experience its joys and problems through another person's eyes and feelings, is a helpful skill to acquire if one is to learn from the life situations of others.

Consider the following situation taken from the book *Nam* by Mark Baker.

> We got into this village and herded all the people together, maybe sixty-seventy people. Women, children, everybody. We burned all their homes to the ground. We thought they were being evacuated.
>
> At the last second I broke squelch. You don't talk on the radio because the enemy can triangulate, they can hear you. You just do not talk on the radio. I broke squelch because I thought they would move these people out, relocate them to a POW camp. Question them, find out who's doing what and release the rest of them.
>
> A guy gets on the radio and says, "Waste 'em."
>
> I wasn't going to talk on the radio. I broke squelch again—twice. The guy goes, "Waste 'em."
>
> I said, "Waste what?"
>
> "Waste everybody that you've got."
>
> "You're talking about sixty-seventy people, some of whom may be friendlies. Are you aware of that?"
>
> He said, "Waste 'em."
>
> "Can I have your name and rank?" I said, because I was not going to kill all those people.
>
> "Sonny boy," he said, "I assure you that I outrank you by five ranks and twenty years. And I'm telling you to waste 'em."
>
> "How do I know you're not a civilian?" I said. "You may be a field agent for the CIA or something. I'm not going to 'waste 'em' until I get somebody on this . . . radio who will tell me who the hell they are and by what authority I'm doing the wasting. At that particular point, I might do something about it."
>
> Two people who claimed to be very, *very* high-ranking officials got on the radio. One of them said to me, "By order of the Commander in Chief of the United States Armed Forces, I'm

telling you that the previous transmission given you is what you are to adhere to."

"I really can't believe what you're telling me."

"We really don't care if you believe. Waste 'em."

So I got with eight of my men. The other two were guarding the villagers. I told them we'd just had an order on the radio to emulsify these people. What should we do? We had to talk for an hour.

It was a double bind. If we did it, we would be very ill at ease with ourselves. If we didn't do it, we'd be in a lot of trouble when we got back. There was no right answer.

But I had a couple of people who really enjoyed killing quite a bit. They were the ones on guard. I told them what the situation was. They couldn't wait. They grinned from ear to ear. They pulled back, made all the villagers lie down on the ground with their hands behind their backs. Then these guys wasted them. The women, the men, the children, everyone.

Excerpt from pp. 176-177, "We got into this village. . .The women, the men, the children, everyone," of NAM by Mark Baker. Copyright © 1981 by Mark Baker. Reprinted by permission of William Morrow & Company.

Instructions:

Try to imagine how the following individuals would react in this situation. What reasons might they give for their actions. Try to imagine and explain their feelings.

The patrol leader

The two soldiers who did the actual killing

The two high-ranking officials on the radio who ordered the killings

The victims

A 19-year-old soldier on his first patrol in Vietnam

A 36-year-old career soldier with two years to go before retirement who is a member of the patrol

The commander in chief, President Johnson

William Mahedy, the author of viewpoint five in this chapter

Peter Marin, the author of viewpoint six in this chapter

You

Periodical Bibliography

The following articles have been selected to supplement the diverse views presented in this chapter.

The American Legion Magazine	"A Lifetime of Nightmares," May 1989.
Judith Coburn	"The Last Patrol," *Mother Jones*, February/March 1987.
Brian Doyle	"You Had to Be There," *Salt*, February 1988. Available from *Salt*, 205 W. Monroe, Chicago, IL 60606.
Janet Gardner	"Answers at Last?" *The Nation*, April 11, 1987.
Bob Greene	"Homecoming," *Esquire*, February 1989.
Kim Heron	"The Long Road Back," *The New York Times Magazine*, March 6, 1988.
Malcolm Jones Jr.	"Is There Life After Vietnam?" *Newsweek*, February 5, 1990.
Joseph R. Kurtz Jr.	"Vietnam Veterans' Nonstop Con Game," *The New York Times*, March 10, 1986.
Marc Leepson	"From Shame to Glory," *Common Cause Magazine*, January/February 1988.
Multinational Monitor	"Agent Orange: Bringing the Battle Home," April 1987.
Newsweek	"Heroes, Past and Present," July 16, 1987.
Andrew Purvis	"Clean Bill for Agent Orange," *Time*, April 9, 1990.
Ellen K. Silbergeld	"Agent Orange Claims Should Be Paid Now," *American Legion Magazine*, December 1989.
Mary Stout	"Lifting the Vietnam Stigma," *U.S. News & World Report*, November 16, 1987.
Joe Stuteville	"'Women Were Casualties, Too,'" *American Legion Magazine*, November 1987.
George C. Wilson	"A Separate Peace," *The Washington Post National Weekly Edition*, April 2-8, 1990.

CHAPTER **5**

What Should U.S. Policy Be Toward Indochina?

Chapter Preface

The Vietnam War had a profound impact on American foreign policy. Haunted by America's defeat in that tiny country, many of today's policymakers are more cautious than they were three decades ago about intervening in another country's struggles against communism. This can be seen in the controversy over U.S. policy toward Cambodia, a country that neighbors Vietnam.

The Communist dictator Pol Pot took over Cambodia shortly after South Vietnam surrendered to North Vietnam in 1975. Pol Pot and his supporters, the Khmer Rouge, killed an estimated two to three million Cambodians—up to one-third of the population—in a vicious reign of terror that lasted three years. Pol Pot was deposed when Vietnam, also Communist, invaded Cambodia in 1978. Cambodia became embroiled in a bloody civil war between the Communist government installed by the Vietnamese and several resistance groups, including the Khmer Rouge and other, non-Communist groups. The war threatened to intensify after Vietnam officially withdrew its troops from Cambodia in 1989. In this complicated situation, U.S. leaders have debated whether to offer aid to the non-Communist resistance groups.

Interestingly, in the course of the debate, people on both sides of the issue use America's tragic involvement in Vietnam to support their positions. Vice President Dan Quayle, who believes that the U.S. should support non-Communist forces in Cambodia, argues, "No great nation can long afford to be paralyzed by a memory" of defeat. Journalist Susan Blaustein, on the other hand, urges the U.S. to establish peaceful relations with Cambodia's Communist, Vietnamese-supported government. She argues that those who oppose such reconciliation have impure motives, specifically, a "desire to get back at Vietnam" for defeating the U.S.

This chapter considers what today's American policy should be toward Cambodia and Vietnam. Memories of the losses suffered and mistakes made during the Vietnam War reverberate throughout the diverse views presented here.

185

"The United States should . . . unilaterally normalize relations with Hanoi."

The U.S. Should Improve Diplomatic Relations with Vietnam

John LeBoutillier

The United States has not had official diplomatic relations with Vietnam since the collapse of South Vietnam in 1975. In the following viewpoint, John LeBoutillier argues that normalizing relations with Vietnam will reduce Soviet Union influence in Indochina, and encourage Vietnam to continue its economic and political reforms. LeBoutillier is a former congressman from New York and runs a private organization which attempts to gather information on American prisoners of war in Vietnam.

As you read, consider the following questions:

1. What is the significance of the anecdote LeBoutillier uses to begin the viewpoint?
2. Why does LeBoutillier call U.S. policy in the Indochinese region inconsistent?
3. According to the author, why would private U.S. investment in Vietnam be beneficial to the U.S.?

Excerpted from *Vietnam Now: A Case for Normalizing Relations with Hanoi,* by John LeBoutillier (Praeger Publishers, an imprint of Greenwood Publishing Group, Inc., New York, 1989), pp. 1-3 passim, p. 83, pp. 91-94 passim. Copyright © 1989 by John LeBoutillier. Reprinted with permission.

186

Before the early 1990s end, the United States of America could bring military forces back to Vietnam, back to the U.S.-built bases at Cam Ranh Bay and Danang. Only this time, the U.S. ships, planes, and soldiers would not be uninvited combatants, but instead would be guests of the new Vietnamese government in Hanoi.

In a stunning policy reversal, the reformist regime in Vietnam wants to move out of its almost total dependency on Moscow and toward a more open, friendly relationship with the United States. As a part of that new move, Hanoi's leaders are offering Washington the opportunity to alter the strategic military balance in the Pacific. At a time when the Soviets are expanding their reach throughout Southeast Asia and the Philippine government has threatened not to renew the leases for the two U.S. bases in the Philippines, Subic Bay, and Clark Field, Hanoi is offering a new alternative: a lease agreement for the United States to use the bases it originally built in Vietnam over twenty-five years ago.

This amazing Vietnamese offer was matter-of-factly presented to me by two high-level Vietnamese foreign ministry officials as we drove outside Hanoi in the back seat of a Soviet Volga limousine. . . .

A Surprising Answer

Amid the horn tooting and the wave of bikes, I casually asked my two Vietnamese escorts, "Do you think the day could ever come when the United States military could have access to Vietnamese military facilities?" I was gently probing. Without hesitation, both officials responded with identical statements: "The day after the United States normalizes relations with Vietnam, we are prepared to open negotiations with Washington to work out an agreement whereby America can have access to Cam Ranh Bay and Danang."

In Vietnam, officials of this level of the foreign ministry never make policy statements unless they have been authorized to do so by their superiors. They are almost robotlike in making statements and in asking questions designed to solicit information. So when two of them made this identical statement, it was obvious to me that it had come from above. I probed further, only to learn that, indeed, this is a genuine new offer from the government in Hanoi. It is an offer that could entirely restructure the superpower balance throughout the Pacific.

Perhaps most surprising about this startling new development is that no one from Washington had ever even bothered to ask Vietnam's leaders about the possibility of the United States returning to the two bases. Why not? Because there are not normalized relations between the United States and Vietnam; there

is no regular dialogue. The only talking between these two former adversaries, infrequent and irregular as it is, concerns matters left over from the war: missing American soldiers, Amerasian children, the release of political prisoners, and the Vietnamese invasion of Kampuchea (Cambodia).

U.S. Policy a Failure

Present U.S. policy is so fundamentally flawed and inconsistent
that it has directly contributed to greatly increased Soviet influence in Southeast Asia. This policy has isolated Vietnam and
forced the Vietnamese into the Soviet orbit. Thus, Moscow has
obtained an invaluable toehold in the world's most rapidly growing region. Furthermore, what has been accomplished? Vietnam,
we see, is still occupying Kampuchea. On the emotionally
charged POW/MIA issue, we see almost no progress. The thousands of Amerasian children remaining in Vietnam continue to
haunt us. The release of Vietnamese political prisoners, many of
whom worked for the United States during the war, continues to
be put off. Clearly, this policy does not serve any U.S.
interest. . . .

The United States should now reassert itself in Southeast Asia.
First, normalize relations with Vietnam. One immediate result
will be competition in the region between the Americans, the
Soviets, and the Chinese. The United States and its free-enterprise allies will win this competition.

John LeBoutillier, *Vietnam Now*, 1989.

Except to consider these issues, none of them of vital U.S.
strategic importance, Washington has deliberately chosen to hide
its head in the sand and relive the war, wrapped up in a combination of guilt, spite, and bitterness.

Meanwhile, Moscow has circled like a vulture and swooped
down on Vietnam, picking it dry and using the remains for its
own strategic design: to become the major player throughout the
Pacific.

Sadly, Washington's failure to act has allowed Moscow to expand its reach. The United States' mistaken policy since the end
of the war in 1975 has driven Hanoi into a position of almost total dependency upon Moscow. In the process, Vietnam's economy and infrastructure have drastically deteriorated. As a result,
Hanoi has removed its hard-line pro-Soviet government and replaced it with a group of pragmatic reformists who are willing to
experiment with free-enterprise innovations. To this new
regime's potentially historic offer to allow the United States to
come back and use the bases in Vietnam, Washington has turned
a deaf ear. . . .

The 1980s have seen a reevaluation of the Vietnam War, the leaders who conducted that effort, and the way the media covered it. Some opinions have changed; others have hardened. Rambo has become a hero, Jane Fonda more of a villain. Even General William Westmoreland has been rehabilitated. The Vietnam Veterans Memorial Wall has been built. Parades finally welcoming home our troops have helped to soften the bitterness of their original return. Movies like *Platoon, Hamburger Hill,* and *Full Metal Jacket* show conflicting accounts of the war itself.

The United States has finally been able to look back on one of the worst periods in our nation's history. While the pain will never leave, it has receded enough to allow rational analysis. However, there is no sense in looking back unless we apply those lessons to the future. The question of normalizing relations with Vietnam and then moving toward a new, warmer relationship with the Hanoi regime is the next logical step in the healing process. If the United States can rebuild both Japan and West Germany, not out of sentimentality or guilt, but because of the strategic significance of both nations, then the United States must also recognize the value of Vietnam in Southeast Asia. To continue to consign Vietnam to the Soviet orbit is bad policy for the United States and for U.S. interests. . . .

The United States needs to arouse itself from its post-Vietnam slumber and realize that the Pacific is the world's fastest growing region. Washington needs to adjust its thinking, remembering that the United States remains the leading economic power in the world. For too long American myopia has consigned Southeast Asia to a competition between the Soviets and the Chinese.

What the U.S. Should Do.

The United States should immediately change policy and focus its diplomatic energy on reentering the competition in Southeast Asia. To do so, Washington should adopt the following measures:

Unilaterally normalize relations with Hanoi, despite short-term protestations from some of our ASEAN [Association of Southeast Asian Nations] friends and allies. In recognizing Vietnam, Washington should not automatically grant full trading privileges to Hanoi, but instead should announce a schedule of increased trade and economic assistance to Hanoi, provided Hanoi announces a schedule of progress on resolving the bilateral issues mentioned above. Included in this announced schedule by Washington should be incentives, such as accelerated assistance, most favored nation trading status, and help with the World Bank and the International Monetary Fund. Also, incentives should be included to encourage Hanoi to use its unique relationship with Laos and Kampuchea to settle once and for all the POW/MIA [prisoner of war/missing in action] situation in those two countries as well.

Future trade schedules and economic concessions should be tied to the three other main bilateral issues, the Amerasian children, the release of political prisoners, and the acceleration of the Orderly Departure Program. Hanoi should be encouraged to repatriate the children of U.S. soldiers and rewarded for allowing citizens to leave. Emigration is, and has been, the central impediment to increased trade with the Soviets; why not the same for Vietnam?

Washington should recognize that the best way to encourage Hanoi to change is not by threatening it, but by offering positive inducements and rewards for actions with which the United States agrees. Furthermore, Hanoi must now be treated not with bitterness, but in the spirit of a new diplomatic relationship that can benefit both sides. The United States should contrast its behavior to that of its "clumsy rival," Moscow.

A Lasting Interest

Although the intention of American policy is to isolate Vietnam, the effect has been to isolate ourselves from a country in which we have a lasting interest. . . .

We need to shoulder some share of responsibility in a region where the United States presence just 15 years ago was a central factor. Our policy of isolation has reached the point of diminishing returns.

Larry Pressler, *The New York Times*, May 23, 1988.

The United States should encourage private U.S. investment in Vietnam. This is especially true in the short term as Congress struggles with a massive federal deficit and a 20 percent cut in the foreign aid budget. Businesses throughout Asia already recognize that Vietnam offers not just a large work force, but a potentially lucrative market, as well. Turning the Vietnamese spirit away from war making and toward product making can only benefit everyone. The success in China in the last decade of adopting semifree market innovations is certain to be duplicated by Hanoi. General Secretary Linh is a pragmatic leader who recognizes that Deng and Gorbachev have already taken huge steps to reform their systems. Linh is also inclined to adopt reforms, especially with U.S. assistance, and, as he does so, he will gradually move away from the Soviet orbit. Hanoi will move because only the United States can satisfy Vietnam's economic and technological needs, ranging from fertilizer to personal computers. Hanoi's change of direction, however, can only occur with constant, positive U.S. prodding, not the bullying, threatening behavior of the Soviets.

The United States, as a superpower, should not surrender in any contest, not even on the terms of the debate. In other words, Washington should compete for a new preeminence in Southeast Asia on its own terms, not those of the Soviets. Thus, U.S. economic might can triumph over Soviet military power, if Washington works hand in hand with the U.S. and Asian business community to encourage a new economic offensive in the region, beginning with Vietnam. Japan [has] unveiled plans for just such an offensive, including a possible $4 billion investment program for Vietnam. (The United States has pressured Tokyo not to trade with Hanoi.). . .

Moscow, struggling today with its own economic restructuring, will not be able to compete in Southeast Asia with a renewed U.S. economic presence. The Soviets, frustrated by their own economic impotence and their suddenly less attractive and less needed military power, will find themselves dealt out of the region. Vietnam, relieved of its Kampuchean burden and profiting by lessened hostility from China, will naturally grow less reliant on Moscow. . . .

Southeast Asia will adopt a new, natural multialignment system, with various nations joining together for certain goals. A shifting equilibrium will result, born of natural competition. The centerpiece of this system must be a free-enterprise system.

This concept of a Pacific community can only succeed with the participation of all the region's nations, including Vietnam. Ultimately, only the United States can welcome Vietnam back into not only the Pacific community, but the world community. It must be Washington's goal, as it is Hanoi's, that Vietnam not be subordinate to either Moscow or Beijing. Only the United States can bring about that result.

One Final Reason

Beyond geopolitical strategies and economic interplay, the other argument in favor of the diplomatic normalization of relations between Washington and Hanoi was best expressed to me in Vietnam by the deputy foreign minister, Nguyen Dy Nien. As we drank traditional Vietnamese green tea, Minister Nien said, "Even though the war is over, the bleeding continues on both sides. Only the normalization of relations can stop the bleeding."

VIEWPOINT

"Granting Vietnam . . . improved diplomatic relations now would be to remove the pressure that is forcing Vietnam's communist government to consider concessions."

The U.S. Should Not Improve Diplomatic Relations with Vietnam

Tran Van Luu

Tran Van Luu was a journalist in Saigon before the fall of South Vietnam in 1975. In 1977 he fled to the United States and now lives in San Diego, California. In the following viewpoint he argues that the United States should not establish diplomatic relations with Vietnam. Refusing to normalize relations shows U.S. opposition to Vietnam's foreign and domestic policies, Luu writes, and pressures Vietnam to modify its communist policies.

As you read, consider the following questions:

1. According to Luu, how have the Vietnamese people suffered under the current leadership?
2. In the author's opinion, why is Vietnam closely linked with the Soviet Union?
3. Why do Vietnamese now residing in the United States have conflicting emotions over U.S. aid to Vietnam, according to the author?

Tran Van Luu, "Is It Time to Normalize Relations with Vietnam?" *San Diego Union,* June 12, 1988. Reprinted with permission.

It has been 13 years since South Vietnam was overrun by the invading North Vietnamese army in the spring of 1975. But it was only after the mass exodus of boat people refugees began and Vietnam's invasion of Cambodia occurred in late 1978 that the American press began focusing upon Indochina's new realities.

The visit to Hanoi in 1987 of an official American delegation led by retired U.S. Army Gen. John Vessey put the issue of Vietnam squarely before the American people. It was after this trip that American commentators began to talk of humanitarian assistance and normalizing, or at least improving, relations with Hanoi.

The stated purpose was to resolve such issues as American military personnel still unaccounted for and to arrange the release of Amerasian children. The larger purpose of weaning Vietnam away from the Soviet orbit might also be served, or so some Americans believe.

Vietnam's Record

But look at what Vietnam's communist rulers have done since the war ended in 1975:

Countless thousands of South Vietnamese were imprisoned without trial in the so-called re-education camps. Many are still there, rotting away. . . .

Hanoi's rule also spread the poverty of North Vietnam throughout South Vietnam. Three successive five-year plans, designed along strict Marxist-Leninist lines, have failed. Vietnam's economy is a ruin. . . .This despite Soviet aid that may total up to $3 billion per year.

Vietnam cannot pay its mounting foreign debt. Inflation rages on, with the communist government seemingly unable to control it.

With an inflation rate of 700 percent per year and per capita income of no more than $150 per year, Vietnam today is one of the poorest countries in the world. Some Vietnamese now cannot write to their relatives abroad because an international postage stamp costs 1,000 Dong, one-fifth of the average monthly salary of 5,000 Dong.

Limited Reforms

Much has been made in the Western press of Vietnam's supposed economic reforms, which coincided with Mikhail Gorbachev's new policies in the Soviet Union. But Vietnam's reforms, pushed by new Communist Party General Secretary Nguyen Van Linh, are very limited. They are probably too limited to have much chance of reviving a bankrupt economy.

Vietnam's government now gives the country's farmers longer leases on their state-owned land. Farmers also are allowed to sell more of their harvests privately after paying their taxes to the government. But farmers are still discouraged by their inability to own land on a permanent basis. And farmers are still leaving the land, moving to the cities and trying to become merchants, or anything else that might offer a better living.

Vietnam's new law intended to encourage foreign investment remains only a piece of paper. It is true that more foreign businessmen visited Vietnam in 1987. But most invested only their spare time, not their money. A socialist economy incompetently managed offers little reason for foreigners to invest.

Vietnam's Foreign Relations

In foreign relations as well, Vietnam continues to be its own worst enemy. Remember that Hanoi chose, in effect, to isolate itself from the Western countries and from most Asian countries in 1978. No one forced Vietnam to ally itself formally with the Soviet Union in 1978. And no one forced Vietnam to invade Cambodia a few months later. Some Americans believe that U.S. policy drove Vietnam into the arms of the Soviet Union. But, in fact, the Vietnam-Soviet Union treaty and the Vietnamese invasion of Cambodia occurred during the Carter administration's attempts to *improve* relations with Hanoi and end Vietnam's diplomatic isolation.

Who Benefits from Normalization?

For Vietnam, the advantages of normalization are obvious. Not only would it re-open Vietnam to lost U.S. trade—along with the inevitable aid programs—it would clear the way for full-scale involvement here from American allies like Japan, hesitant to defy the U.S. embargo openly. Politically, too, normalization would be a boon for Vietnam, a sign of acceptance within the ranks of nations.

From the White House window, by contrast, the benefits of normalization are by no means self-evident. "That's a very American question," complains one Vietnamese woman. True perhaps, but it doesn't change the fact that the answers from a round of her government's officials are at best hazy: "in the U.S. interest to be involved here". . . "fosters dialogue" . . . "better for the region," and so on.

William McGurn, *The Wall Street Journal*, April 12, 1989.

Also, Ho Chi Minh's biography and many books about the Vietnamese Communist Party testify that Ho and his fellow revolutionaries in the party leadership sold themselves to communism since the 1920s.

When will Americans learn that Vietnam is communist today

not because the Vietnamese revolution was driven to communism but because it embraced communism and sought to impose communism on all Vietnamese?

Officially, the policy of the U.S. government today sets two conditions for normalizing relations with Hanoi: Vietnam must fully resolve the MIA [missing in action] question and withdraw completely from Cambodia.

Resolving the first question is long overdue. There is no excuse for Hanoi to be holding remains of American military dead more than a decade after the war. There is no excuse for Hanoi to release a few sets of remains every so often as a form of diplomatic and political extortion. Hanoi is still trying to barter its MIA remains for American aid and formal diplomatic relations.

The Paris Peace Accords of 1973 require Hanoi to make the fullest possible accounting of Americans missing in action. Allowing even private, humanitarian aid to Vietnam now and extending closer diplomatic relations would be to reward Hanoi's cruel, cynical extortion on the MIA question.

And what about Vietnam's continued military occupation, and colonialization, of Cambodia? . . . America should join with the other non-communist nations of Southeast Asia in demanding that Vietnam withdraw now. . . .

Overseas Vietnamese

The Vietnamese overseas are caught in conflicting emotions on the subject of normalizing relations between Washington and Hanoi. More than anyone else, they are thinking of their relatives and friends who must carry on life in the shadow of totalitarianism and poverty.

On the one hand, overseas Vietnamese want to see international resources made available to the people at home in Vietnam. They want to see capital and technology provided to help the Vietnamese rebuild their country. The overseas Vietnamese also respect America's traditional generosity in helping with the economic reconstruction of former enemies.

But overseas Vietnamese also agree with the many Americans here who question why America should improve relations with Vietnam now. Who would benefit once such improved relations were established? Should America want to jump in to Vietnam's economic mess and begin footing the bills now paid by the Russians? Generosity has its limits.

Will America agree to recognize a country, Vietnam, that is sending its soldiers to occupy neighboring countries, Cambodia and Laos? Will America agree to give economic or food aid to a country that maintains a 1 million-man army, the sixth largest army in the world, plus keeps another million or so persons in communist party jobs that contribute nothing to the economy?

Would American food aid sent to Vietnam feed the people of Vietnam first, or the Vietnamese army and communist party cadre first?

False Hopes

[There] is the assertion that through normalization the US can wean Vietnam from the Soviet bloc. If billions of dollars and more than 50,000 American lives could not change Hanoi's mind before, why should a far smaller amount of aid plus one ambassador do so now? The fantasy of American leverage over Vietnam has proven costly enough not to be rebelieved.

I put the question to a ranking official in the Ministry of Foreign Affairs: If the United States were to normalize relations with Vietnam, would your government try to reduce Soviet influence in the region—for example by asking Soviet forces to quit the naval base at Cam Ranh Bay? He refuses to give me any reason to think this would occur. Vietnam attaches no preconditions to normalization, he says; nor will we promise you anything, he implies. Given the high rate of failure of previous agreements between the two countries, I appreciate his refusal to raise US expectations.

Donald K. Emmerson, *The Christian Science Monitor,* December 30, 1987.

Most overseas Vietnamese believe Hanoi should help itself first by cleaning up its own mess. The most serious problem Vietnam faces today is not diplomatic isolation or a lack of aid. Vietnam's most serious problem is a political ideology that smothers human rights and kills the incentives needed to develop a healthy, growing economy.

Granting Vietnam aid, trade, and improved diplomatic relations now would be to remove the pressure that is forcing Vietnam's communist government to consider concessions. Now that the pressure is beginning to work, keeping it on makes more sense than granting Hanoi a reprieve.

"The families of our POWs/MIAs deserve better than the treatment they have been given by the United States government."

The U.S. Should Keep Searching for Vietnam War Prisoners

Robert C. Smith

In 1973 North Vietnam released 591 American prisoners of war (POWS), some who had been imprisoned for over five years. Over 2500 American soldiers remain unaccounted for, however. In the following viewpoint, Robert C. Smith argues that there might still be live American prisoners in Vietnam, and states that the U.S. government should be doing more to secure their release. Smith is a Republican congressman from New Hampshire, a member of the House Veterans Affairs Committee, and a Vietnam veteran.

As you read, consider the following questions:

1. Why has the Vietnam War not ended for many families, according to Smith?
2. Why does the author believe there still might be American prisoners in Vietnam and Laos?
3. What in Smith's opinion is America's moral obligation to U.S. soldiers missing in Vietnam?

Robert C. Smith, "Where Are They?" *The Manchester Union Leader,* September 29, 1987. Reprinted with permission.

For most people, the Vietnam War is an event of the past. Something you remember when watching *Platoon*, or *Coming Home*, or the *Deer Hunter*. Or maybe you know a friend of a friend's brother who did a tour of duty.

But for over 2,400 American families, the war that officially ended 15 years ago is not yet over. Those families have fathers, brothers, uncles, and sons still listed as missing in Southeast Asia, relatives who did not come home to American soil during "Operation Homecoming.". . .

I have been actively working to discover the truth about our missing American servicemen. I have poured over countless Defense Intelligence Agency reports detailing live sightings over the past 20 years—some as recent as 1986. There are file cabinets full of reports, which most Americans don't even know exist.

In 1986, I traveled to Hanoi with my colleagues on the House POW/MIA [Prisoners of War/Missing in Action] task force, where we discovered information confirming that all live sighting witnesses are not, as the bureaucrats say, "fabricators." From the extensive research we have done, the witnesses and refugees we have talked to, and the classified reports and maps we have looked at, I believe we can confirm the existence of men still alive in Southeast Asia.

Unanswered Questions

In 1973, the United States pulled out of Southeast Asia from an unpopular war—most people felt that our boys had been sent to a foreign land to fight "someone else's war." The closing of the war left too many open, unanswered questions concerning our POWs since the conclusion was handled so shabbily.

Some 569 American men were shot down over Laos and not one of those men were ever returned alive, even though 39 percent of all American pilots shot down over Vietnam came back. The soldiers in Laos used the same ammunition, the same aircraft, and flew over similar terrain—if we follow our logical instincts, surely someone survived over Laos.

When our negotiators went to Paris to sign the Paris Peace Accords, they brought with them a longer list of POWs and MIAs than the Vietnamese list. They returned without a full accounting of those on our list. This "long list/short list" controversy was further exacerbated by the fact that, even though we were bombing Laos and were at war with Laos, that country never signed the Paris Peace Accords. Contemporary news reports, however, referred to comments by Laotian and United States officials—including former Secretary of State Henry Kissinger and former President Richard Nixon—alluding to prisoners held captive in Laos. Kissinger and Nixon said "the United

States would not leave Southeast Asia until those men were accounted for." The fact is, they were not accounted for.

At the termination of this tragic era, the government of Vietnam said "we have no more live Americans here." An executive commission, The Woodcock Commission, and a congressional commission, The Montgomery Commission, essentially confirmed that statement upon visits to Southeast Asia. Both the Vietnamese and the commissions were proven wrong when, in 1979, Marine Private Robert Garwood walked out of Vietnam. Bob Garwood had, allegedly, "collaborated with the enemy" and when he returned to the States he was immediately court martialed and found guilty. But whether he is a "collaborator" or not is another issue. What is crucial is that he claims to have seen live men, our men, still being held captive in Southeast Asia.

Mike Shelton, *The Orange County Register*. Distributed by King Features Syndicate. Reprinted with permission.

Incredibly, key officials in the Vietnam negotiations—like Henry Kissinger and Richard Nixon—have never been asked to testify before any congressional committee on this matter.

Former Defense Intelligence Agency Director General Eugene Tighe and former National Security Council Adviser Robert McFarlane, have also both said they believe there are live men in Southeast Asia.

Instead of thoroughly investigating reports of live men, the trend of our government agencies on POWs is to debunk and debase rather than debrief and deliver.

The families of both the deceased and the missing have been denied the full truth for too many years. Although I am not one that has alleged a coverup, it is understandable how that term could come in to focus in this situation. . . .

For too long, there has been a pattern of mismanagement and "old blood" working to resolve this issue, in the areas of both live men and remains. It is time for a serious change—for the sake of American pride, dignity and honor to those men who served our country with distinction. The families of our POWs/MIAs deserve better than the treatment they have been given by the United States government.

Hugh Fanning

On Oct. 31, 1967, Air Force Major Hugh Fanning was shot down over North Vietnam while flying an A-6 Intruder. His wife, Kathryn Fanning, was told by the government that he could "probably not survive" the crash. For 17 years she was given limited information, and then, in 1984, she received a small package of bones which she buried in August of that year.

On Oct. 23, 1985, Kathryn Fanning exhumed what she had been led to believe were her husband's remains. Upon bringing them to two board-certified anthropologists, she was told there was no way those bones could be identified as her husband.

Now, 20 years later, Kathryn Fanning has finally received a signed notice from the Armed Services Graves Registration Office (ASGRO) that rescinded identification of Major Fanning. She has since learned that her Military Assistance Officer had hidden reports in his home, and that a photo of a dead pilot had appeared in a North Vietnamese newspaper the day after Major Fanning went down. It took her nearly 20 years to get that photo, why wasn't she told? She is returning those remains to ASGRO, but now the question lingers . . . whose bones are they?

The government's practice of spurious identification of bits of remains is reprehensible. The Armed Services Graves Office is over-eager to make these often doubtful identifications so they can cross names off the MIA list. It is beyond the dignity of the United States and an inexcusable ploy to deceive the families.

Secret Reports

I [have] introduced H.R. 2260 to declassify all live sighting case files and make available to the families information about their loved ones, so cases like Kathryn Fanning's do not occur. The names of POWs and their families, and the sources, and methods of intelligence collection in these reports would not be released for public consumption to protect the privacy of the families and government intelligence.

During the past several years, I and a number of my colleagues have read overwhelming numbers of these reports—currently classified as secret in the DIA file. Upon thorough review, it is my conclusion that there is evidence to substantiate that we left men behind. The facts are staggering.

Although many of these reports have been proven false by the DIA, there are over 100 that have not been proven inaccurate despite the toughest scrutiny. Some of the live sighting information has been turned over to the Communist government of Vietnam, yet the American public and the families of these men cannot see it! Until 1978, this live sighting information was not classified as secret.

Donald Sparks

Pfc. Donald Sparks was "killed" in an ambush near Chu Lai on June 17, 1969. Fellow infantrymen saw Sparks and Cpl. Larry Graham get hit. As they withdrew, North Vietnamese Army soldiers were stripping Sparks's body. The next day, the platoon recovered Graham's body, but Sparks was gone.

In May 1970, two letters, dated April 11, 1970, were found on the body of a dead Viet Cong soldier in Quang Tri Province. Handwriting experts confirmed that Donald Sparks wrote both, ten months after his "death." Sparks wrote his parents, "I have not heard or seen another American in nearly ten months now." His status was changed to POW, but he never returned.

The Other Side, September/October 1989.

It seems to me that we are in a gridlock. The DIA says the information is not valid; many of us who have seen the reports believe the opposite. We must let the public break this gridlock by de-classifying the reports. There is no one more deserving of reviewing that information than the 2,400 families of our American MIAs. No departmental bureaucrat should have knowledge that the families do not.

It is our moral obligation to sanctify and respect the dignity of those men who risked life and limb to protect American freedoms, who may still be alive in a Vietnamese prison camp, and whose families may still be wondering "whose bones are they?" The efforts thus far to bring home MIAs, remains, or men still alive, have reflected the epitome of ineffectiveness, ineptitude, and bureaucratic bungling. . . .

Our POWs and MIAs are great patriots. They deserve recognition, and the rights to freedom and democracy guaranteed by this government of the people, by the people, and for the people.

"The prisoners of war who did not return in 1973 have probably long since perished."

There Are No Surviving Vietnam War Prisoners

Alan Pell Crawford

Alan Pell Crawford is a private investigator and author of *Thunder on the Right: The New Right and the Politics of Resentment.* In the following viewpoint, he debunks the notion that Americans are still being held prisoner in Indochina. Americans still missing in action are probably no longer alive, Crawford writes. He argues some people are exploiting the hopes of the families of missing soldiers for money and publicity.

As you read, consider the following questions:

1. Why do many people continue to believe there are surviving American prisoners of war in Vietnam, according to Crawford?
2. According to the author, why are live sightings of Americans in Vietnam inconclusive evidence that prisoners of war are still kept there?
3. How does Crawford account for the American soldiers whose bodies have never been found?

Alan Pell Crawford, "The POW/MIA Rescue Hustle," *The Nation,* October 31, 1988, © 1988 The Nation Company, Inc. Reprinted with permission.

For years, activists like Navy Captain Eugene (Red) McDaniel have been trying to locate and rescue the "hundreds" of Americans they insist are held in Southeast Asia internment camps. They've been unsuccessful because the prisoners of war who did not return in 1973 have probably long since perished. This is a fact neither the P.O.W. lobby nor Ronald Reagan will face, allowing the families of the 2,500 Vietnam-era Americans listed as missing in action to believe, against all evidence, that their loved ones are alive. In 1983 the President said that he considers return of the prisoners "the highest national priority," and, with such encouragement, the P.O.W. lobby has run amok. Its activities, which range from shameless fund-raising to illegal forays across borders, have disrupted official efforts to recover remains and exploited families of the M.I.A.s.

Ironically enough, their efforts have intensified just as diplomatic initiatives have begun to pay off. In October 1988, Vietnam allowed U.S. officials to comb the countryside for the first time, and searchers retrieved two sets of human remains, one of which they think may be an American's. . . .

Private Initiatives

McDaniel's Home Free! project . . . seeks to raise $1 billion in pledges to be paid as reward money to the first Southeast Asian to escape with an American prisoner. In September 1987, Billy Hendon, a former U.S. Representative who works with McDaniel, went to Thailand to release balloons that included notices of the reward. When the Thai government told him he could not, he packed the fliers into sandwich bags and floated them down the Mekong River. The reward money notion seems to be catching on. Laotian police arrested two Americans in October 1988 who said they represented the "National Steering Committee for American War Veterans" and that they were in Laos to advertise their own $2.4 million pot for P.O.W. rescuers.

Former Representative John LeBoutillier, who runs a tax-exempt operation called Skyhook II, isn't waiting for the P.O.W.s to return to dole out dollars. He says his organization distributes "about $10,000" each month to its operatives in Southeast Asia. At this stage the money is used to locate P.O.W.s. Ultimately, it will bribe their captors to release them, which can be accomplished for "$2 million to $5 million."

Jack Bailey of Operation Rescue takes yet a different tack. A retired Air Force colonel, Bailey is the skipper of a ship, the *Akuna*, that rescues Vietnamese refugees. Those refugees, Bailey claims, provide intelligence about P.O.W.s that will in time lead to their release. Bailey says he spends "every nickel I can keep my hands on" to keep the *Akuna* afloat, which must mean he carries a lot of loose change. Operating the boat costs "over \$20,000 a month," its skipper announced back in 1983. The figure rose to "over \$40,000 a month" the next year.

There are problems with Bailey's stories, as there are with those of other P.O.W. activists. He says the *Akuna* has been "patrolling South China seas—saving lives—since 1979," but local fishermen call it "the ship that never sails." In November 1984, claiming he had evidence of P.O.W.s, he delivered to the U.S. Joint Casualty Resolution Center a dog tag and what he said were the remains of three Americans. The Central Identification Laboratory, however, said that what Bailey had given it was "a mixture of commingled human and nonhuman (pig bone fragments)," which precluded "an identification of race data," and that "no association could be made to the dog tag provided or to any missing American."

Whatever else P.O.W. hunting may be, it is a sure-fire money-maker. The American Defense Institute, Captain McDaniel's umbrella organization, operated on $53,000 when it began in 1983, but raised $1.85 million in 1987. In 1983 and 1984, Skyhook II used tape-recorded telephone messages in which Charlton Heston asked Americans to send money; they brought in, LeBoutillier recalls, "several hundred thousand" dollars. Though it cost more than that to conduct the campaign, LeBoutillier says he did "get a lot of names from that project," and those now bring in "about $500,000 a year."

While direct mail or telephone solicitation is effective, person-to-person persuasion rakes in the dollars too. Former Green Beret James (Bo) Gritz, who claims the Pentagon once asked him to lead a covert mission to find P.O.W.s and has attempted three cross-border forays of his own in Southeast Asia, convinced George Brooks, whose son disappeared in 1970, to put up more than a year's salary to bankroll one of his rescue raids. The family of Air Force Lieut. Morgan Donahue, lost in 1968, has spent what Donahue's brother Jeff says is "a fortune, literally," to find the pilot. Instead, they've found a black market in gruesome relics—dog tags, animal bones and blurry snapshots—proffered by what Donahue calls "the worst type of people on this planet." He says they will "disinter a body of a pilot and inject water under a finger with a hypodermic. And roll a fingerprint and bring it out to a grieving wife or mother or whatever and say, 'Here's proof that your father, son, husband, brother or whatever is alive and in captivity.' "

Morgan and Jeff's father, Vincent Donahue, who is close to Cap'n Red, held a press conference in September 1987 to claim the two had evidence that Morgan is being held in Laos. Pentagon investigators viewed this report as they do most such pronouncements: The Defense Intelligence Agency (D.I.A.) says McDaniel's evidence is inconclusive and contradictory and "nothing can be verified or substantiated." The agency also notes that fliers seeking information about Morgan have circulated "for many years." Refugees, aware of the family's willingness to pay for information, have been only too happy to oblige.

Hard Evidence?

Even so, Cap'n Red took the opportunity to kick off a fund-raising campaign in which he claimed that he had obtained "hard evidence" that Donahue "recently risked his life to send us a signal that he is still alive." LeBoutillier's direct mail letters are similarly explicit:

> Starved and clad only in filthy rags, American soldiers and airmen are kept chained in tiny bamboo cages . . . made to work like animals pulling heavy plows. . . forced to toil from

daybreak to nightfall in steaming tropic heat . . . kicked and beaten constantly for their guards' amusement.

Reviewing such fund drives, the D.I.A. found they include "little or no substantive data which would lend itself to serious intelligence analysis," but instead are "rambling discourses filled with inflammatory rhetoric." While the approaches in these letters vary, they all share some common themes, "one of the strongest being that the organization is on the verge of rescuing a [P.O.W.], and if the recipient does not send money promptly, American servicemen will die."

No Surviving Prisoners

Of the 63 P.O.W.'s still unaccounted for, there is no credible evidence that any of them are being held against their will. Fifteen are listed as having died in captivity by the Vietnamese (all in South Vietnam). Information on half of the remaining 48 indicates that they, too, probably died after capture.

Thus, there is no information that any of these men are alive. By contrast, there are strong indications that other Americans may be living in Southeast Asia of their own free will.

Numerous cases have been reported in the news. For example, McKinley Nolan of Washington, Tex., was serving with the 1st Infantry Division when he disappeared, along with his Cambodian wife, in November 1967. He later turned up in Hanoi doing broadcasts for Radio Hanoi and writing leaflets that were circulated among American P.O.W.'s. He is believed to be alive and living in Vietnam.

Walter F. Wouk, *The New York Times*, January 23, 1989.

Skyhook II's LeBoutillier even tells his marks how the men are to be rescued:

> Late one evening, as prison-camp guards kick and flog a group of our boys along the trail back to their cages, the last few Communists in line might be swiftly and quietly dragged into the jungle. Then, a few seconds later, the bedraggled American P.O.W.'s they were guarding might also vanish suddenly from the rear of the plodding group. The Americans, of course, would now be in friendly hands. (We won't talk about the guards' fate.) In a matter of just a day or two, the rescued Americans would be smuggled across the border to our SKY-HOOK II Project group in Thailand. . . .
>
> In just a few weeks—for a relatively few thousands of dollars—six, ten, perhaps dozens of these abused and forgotten American servicemen could be brought back to America *and allowed to tell their story to the world!* [Emphasis in original.]

There are good reasons Americans are suckers for such stuff.

After the P.O.W.s came home fifteen years ago many families of the M.I.A.s feared that their fellow citizens, eager to put the war behind them, would soon forget the soldiers who remained behind. They felt exploited by the Administrations of both Lyndon Johnson and Richard Nixon during the war, and grew cynical about whatever the government told them regarding their missing relatives. The endless trickle of reports of Westerners in Southeast Asia—Americans who, listed as M.I.A.s, might in fact be P.O.W.s—only contributed to the widespread distrust. Finally, the desire of right-wingers like LeBoutillier to reclaim America's "lost honor" by rescuing P.O.W.s plays to a thwarted patriotism.

Besides dog tags and pig bones, there are the "live sightings," none of which have withstood serious examination. As Lieut. Gen. James Williams, a former D.I.A. director, told Congress, "A lot of these people who talk about live sightings say they have seen an individual who was a Caucasian, who they think was an American, who was white, who looked like he was under guard. . . . Sometimes sources can't pin down exactly where they were, and can't remember the date of observation."

No New Sightings

In January 1986, the Defense Department reported that there had been 806 reports of firsthand, live sightings in Vietnam, Laos and Cambodia since 1975. Some of these reported sightings, however, took place well before 1975 and in no way constituted new evidence. One-third of them, in fact, occurred before Saigon fell. "Only one first-hand case reporting a sighting of Americans in captivity since 1980 is unsolved," says Commodore Thomas Brooks, another former D.I.A. official, adding that there has not been a new one in more than three years.

Of the original 806 live sightings, the Pentagon found, 24 percent (about 194) are "known or suspected fabrications" and 64 percent (about 517) have been correlated to Americans who have since returned and are thus accounted for. That leaves 12 percent, or about 95 reports; 47 of those were of men who appeared to be Americans but did not seem to be prisoners and 48 involved men who appeared to be Americans under guard. Those not under guard, Brooks says, "could be Soviet advisers, West European diplomats or press or other Caucasians." They could also be defectors. No one disputes that many non-Asians now live in Southeast Asia; some of them, according to Congressional testimony, "simply walked away from their units to live with tribes in the mountains, or became addicted to drugs and stayed behind after the American departure." McDaniel suggests there may be "eighteen or nineteen" of these.

The numbers do not add up. As already stated, some 2,500 Americans are designated as missing in action. Before the fall of Saigon, however, the Pentagon listed only 800 as either P.O.W.s or M.I.A.s. After the war, those killed in action but whose bodies were not returned (those designated K.I.A./B.N.R.) were added, bringing the total to 1,180. More than 430 of the K.I.A./B.N.R.s were pilots whose planes were shot down over water and are considered nonrecoverable. In another 647 cases, a "presumptive finding of death" was made at the time the servicemen disappeared. Well over half—more than 1,900—are therefore known or presumed to be dead. This leaves fewer than 600 who, theoretically, might be alive.

Inflated Numbers

That number, too, is inflated. The House Select Committee on Missing Persons in Southeast Asia, noting that 81 percent of M.I.A.s were airmen, concluded that the circumstances of their disappearance indicate that the "possibility [of any of them surviving] is very slight." A pilot lucky enough to parachute to the ground was more likely to survive if captured than if left on his own. Marine Lieut. Pat Caruthers, who headed the corps' survival training program, says a soldier who got lost on the ground faced such severe difficulties that safe return to his unit was highly unlikely. Some 10 percent of those who were captured died in captivity. How many more perished before entering the prison gulag is unknown. Navy Commander George Coker, a former P.O.W. himself, told Congress that "maybe 3, 4, 5 percent" of prisoners either committed suicide, quit eating or stopped attending to their hygiene and died.

Vietnam's record of returning the remains of U.S. servicemen—three one year, two the next, and whenever it suited that government's diplomatic ends—suggests that Hanoi has systematically warehoused the remains of American servicemen. In 1980, the D.I.A. investigated a Vietnamese refugee's claim that he had prepared the bodies of more than 400 Americans that were then stored in a former P.O.W. camp and concluded that the man's story was accurate.

Start substracting these sums from the 2,500 figure, and the bottom line is pretty obvious: There are precious few, if any, Americans left to rescue, and nothing like the "several hundreds" McDaniel refers to in a Home Free! flier.

To think the prisoners are there, one most believe that, of the 200 or so who theoretically could be alive, every last one in fact is—and has managed to survive under what McDaniel, LeBoutillier and others describe as almost unbearably brutal conditions. None of which perturbs McDaniel in the least. "Of course the conditions are brutal," Cap'n Red responds, "which is why we don't have a moment to waste."

5

VIEWPOINT

5

5

"We must not permit the Non-Communist Resistance in Cambodia to become the last casualty of the Vietnam war."

The U.S. Should Aid Cambodia's Resistance Forces

Dan Quayle

Dan Quayle was elected vice president of the United States in 1988. The following viewpoint is excerpted from a speech he made following a 1989 trip to Asia. Quayle argues that the U.S. should continue to play an active role in Indochina. He believes the U.S. should aid non-Communist resistance forces in Cambodia who are battling the communist government. Quayle asserts that critics of Cambodian aid believe the U.S. should avoid all involvement in Indochina, which he argues is the wrong lesson from the Vietnam War.

As you read, consider the following questions:

1. According to Quayle, what role should the U.S. play in Asia?
2. What does Quayle believe would be the best way to prevent Pol Pot from returning to power?
3. Does the author support the use of U.S. troops in Cambodia? Why or why not?

5
Dan Quayle, speech delivered June 12, 1989 at The Heritage Foundation Asian Studies Center Conference, Washington, D.C.

209

Since World War II, the United States has been deeply engaged in Asia, helping to defend our Allies while promoting peace and stability throughout the region. Formal bilateral security relationships with Japan, the Republic of Korea, Thailand, the Philippines and Australia, along with informal cooperation with other free world nations, have made an immense contribution to the stability of the region, and have been a vital factor in our global deterrence posture.

The Soviet Threat

One of the key themes I stressed in both my public and private remarks in Asia was the need for the United States and our Asian allies to maintain our commitment to collective security. As the Soviet Union takes its first faltering steps to democracy, as it begins to be interested in contributing constructively to settling international disputes, there may be a tendency to neglect our common defense, and to ignore the need to nurture our Alliance relationships.

I am firmly convinced that we must resist the temptation to dispense with our defense capabilities. Rather, we must prudently watch to see if Gorbachev's peace rhetoric in the Pacific is matched by deeds that lessen the Soviet threat. We must adopt a long range perspective on the Soviets that is hopeful, yet cautious. Although there are encouraging signs of change in Soviet policies, these changes have not been uniform and, with the exception of the Sino-Soviet border, there has been no substantial reduction in the overall Soviet threat, especially in the military capabilities in the Northwest Pacific. The Soviet Pacific Ocean fleet still numbers 871 ships and craft. As long as this threat remains, so does the need for preparedness. . . .

The United States must continue to maintain an active role and presence in the Pacific. The U.S. must remain a Pacific power, the fundamental guarantor of regional stability. . . .

The Situation in Cambodia

I would like to talk about Cambodia, and about the Administration's policy in support of peace and democratic development in Southeast Asia. As you know, Vietnam invaded and occupied Cambodia in late 1978. At the time, it seemed doubtful that the victorious Vietnamese could ever be induced to go home. Now, however, Vietnam has indicated that it will withdraw its forces from Cambodia by September 30, 1990. We continue to hope that progress can be made in negotiations among the Cambodian factions toward agreement on an interim coalition government under Prince [Norodom] Sihanouk which will lead to free elections and genuine stability in Cambodia, and prevent the return to the Khmer Rouge "killing fields."

In the past, the U.S. has worked closely with the ASEAN [Association of Southeast Asian Nations] nations as well as with China to bring home to Vietnam the diplomatic and economic consequences of its domination of Cambodia. The ASEAN leaders agree with our position that the Vietnamese-installed Hun Sen regime cannot be allowed to monopolize power after Vietnamese forces have withdrawn. A one-sided settlement would make continued civil war almost inevitable. At the same time, the communist Khmer Rouge, who are responsible for the deaths of 20 percent of Cambodia's 1975 population—some million and a half persons—must not return to dominance. The only realistic and satisfactory alternative is a transitional coalition government headed by Prince Sihanouk, in which the Non-Communist Resistance—the groups headed by Sihanouk and Son Sann—would play a key role. This coalition would establish the framework of a new, non-communist state and organize elections that would offer the Cambodian people an opportunity to decide their own future.

The Purpose of Military Aid

Those who suggest that providing arms to the non-communist resistance would obstruct a political settlement miss the point of the proposal. The purpose is not to increase the level of violence in Cambodia, but to enhance the prospects for a political settlement that will bring the violence to an end.

It is possible, of course, that the negotiations will break down and that no political settlement will be reached. In that case, military assistance to the non-communists also would constitute a further hedge against the return to power of the Khmer Rouge, who still field a fierce and formidable force of 30,000 to 40,000 men under arms.

Stephen J. Solarz, *Los Angeles Times*, May 31, 1989.

To deal with the twin dilemmas of the Khmer Rouge and the Hun Sen regime, virtually every government supports an international presence under United Nations auspices to verify the Vietnamese withdrawal, police a ceasefire, and supervise democratic elections in Cambodia. The only exceptions are Vietnam and its Cambodian client. Even Moscow at times has appeared willing to accept an international presence, with the caveat that it must be acceptable to Hanoi and Phnom Penh.

The U.S., ASEAN, China and our Allies in Europe and Japan welcome steps that will hasten a true, complete, and internationally verified withdrawal as a real contribution to a comprehensive political settlement in Cambodia. U.S. policy towards

Cambodia has consistently called for such a withdrawal, along with effective measures to prevent the return to power of the Khmer Rouge. And the U.S. looks forward to eventual normalization of relations with Vietnam in the context of a genuine withdrawal and an acceptable settlement in Cambodia. The pace and scope of the normalization process, of course, will be affected by Vietnam's cooperation with us on humanitarian issues, including the prisoner-of-war/missing-in-action issue.

The best opportunity for preventing a return to power by the Khmer Rouge is a comprehensive settlement that includes a Sihanouk-led interim coalition government and an international presence to monitor and supervise elections and keep the peace. No single element can do the job alone. Our policy is designed to create the full range of stabilizing and restraining elements needed for a comprehensive settlement. However, the most important single element is strengthening the Non-Communist Resistance in as many ways as possible. For this reason, the Administration has asked Congress to authorize additional aid to the Non-Communist Resistance. The purpose of such assistance is to increase the political strength of the Non-Communist Resistance in the peace process while simultaneously giving it the strength to hold its own in the event of a Khmer Rouge attempt to seize power.

Supporting the Resistance

Yet instead of endorsing greater assistance to the Non-Communist Resistance, some in Congress have opposed it. They have challenged the Administration to make the case for more assistance in a public forum. Well, this *is* a public forum, and I would like to lay out the case for strengthening the Non-Communist Resistance in Cambodia.

The basic rationale for such a policy is straightforward. At this moment, the forces of the murderous Khmer Rouge are heavily armed, thanks to China's assistance. The forces of the Hun Sen regime are even more heavily armed, thanks to Soviet and Vietnamese assistance. Under these circumstances, surely the non-communist forces deserve the assistance of the West. Surely we should act to prevent the Khmer Rouge from returning to power. Surely, as Americans, we have a compelling moral responsibility to do what we can, short of direct intervention, to provide the wherewithal for the Cambodian people to have a genuine choice in determining their future. . . .

By strengthening the Non-Communist Resistance, we would be *increasing* the prospects for a successful political, *negotiated*, outcome; by doing nothing, we would increase the likelihood of continued civil war and the potential for a return to power by the murderous Khmer Rouge. Unless Sihanouk is strong enough militarily and politically, he will not be able to hold the center of the Cambodian political stage long enough to ensure a free and fair election.

We have seen many reports portraying Hanoi's invasion-installed PRK [People's Republic of Kampuchea] regime as beneficent, reforming and popular. If Hun Sen—a former Khmer Rouge commander—is as popular as his press reviews claim, he has nothing to fear from going to the polls and substituting ballots for bullets in an internationally supervised, properly prepared election. If the PRK is as strong as it claims, an election victory will give it the legitimacy it so visibly lacks and badly needs.

Let there be no mistake about this crucial point: it is the absence of a negotiated agreement, not our assistance to the Non-Communist Resistance, that increases the prospects of civil war. By aiding Prince Sihanouk and the Non-Communist Resistance, we will be encouraging a political process that will bring Cambodia's civil war to an end. By withholding aid, we will only make continued civil war more likely.

Answering the Critics

But our Congressional critics accuse the Administration of seeking to promote "instability" in Cambodia. They forget that the best guarantee of stability is a negotiated settlement, and that aid to the Non-Communist Resistance will help bring about such a settlement. They claim that by aiding Prince Sihanouk and the Non-Communist Resistance forces, we become indirect accomplices of his Khmer Rouge partners. They forget that our assistance to Prince Sihanouk is designed to make it possible for him to be *independent* of the Khmer Rouge *without* becoming a prisoner of the Vietnamese sponsored puppet government. Prince Sihanouk's children were murdered by the Khmer Rouge. Does anyone seriously think that he needs instruction on how dangerous and odious these people are?

Critics claim that anything given to the Non-Communist Resistance will fall into the hands of the Khmer Rouge. In a single instance in the past, when the Non-Communist Resistance was dreadfully weak, a larger Khmer Rouge unit surrounded and disarmed a woefully outnumbered Non-Communist unit. However, this no longer happens—not because the Khmer Rouge have suddenly become genteel but because the Non-Communist units are now large enough and well armed enough to defend themselves in most cases while operating inside Cambodia.

Critics warn that by strengthening the Non-Communist Resistance we are headed down a "slippery slope." They forget that we have in fact been providing substantial amounts of assistance to the Non-Communist Resistance for years. This assistance has not led us back into direct involvement in Indochina. It has contributed to a policy of seeking a comprehensive, political settlement for Cambodia. Further assistance is a means to bringing about such a political settlement. . . .

Fearing Another Vietnam

But, in fact, what underlies all these criticisms of our policy and to the Non-Communist Resistance is a deeper fear—the fear of "another Vietnam." The unacknowledged but all too tangible presence in the debate over Cambodia is the ghost of Vietnam. But, my friends, it is now time to lay this ghost to rest. President [George] Bush noted in his Inaugural Address: "No great nation can long afford to be sundered by a memory." Similarly, *no great nation can long afford to be paralyzed by a memory. We must not permit the Non-Communist Resistance in Cambodia to become the last casualty of the Vietnam war.*

The situation in Southeast Asia today is very different from that of the late 1960s or the early 1970s. We have learned many things since 1975, the year Saigon fell to the armies of the North Vietnamese communists. We have learned that the coming of "peace," so-called, to Southeast Asia did not bring an end to suffering and injustice for the people of that region. Few of the critics of American involvement in the Vietnam War later found the time to pay much attention to the horrors inflicted on the people of Indochina by the communist regimes in Hanoi and Phnom Penh. Few had the courage to admit they may have been wrong in their assessment of the moral calculus of the situation in Southeast Asia.

At the same time, we have learned that there are limits to America's ability to assist others to achieve and defend free government. We have learned that America cannot fight others' battles for them.

But we have also learned that we have every reason to be confident in the ultimate triumph of freedom. The Vietnam experience damaged our confidence in American values and institutions. But over the last years, our confidence has been restored. And indeed, as we look at Asia and the world today, it is clearer than ever before that the future does not lie with Soviet communism or its Asian variants. To a degree that would have seemed astonishing even a decade ago, democratic ideals are on the march in Asia.

Let me conclude by reaffirming this Administration's determination to remain engaged in Asia—engaged for peace, for freedom, and for democracy. Our role in Asia's attainment of these goals remains vital. And that is why it must continue.

VIEWPOINT

"It is time for the United States to re-examine its position."

The U.S. Should Not Aid Cambodia's Resistance Forces

Susan Blaustein

Debates similar to those heard during the Vietnam War are being waged today over whether or not the U.S. should aid guerrillas fighting the communist government of Cambodia. In the following viewpoint, Susan Blaustein criticizes U.S. plans to help resistance forces. She argues that such aid would increase the chances of former dictator Pol Pot returning to power in Cambodia. Blaustein is a free-lance writer living in Southeast Asia. Her articles have appeared in *The Nation* and *The New Yorker*.

As you read, consider the following questions:

1. What three motivations does Blaustein believe are behind current U.S. policy toward Cambodia?
2. According to the author, how have memories of the Vietnam War affected U.S. policy in Cambodia?
3. Why does Blaustein contend the U.S. should support the Hun Sen government in Cambodia?

Susan Blaustein, "Old War, China Card & Sihanouk," *The Nation*, October 30, 1989, © 1989 The Nation Company, Inc. Reprinted with permission.

After ten years of letting Khmer Rouge communists and Vietnamese-backed communists shoot it out among themselves, the United States is now rooting around for a policy on Cambodia. But . . . Washington's current views on the subject perpetuate the same reactive thinking that has guided its action—and inaction—for more than ten years. Since 1978, when Vietnam invaded Cambodia and toppled the Khmer Rouge regime, the United States has followed the lead of China, Prince Norodom Sihanouk of Cambodia and their Southeast Asian allies in condemning the Vietnamese occupation and denying recognition and reconstruction assistance to the Vietnamese-installed Phnom Penh government. Instead, the United States has recognized the loose coalition of two noncommunist resistance forces and the Khmer Rouge, which is led by the infamous Khieu Samphan.

U.S. Motivations

United States policy toward Cambodia seems to have three motivations, none of which have much to do with Cambodia but all of which have been adhered to with remarkable stubbornness through four administrations: antagonism toward Vietnam; unwillingness to upset China, the main supplier of the Khmer Rouge; and insistence on Sihanouk as central to any political solution.

Since the Vietnamese invasion of Cambodia, some mixture of resentment and desire to get back at Vietnam for "winning" what Vietnamese call "the American War" has fueled the persistent U.S. condemnation and economic boycott of both Cambodia and Vietnam—all in the name of securing Cambodian sovereignty. Now the Vietnamese and Cambodian governments claim that Vietnam's last 26,000 troops have left Cambodia. For almost eleven years the United States has insisted that the Vietnamese must get out if they want the embargo ended, and that their withdrawal be verified by an international force. But when Vietnamese and Cambodian officials finally agreed to allow an international monitor inside Cambodia, the United States refused to agree to such a force in the absence of "a comprehensive diplomatic settlement." Without a verified withdrawal, charges that Vietnam has left behind troops disguised as Cambodians are impossible to disprove, and the Bush Administration can continue to rationalize the decade-long U.S. embargo that strangles Vietnam.

According to the peculiar logic of U.S. Indochina policy, the Vietnamese have been more oppressive than the Khmer Rouge. While Vietnam has been condemned by the United States and its Asian allies as the invader and aggressor, since 1982 the Khmer Rouge have occupied Cambodia's seat at the United

Nations as part of the coalition with Sihanouk and a second noncommunist faction, Son Sann's Khmer People's National Liberation Front. Now that the Vietnamese claim to have left, the relative threats to Cambodians posed by what Richard Solomon calls the two "elements" of the "split Khmer-communist movement" must be freshly evaluated. Prime Minister Hun Sen and President Heng Samrin, who left the Khmer Rouge for Vietnam in the late 1970s, have governed Cambodia creditably since 1979 and are not mass murderers, whereas the tyrannical Khmer Rouge regime left over a million dead and the country in ruins. These are not subtle distinctions.

U.S. Must Leave

Vietnam and Cambodia have both suffered long enough. It is time for the United States—the primary nation responsible for the misery and terror that both peoples have endured—to leave them in peace. That can be done only by stopping all aid to the Sihanouk coalition and by recognizing the Hun Sen government, de facto if not officially. In short, the time has come, as part of the ending of the Cold War, to end our war against the people of Indochina.

In These Times, October 4-10, 1989.

But Washington would rather not hear any good news about Vietnam or the government it put into place in Phnom Penh. The Bush Administration not only opposed credible verification of the troop withdrawal but it has blocked the U.S. Agency for International Development and even prevented the U.N. [United Nations] Development Program from carrying out recent fact-finding missions inside Cambodia to assess the state of the country's infrastructure. Rather than let new information interfere with their long-held beliefs about the threat to Cambodia of "Vietnamese hegemony," U.S. officials prefer to continue on their old course. . . .

Supporting China

Maintaining smooth relations with China is the second concern that has driven Washington's Cambodia policy for the last fifteen years. Although reports of Khmer Rouge atrocities reached the United States as early as mid-1975, throughout the four years of the Khmer Rouge regime—indeed, throughout the rest of the Ford, Carter and Reagan Administrations—normalizing relations and forging a strategic alliance with China always precluded demanding that China stop bankrolling its murderous Khmer Rouge allies. . . .

The third force steering U.S. policy in Cambodia is Prince

Sihanouk. He was "our horse in this race," declared Solomon in his testimony about the Paris talks, "and we tried to build the peace process around him." Washington's choice has refused Hun Sen's overtures to forge a bilateral agreement and, like the Chinese, insists on including the Khmer Rouge in any transitional government. . . .

Who is this old horse on whose good sense the United States is ready to stake Cambodia's future? Despite his royal name, and gilded memories of his rule in the time before Pol Pot, Sihanouk has not demonstrated his ability to deliver anything the country needs. After ten years as the opposition leader with the strongest international support, he has yet to harness that support to design and finance a practical program for rebuilding his ravaged country. When he was overthrown in 1970, probably with U.S. acquiescence, Sihanouk displayed the quality of his judgment by allying himself and sticking with the Khmer Rouge. These unlikely allies share a virulent hatred for Vietnam that no doubt pleases their superpower backers. In the name of Khmer nationalism, U.S. officials persist in basing critical policy decisions on a leader who hates the Vietnamese as much as they do, but whose only presence inside Cambodia in the past nineteen years was as a puppet and prisoner of the Khmer Rouge from 1975 to 1979. . . .

Even so, the Prince's erratic behavior has not deterred the Bush Administration from doggedly supporting him. The United States wants "to strengthen the noncommunists as much as we can," Solomon said. "We would not like to see Sihanouk dependent on the Khmer Rouge." In 1989 the Administration obtained Congressional approval to send lethal reinforcements to Sihanouk, a move initially designed to strengthen his bargaining power in negotiations and subsequently used, Administration officials claim, to try to pry him loose from the Khmer Rouge. So far this move has yielded no results. . . .

No Political Settlement

With . . . an imminent political settlement unlikely, and with Sihanouk's refusal to distance himself from the Khmer Rouge, the Bush Administration will now have to decide how far it is willing to go to bolster the Prince and his noncommunist allies. Having publicly objected to a possible Khmer Rouge return to power, can the Administration continue to countenance lethal aid to Sihanouk if it means following him all the way back to Phnom Penh, arm-in-arm with the Khmer Rouge? . . .

With Vietnam's troops gone, Hun Sen's army largely untested and the Khmer Rouge moving into Cambodia's northwest provinces, it is time for the Bush Administration to take a more principled role in resolving Cambodia's crisis. First, it must insist that China stop supplying the Khmer Rouge, that Thailand

219

stop providing them sanctuary and that Sihanouk cut his ties with them. If Sihanouk continues to refuse to do so, the Bush Administration must stop putting its money on the dotty Prince simply because he is the best-known noncommunist contender.

U.S. Interests

The US has three basic interests in Cambodia: the prevention of a return to power by the genocidal Khmer Rouge; the establishment of a pluralistic society that will uphold the human and civil rights of the Cambodian people; and the creation of stability, which will foster the conditions for social and economic reconstruction and development.

The suggestion that the US just increase its political, economic, and military support of the noncommunist forces does not adequately reflect American interests in Cambodia or the complexities of the situation there. Rather, it continues the cold-war, oppose-communism-at-any-cost mentality.

Michael Chambers, *The Christian Science Monitor*, November 29, 1989.

Second, it is time for the United States to re-examine its position vis-à-vis the Hun Sen government. If the Administration means what it says about self-determination for the Cambodian people, it should look beyond the "Made in Hanoi" label still attached to the government in Phnom Penh to see exactly what it has been able to accomplish and how it rates with Cambodians. Even with an ongoing war and negligible Western assistance, Hun Sen has shown flexibility in his economic policies and made progress in restoring the country's public works and human services from the wreckage left in 1979 by the Khmer Rouge. In so doing he seems to have garnered a significant amount of public confidence. He is, in fact, precisely the kind of Third World leader that the United States should be willing to deal with if it is serious about breaking with its anachronistic cold war world view.

Finally, the Administration should consider resuming reconstruction and humanitarian assistance as a means of encouraging Hun Sen into guaranteeing internationally supervised elections for a truly "sovereign" Cambodian government. . . .

Now, with Vietnam's departure, is the logical time for the Bush Administration to drop the tired and ineffective Cambodia policy of the last decade—a policy primarily based on fear of offending China and the sting of Vietnam War wounds. To hold to it out of habit and cowardice will cost many more Cambodian lives.

a critical thinking activity

Lessons to Be Learned from Vietnam

It is said that experience is life's best teacher. One must actively reflect on past experiences to derive lessons for the present and future, however. The purpose of this activity is to examine the reasons for America's failure in Vietnam and to see if there are lessons to be learned that can be helpful in directing America's foreign policy toward Vietnam and Cambodia today.

Part I

Step 1. The class should break into groups of four to six students. Working individually within each group, each student should rank the reasons listed below for America's failure in Vietnam. *Assign the number 1 to the reason most responsible for American failure, the number 2 to the second most important reason, and so on, until all the reasons have been ranked. Add any reasons, not listed, that you think should be included.*

Step 2. Students should compare their rankings with others in their group, giving the reasons for their rankings.

Reasons for America's Failure in Vietnam

1. U.S. failure to declare war
2. Unexpected determination of the enemy
3. U.S. peace movement that undermined public support
4. Russian and Chinese support of the enemy
5. Lack of U.S. determination
6. Critical press accounts that undermined public support
7. Poorly planned U.S. military strategy

221

8. Incompetence of U.S. political leaders
9. An unjust cause
10. Lack of support by America's allies
11. Lack of support of the South Vietnamese people
12. _____
13. _____
14. _____

Part II

Step 1. Each small group should draft a *Statement of Vietnam Lessons* that current U.S. leaders should study in planning American policy toward Vietnam and Cambodia. Include a minimum of four lessons in each draft.

Lesson 1. _____

_____

Lesson 2. _____

_____

Lesson 3. _____

_____

Lesson 4. _____

_____

Step 2. Each small group should compare its draft and rankings from Part I with others in a classwide discussion.

Step 3. The entire class should draft a *Statement of Vietnam Lessons*. Include a minimum of six lessons in the classwide draft.

Step 4. Send a copy of the classroom draft to appropriate government officials:

   the president of the United States

   the two U.S. senators representing your state

   your congressman or congresswoman

   the U.S. secretary of state

   the U.S. secretary of defense

   others the class considers appropriate

Periodical Bibliography

The following articles have been selected to supplement the diverse views presented in this chapter.

Robert Sam Anson	"Again, the Indochina Quagmire Beckons," *The New York Times*, October 18, 1989.
Alan Berlow	"Never Again?" *Harper's Magazine*, October 1989.
George Black	"Republican Overtures to Hanoi," *The Nation*, June 4, 1988.
Stanley W. Cloud	"Still a Killing Field," *Time*, April 30, 1990.
Seth Cropsey	"Moscow in the Pacific," *National Review*, June 5, 1987.
William J. Duiker	"Is It Time to Recognize Vietnam?" *The World & I*, July 1988.
In These Times	"As Vietnam Withdraws from Cambodia, the U.S. Should Follow Suit," October 4-10, 1989.
James A. Kelly	"The United States in Southeast Asia: A Political-Security Agenda," *The Washington Quarterly*, Autumn 1989.
Kirk Kidwell	"Bring Them Home!" *The New American*, February 2, 1987.
John LeBoutillier	"Coming to Terms with Vietnam," *The New York Times Magazine*, May 1, 1988.
Todd L. Newmark	"Strange Alliance," *Commentary*, March 1990.
Nguyen Co Thach, interviewed by Stanley W. Cloud	"'It's Time to Heal the Wounds,'" *Time*, April 30, 1990.
Lionel A. Rosenblatt	"Arms Won't Defeat the Khmer Rouge," *The New York Times*, June 2, 1989.
Jill Smolowe	"Will It Ever End?" *Time*, October 9, 1989.
Steven J. Solarz	"Cambodia and the International Community," *Foreign Affairs*, Spring 1990.
Richard H. Solomon	"Cambodia and Vietnam: Trapped in an Eddy of History?" *Department of State Bulletin*, November 1989.
John R. Thomson	"Holiday in Cambodia," *National Review*, October 13, 1989.
Lesley Wischmann	"When the War Never Ends," *The Other Side*, September/October 1989.
Walter F. Wouk	"Will the Vietnam War Ever End?" *The New York Times*, January 23, 1989.

Chronology of U.S. Involvement in Vietnam

February 1930	The Indochinese Communist Party is formed under the leadership of Ho Chi Minh. The party opposes French colonial rule.
September 22, 1940	The French government agrees to allow the Japanese to use Vietnam to station troops. The Japanese troops, allegedly ignorant of the Franco-Japanese agreement, cross into Vietnam from China and take French-held cities. Japan continues to occupy more and more of Indochina but permits French administration to continue.
May 1941	Ho Chi Minh forms the Viet Minh during the meeting of the Central Committee of the Indochina Communist Party. The Viet Minh's purpose is to fight the French and Japanese.
September 2, 1945	Ho Chi Minh announces the foundation of the Democratic Republic of Vietnam (DRV).
September 13, 1945	British forces arrive in Saigon to begin disarmament of the Japanese and to assume control of Vietnam.
September 26, 1945	Lieutenant Colonel A. Peter Dewey, head of the Office of Strategic Security (OSS) mission in Vietnam is the first American killed there. The OSS is the precursor of the Central Intelligence Agency.
December 1946	Viet Minh attack French positions and the Franco-Vietnamese War begins.
June 1948	Bao Dai becomes chief of state of Vietnam under French control.
July 1949	Bao Dai decrees the establishment of the State of Vietnam.
January 14, 1950	Ho Chi Minh proclaims the Democratic Republic of Vietnam as the only legal government of Vietnam.
January 18, 1950	China recognizes the DRV as the legal government of Vietnam.
February 7, 1950	The United States and Britain recognize Bao Dai's government.
June 27, 1950	U.S. President Harry S. Truman announces that he is sending military aid to French forces and he will send a military mission to Vietnam.
December 23, 1950	Mutual Defense Assistance Agreement is signed by the United States, Vietnam, France, Cambodia, and Laos.
May 7, 1954	Viet Minh forces defeat the French at Dien Bien Phu, the village the French had chosen as a bulwark against the Viet Minh. The French held Dien Bien Phu from November 1953 until the defeat.
June 16, 1954	Bao Dai selects Ngo Dinh Diem as prime minister of the State of Vietnam.

July 21, 1954	Geneva conference calls for a cease-fire in Vietnam and divides it at the seventeenth parallel. Ho Chi Minh assumes control of North Vietnam and Bao Dai rules South Vietnam. Bao Dai's government denounces the agreement and the United States declines to sign it.
September 8, 1954	The Southeast Asia Treaty Organization (SEATO) is formed by the United States, France, Britain, Australia, New Zealand, Pakistan, Thailand, and the Philippines.
January 1, 1955	United States begins to send aid directly to Bao Dai's government in Saigon.
February 12, 1955	U.S. advisory group begins training the South Vietnamese army.
October 26, 1955	Diem, after defeating Bao Dai in a referendum, announces the formation of the Republic of Vietnam in the south. He becomes South Vietnam's first president.
May 8-19, 1957	President Diem visits the U.S., addressing a joint session of Congress and receiving a declaration of support from U.S. President Dwight D. Eisenhower.
May 1959	U.S. advisers are ordered to Vietnam to assist South Vietnamese infantry, artillery, armored, and marine forces.
December 20, 1960	National Liberation Front (NLF) is formed in South Vietnam with Hanoi's support to overthrow the Saigon government.
May 5, 1961	U.S. President John F. Kennedy announces it may be necessary to send U.S. troops to Vietnam.
December 8, 1961	U.S. State Department publishes a "white paper" claiming that South Vietnam is threatened by "clear and present danger" of Communist aggression.
February 7, 1962	Two U.S. Army air support companies arrive in Saigon, bringing total of U.S. troops in South Vietnam to four thousand.
February 24, 1962	China demands a withdrawal of U.S. troops from Vietnam, claiming its security is threatened.
May 1, 1963	Buddhists gather in the city of Hue to protest a decree prohibiting them from flying their flag. Several months of rioting break out.
May 8, 1963	President Diem's troops fire on twenty thousand Buddhists gathered in the city of Hue to celebrate the Buddha's birthday. Diem's troops kill eight children and one woman.
August 24, 1963	Washington cables the Saigon embassy, recommending that President Diem be removed.
November 1, 1963	A military coup overthrows the Diem government. Diem attempts to flee, but is caught and executed the next day. He is replaced by Vice President Nguyen Ngoc Tho and General Duong Van Minh.
November 22, 1963	President Kennedy is assassinated.

November 23, 1963	U.S. President Lyndon B. Johnson announces continued U.S. support for the South Vietnamese government.
January 30, 1964	In another military coup, General Khanh, a South Vietnamese Army commander, overthrows the government of General Minh.
June 12, 1964	General Khanh and another South Vietnamese, Air Marshall Nguyen Cao Ky, call for air strikes against North Vietnam.
August 2, 1964	North Vietnamese patrol boats attack the U.S. destroyer *Maddox*. The *Maddox* sinks one of the three attacking boats and cripples the other two. Two days later the *Maddox*, along with another U.S. destroyer, the *Turner Joy*, reports a second North Vietnamese attack, with the U.S. sinking more North Vietnamese boats. The U.S. retaliates with an air strike in North Vietnam.
August 7, 1964	U.S. Congress passes the Gulf of Tonkin Resolution (98-2 in Senate and 416-0 in House), giving President Johnson the authority to use "all necessary steps, including the use of armed force" in Southeast Asia.
February 7, 1965	President Johnson orders bombing of North Vietnam after eight American soldiers are killed in a Viet Cong attack.
February 27, 1965	U.S. State Department issues a "white paper" accusing North Vietnam of aggression.
March 8, 1965	Thirty-five hundred American marines land at Da Nang. They are the first U.S. combat troops sent to Vietnam.
April 7, 1965	President Johnson offers a one-billion-dollar Southeast Asia aid package if the North Vietnamese will participate in "unconditional discussions."
June 8, 1965	U.S. State Department publicly authorizes U.S. troops to participate in combat.
October 15-16, 1965	The National Coordinating Committee to End the War in Vietnam sponsors nationwide demonstrations in the U.S.
April 12, 1966	American B-52s bomb North Vietnam for the first time in response to a Viet Cong attack on U.S. sodiers.
October 25, 1966	U.S. offers to withdraw its troops six months after Hanoi withdraws its forces.
January 10, 1967	President Johnson requests a 6 percent income tax surcharge to finance U.S. involvement in Vietnam.
April 15, 1967	Over 100,000 people in New York and San Francisco demonstrate against the war in Vietnam.
January 31, 1968	As the Vietnamese New Year begins, North Vietnam launches the Tet Offensive, a massive surprise attack against South Vietnam's cities. The U.S. and South Vietnam defeat the North after twenty-six days of fighting.

March 16, 1968	As President Johnson's popularity plummets, Senator Robert Kennedy announces that he will run for president. On the same day in Vietnam, Lieutenant William Calley orders his men to fire on the village of My Lai, killing between 200 and 500 unarmed villagers.
March 31, 1968	President Johnson announces his decision not to seek reelection.
April 3, 1968	North Vietnam offers to participate in peace talks.
June 5, 1968	After winning the California primary, Robert Kennedy is shot. He dies the next day.
August 26-29, 1968	The Democratic National Convention opens in Chicago. The convention is marked by divisions in party policy regarding Vietnam. Outside the convention hall, protests against U.S. involvement in Vietnam are forcibly dispelled by the Chicago police.
October 31, 1968	President Johnson halts bombing of North Vietnam.
November 6, 1968	Richard M. Nixon defeats Hubert H. Humphrey to become the U.S. president.
March 15, 1969	President Nixon orders the bombing of Viet Cong sanctuaries in Cambodia. Three days later U.S. B-52s attack. The bombings continue through April 1970. All bombing of Cambodia remains secret from the U.S. public.
May 14, 1969	President Nixon proposes simultaneous withdrawal of U.S. and North Vietnamese troops.
June 8, 1969	President Nixon announces first U.S. troop withdrawal of twenty-five thousand soldiers.
July 25, 1969	The president announces the "Nixon Doctrine. He calls for sending more economic and military aid to South Vietnam to strengthen the South Vietnamese military. This policy of Vietnamization would prevent a North Vietnamese victory while also allowing the U.S. to gradually withdraw itroops, according to Nixon.
September 3, 1969	Ho Chi Minh dies.
October 15, 1969	Thousands of Americans participate in demonstrations in opposition to the Vietnam War.
November 3, 1969	President Nixon appeals to what he calls the "silent majority," Americans who support the war in Vietnam. He claims that withdrawing from Vietnam would harm U.S. interests.
November 12, 1969	U.S. Army announces that U.S. troops allegedly killed over one hundred civilians in March of 1968 in the Vietnamese village of My Lai.
April 29, 1970	U.S. troops invade Cambodia to attack North Vietnamese and Viet Cong sanctuaries.
May 4, 1970	Ohio national guardsmen kill four Kent State University students during a campus antiwar demonstration.
June 24, 1970	Senate repeals 1964 Gulf of Tonkin Resolution by a vote of eighty-one to ten.
March 29, 1971	Lieutenant Calley convicted of murdering South Vietnamese civilians at My Lai.

June 13, 1971	*The New York Times* begins publication of leaked portions of *The Pentagon Papers*, the Pentagon's analysis of how the U.S. commitment in Indochina grew over a period of three decades. Their publication leads to a legal battle between the government and the press.
January 25, 1972	President Nixon reveals that Henry Kissinger, his national security adviser, has been engaged in secret peace talks in Paris since August 1969.
May 8, 1972	President Nixon announces that the U.S. will mine North Vietnamese harbors.
October 21, 1972	Henry Kissinger and North Vietnamese military leader Le Duc Tho reach a cease-fire agreement.
December 1972	U.S. B-52s and other aircraft bomb North Vietnam.
January 27, 1973	The U.S., South Vietnam, North Vietnam, and the Viet Cong sign peace agreements, including an agreement to cease firing and to withdraw U.S. troops.
March 29, 1973	North Vietnamese release sixty American prisoners of war, who leave Vietnam along with the last remaining U.S. troops.
August 1974	President Nixon resigns to avoid being impeached for his role in the Watergate scandal. Vice President Gerald Ford assumes the presidency.
Spring 1975	North Vietnamese launch final offensive of the Vietnam War, capturing half of Vietnam and killing or capturing one-third of the South Vietnamese army.
April 23, 1975	President Ford declares the war "finished."
April 30, 1975	The city of Saigon surrenders to North Vietnamese Communists. The remaining Americans are evacuated from the roof of the U.S. Embassy.
1975-1978	The Khmer Rouge under Pol Pot kills two million to three million Cambodians, one-third of the population.
January 21, 1977	U.S. President Jimmy Carter pardons most Vietnam War draft evaders.
Spring 1978	Veterans Administration first reports health problems in Vietnam veterans related to the herbicide Agent Orange. Agent Orange was dropped from U.S. planes to kill the vegetation in Vietnam.
December 1978	Vietnam invades Cambodia following Cambodian attacks on Vietnam. Vietnam overthrows Pol Pot and the Khmer Rouge and installs the Hanoi-backed Cambodian National United Front for National Salvation. Cambodia is renamed the People's Republic of Kampuchea.
February 17, 1979	China attacks Vietnam to protest Vietnam's invasion of Cambodia. Sixteen days later, China witdraws.
1981	The U.S. provides two million dollars to protect the "boat people," Indochinese refugees who fled the war-torn region. After pirates attack more than three-quarters of the boats carrying the refugees, the U.S. and Thailand announce a joint force to protect the boat people.

1981-1983	Sixteen thousand Vietnam veterans and their families file a class-action lawsuit against seven major chemical companies for Agent Orange poisoning.
July 1982	The coalition government of Democratic Kampuchea forms and includes both Communist and non-Communist factions.
November 11, 1982	The Vietnam Veterans War Memorial is dedicated in Washington, D.C.
May 7, 1984	After 16,000 families announce they are suing the manufacturers of Agent Orange, seven chemical companies agree to pay 180 million dollars to settle the families' claims hours before the trial starts.
November 5, 1985	The United Nations passes a resolution ordering Vietnam to withdraw from Cambodia. Vietnam resists U.N. pressure.
September 30, 1986	A Pentagon panel concludes there are Americans still held prisoner in Southeast Asia.
July 1987	General John Vessey, President Ronald Reagan's special envoy to Vietnam, visits Hanoi to discuss the status of American prisoners of war and other humanitarian issues.
January 1988	U.S. Congress passes the Amerasian Homecoming Act. This allows Vietnamese children whose fathers were Americans to come to the U.S. with their mothers.
Spring 1988	Vietnam bows to pressure from the U.N. and agrees to withdraw troops from Cambodia, with all troops gone by 1990.
June 15, 1988	Hong Kong declares that it will no longer accept Indochinese refugees. Acting on orders from England, the government says that any refugees will be declared illegal immigrants and will be returned to their countries.
November 4, 1988	Vietnam returns the remains of twenty-three service people missing in action since the Vietnam War. During President Reagan's two terms in office, Vietnam returns the remains of 196 service people.
July 30, 1989	The U.S. and the Socialist Republic of Vietnam sign an agreement to resettle Cambodians and their families in the U.S.
Fall 1989	Peace talks between the Indochinese countries, the permanent members of the U.N. Security Council, and the Khmer Rouge take place in Paris.
September 1989	Vietnamese troops withdraw from Cambodia, ending a decade of occupation. Some advisers remain.
April 1990	A U.S. Centers for Disease Control study concludes that the herbicide Agent Orange did not injure soldiers who fought in Vietnam.
April 30, 1990	Vietnamese Communist Party leader Nguyen Van Linh appeals for friendship and economic cooperation with the United States.

Annotated Book Bibliography

Mark Baker	*Nam.* New York: Quill, 1982. Graphic descriptions of the war in short statements by those who fought. Very powerful.
Larry Berman	*Lyndon Johnson's War.* New York: W.W. Norton & Company, 1989. A historical examination of U.S. policies between 1965 and 1968. Berman blames poor decisions by President Johnson for U.S. failure in Vietnam.
William Broyles Jr.	*Brothers in Arms.* New York: Alfred A. Knopf, 1986. A moving personal account of a Vietnam veteran turned *Newsweek* editor who revisits Vietnam in 1984 to meet his former enemies.
Barthy Byrd	*Home Front: Women and Vietnam.* Berkeley, CA: Shameless Hussy Press, 1986. Portrayals of nine different women whose lives were changed by the Vietnam War.
Philip Caputo	*A Rumor of War.* New York: Holt, Rinehart & Winston, 1977. Personal account of a young Marine officer in his first, disillusioning year of battle. One of the first widely distributed books to seriously examine the war.
David Chanoff and Doan Van Toai	*Portrait of the Enemy.* New York: Random House, 1986. The story of the Vietnam War told by the "other side." Interviews with Vietnamese soldiers, generals, spies, villagers, draft-dodgers, and others.
William Colby	*Lost Victory.* New York: Contemporary Books, 1989. Colby, who worked for the Central Intelligence Agency in Vietnam, and was CIA director when South Vietnam fell in 1975, argues that in the 1970s the U.S. had succeeded in developing effective tactics for defending South Vietnam, only to have U.S. support withdrawn.
Peter Collier and David Horowitz, eds.	*Second Thoughts: Former Radicals Look Back at the Sixties.* New York: Madison Books, 1989. A book taken from a conference of former sixties radicals and leftists who reexamine social issues. A chapter on Vietnam is critical of the antiwar movement.
David Dellinger	*Vietnam Revisited.* Boston: South End Press, 1986. A history of the Vietnam War from the perspective of a U.S. antiwar activist. Includes descriptions of his visits to Vietnam in 1966 and 1985.
Doan Van Toai and David Chanoff	*The Vietnamese Gulag.* New York: Simon & Schuster, 1986. An autobiographical account of a Vietnamese person caught in the war. Tells of his political activism against U.S. involvement in Vietnam, his visits to U.S. colleges during the antiwar movement, his 1975 arrest and two-year imprisonment under Vietnam's Communist rulers, and his eventual resettlement in America.

Bernard Edelman	*Dear America: Letters Home from Vietnam.* New York: Pocket Books, 1986. Moving anthology of letters from soldiers, with information provided on their past and present circumstances.
James A. Freeman	*Hearts of Sorrow: Vietnamese-American Lives.* Stanford, CA: Stanford University Press, 1989. The author, an anthropologist, records accounts of fourteen Vietnamese people. The narrators tell of their lives in Vietnam during and after the war, and of moving to the U.S.
Ellen Frey-Wouters and Robert S. Laufer	*Legacy of a War.* Armonk, NY: M.E. Sharpe, 1986. A survey of over a thousand men, both veterans and nonveterans, which examines how the war changed their lives and their beliefs.
James William Gibson	*The Perfect War.* Boston: The Atlantic Monthly Press, 1986. Argues that U.S. strategy in Vietnam reflected confident opinions that America could overwhelm the Vietnamese with superior technology and fire power. Concludes that the U.S. has not fully learned its lessons from Vietnam, and that other such wars are possible.
Mike Gravel, ed.	*The Pentagon Papers,* five volumes. Boston: Beacon Press, 1971. A secret study of U.S. involvement in Vietnam commissioned by Secretary of Defense Robert McNamara in 1967. Revealed a continuing pattern of the U.S. government's attempts to deceive the public about America's military involvement in Vietnam. In 1971 the study was leaked to *The New York Times,* which, after a controversial Supreme Court ruling, made it available to the public.
Bob Greene	*Homecoming.* New York: G.P. Putnam, 1989. Accounts of Vietnam veterans' experiences upon returning to the U.S. and the public's response to them.
Lawrence E. Grinter and Peter M. Dunn, eds.	*The American War in Vietnam.* Westport, CT: Greenwood Press, 1987. A collection of essays by scholars and military officials examining what lessons the Vietnam War holds for U.S. foreign policy.
David H. Hackworth and Julie Sherman	*About Face.* New York: Simon & Schuster, 1989. Memoirs of a decorated and controversial army colonel, who in 1971 quit the army and left the U.S. after publicly criticizing U.S. policy in Vietnam. Highly opinionated accounts of the Vietnam War from a soldier's perspective, critical of the U.S. military bureaucracy.
Norman B. Hannah	*The Key to Failure: Laos and the Vietnam War.* New York: Madison Books, 1987. Examines military operations in Laos, a small neighboring country officially neutral during the Vietnam War. Includes how the U.S. recruited the Hmong, a tribal people, into the war effort.
Le Ly Hayslip with Jay Wurts	*When Heaven and Earth Changed Places.* New York: Doubleday, 1989. Autobiography of a Vietnamese woman. Describes her family, her encounters with the Viet Cong and American soldiers, her marriage to a soldier and move to the U.S., and return visit to Vietnam.

John Hellman	*American Myth and the Legacy of Vietnam.* New York: Columbia University Press, 1986. An examination of novels, memoirs, and films about Vietnam. Among the films examined are *Apocalypse Now, The Deer Hunter,* and the *Star Wars* trilogy.
Anthony James Joes	*The War for South Viet Nam, 1954-1975.* New York: Praeger Publishers, 1989. History of the Vietnam War. Argues that South Vietnam could have been saved if the U.S. had used better tactics, and not abandoned the war in the 1970s.
Paul Joseph	*Cracks in the Empire: State Politics in the Vietnam War.* New York: Columbia University Press, 1987. A self-described radical interpretation of the Vietnam War. Argues that U.S. involvement in Vietnam was not an aberration or a result of blunders, but rather part of a deliberate U.S. strategy to maintain world dominance and prevent social revolutions from succeeding.
Rod Kane	*Veteran's Day.* New York: Orion Books, 1990. A personal memoir of the struggles a Vietnam veteran faces after returning to the U.S.
Stanley Karnow	*Vietnam: A History.* New York: Viking, 1983. Companion volume to the thirteen-part public television documentary series. Karnow's is one of the most comprehensive books available on the war.
Ron Kovic	*Born on the Fourth of July.* New York: McGraw-Hill, 1977. Touching memoir of a young patriot who not only becomes disillusioned but becomes a paraplegic as a result of his Vietnam service.
Andrew F. Krepinevich Jr.	*The Army and Vietnam.* Baltimore: The Johns Hopkins University Press, 1986. Analyzes performance of the American army in Vietnam. Concludes that U.S. military leaders used strategies and methods from World War II that were inappropriate in Vietnam.
Guenter Lewy	*America in Vietnam.* New York: Oxford University Press, 1978. A history that examines the charges against U.S. military policy in the war and finds most of them unjustified.
Bill McCloud	*What Should We Tell Our Children About Vietnam?* Norman, OK: University of Oklahoma Press, 1989. A junior high school teacher and Vietnam veteran asked this question and got replies from 128 people. Among the contributors are George Bush, Henry Kissinger, J. William Fulbright, and Tom Hayden.
Robert J. McMahon, ed.	*Major Problems in the History of the Vietnam War.* Lexington, MA: D.C. Heath, 1990. An anthology of both primary source documents and historical essays on issues surrounding the Vietnam War.
Myra MacPherson	*Long Time Passing: Vietnam and the Haunted Generation.* New York: Doubleday, 1984. The result of five hundred interviews with people who came of age during the Vietnam War. Argues that both those who served in Vietnam and those who resisted or evaded military service were deeply affected by the war.

232

William P. Mahedy	*Out of the Night.* New York: Ballantine Books, 1986. Written by a chaplain in the Vietnam War and counselor to veterans. Describes the emotional, spiritual, and theological problems created by the Vietnam War.
Kathryn Marshall	*In the Combat Zone.* Boston: Little, Brown, 1987. Personal accounts of Vietnam by women veterans, including nurses, clerks, and civilians.
Patience H.C. Mason	*Recovering from the War.* New York: Viking, 1990. A self-help book for wives and relatives of Vietnam veterans who have problems coping with life after the war. Written by the wife of a Vietnam veteran.
Richard M. Nixon	*No More Vietnams.* New York: Arbor House, 1985. Nixon, U.S. president from 1969 to 1974, presents his views on the Vietnam War and its lessons for American foreign policy. Argues that myths have developed about the war, including the beliefs that the war was immoral and unwinnable.
Frederick Nolting	*From Trust to Tragedy.* New York: Praeger Publishers, 1988. The memoirs of the U.S. ambassador to South Vietnam from 1961 to 1963. Describes how the U.S. became entangled in Vietnam, and appraises John F. Kennedy and Ngo Dinh Diem, presidents of the two countries, who were both killed in 1963.
Michael Norman	*These Good Men.* Iowa City, IA: Crown Publishers, 1990. A former *New York Times* reporter tracks down veterans he served with in Vietnam to find out how the war affected them.
Tim O'Brien	*The Things They Carried.* Boston: Houghton Mifflin/ Seymour Lawrence, 1990. Collection of stories set in Vietnam by the author of the National Book Award-winning novel *Going After Cacciato.*
Bruce Palmer Jr.	*The 25-Year War: America's Military Role in Vietnam.* New York: Simon & Schuster, 1985. Comprehensive history of the Vietnam War by a general who served as a deputy to General William C. Westmoreland, the commander of all U.S. military forces in Vietnam. Especially informative on the bureaucratic politics of the U.S. military.
F. Charles Parker IV	*Vietnam: Strategy for a Stalemate.* New York: Paragon House Publishers, 1989. Examines the Vietnam War in the context of relations between the U.S., China, and the Soviet Union. Argues that U.S. fears of Chinese intervention were largely unfounded.
Norman Podhoretz	*Why We Were in Vietnam.* New York: Simon & Schuster, 1983. A conservative defense of U.S. involvement in Vietnam.
Morley Safer	*Flashbacks.* New York: Random House, 1990. Noted television journalist who covered Vietnam during the war returns there and describes the land and the people twenty years later.
Al Santoli	*To Bear Any Burden.* New York: E.P. Dutton, 1985. Oral history of the Vietnam War, edited with a generally conservative slant. Includes interviews with Vietnamese and Cambodian participants in the war.

233

Jonathan Schell	*The Real War*. New York: Pantheon Books, 1987. Anthology of acclaimed articles on U.S. military operations that first appeared in *The New Yorker*, plus a new essay in which the author examines why America lost the Vietnam War.
Peter H. Schuck	*Agent Orange on Trial*. Cambridge, MA: Harvard University Press, 1986. A comprehensive description of the Agent Orange controversy.
Grace Sevy, ed.	*The American Experience in Vietnam: A Reader*. Norman, Okla.: University of Oklahoma Press, 1989. Anthology of articles and documents from the Vietnam War era.
Neil Sheehan	*A Bright Shining Lie*. New York: Random House, 1988. A Pulitzer Prize-winning biography of John Paul Vann, a U.S. army colonel who arrived in Vietnam in 1962 and was killed there in 1972. The book becomes a history of U.S. involvement in Vietnam.
Anthony Short	*The Origins of the Vietnam War*. New York: Longman, 1989. A British account of the history of the Vietnam War. Examines the origins of the Communist movement in Vietnam and their fight against the Japanese, French, and Americans.
Uwe Siemon-Netto	*The Acquittal of God: A Theology for Vietnam Veterans*. New York: The Pilgrim Press, 1990. Addressed to and about Vietnam veterans who feel rejected by God and the church, and betrayed by the nation.
Stephen M. Sonnenberg, Arthur S. Blank Jr., and John A. Talbott, eds.	*The Trauma of War: Stress and Recovery in Vietnam Veterans*. Washington, DC: American Psychiatric Press, 1985. Examination of post-traumatic stress syndrome from a medical perspective.
Harry G. Summers	*On Strategy*. Novato, CA: Presidio Press, 1983. U.S. army colonel examines the Vietnam War and faults U.S. strategy. He believes American strategic emphasis on guerrilla warfare was mistaken and led to U.S. defeat.
David F. Trask, ed.	*United States Army in Vietnam*. Washington, DC: Center of Military History, United States Army. A series of books the U.S. Army published which gives an official account of U.S. military involvement in Vietnam. The multivolume history examines strategy, relations with the press, combat operations, and other topics.
Barbara Tuchman	*The March of Folly*. New York: Alfred A. Knopf, 1984. Devotes a long section to American involvement in Vietnam in a book exploring why governments pursue policies harmful to their national interests.
James Webb	*Fields of Fire*. New York: Bantam Books, 1979. A novel showing a Marine platoon which experiences a month of combat during which most are killed.
Louis A. Wiesner	*Victims and Survivors*. Westport, CT: Greenwood Press, 1988. An in-depth scholarly study by a retired Foreign Service officer on the millions of Vietnamese people who were displaced from their homes during the Vietnam War.

Kim Willenson	*The Bad War: An Oral History of the Vietnam War.* New York: NAL Books, 1987. A series of interviews with people involved with the Vietnam War, including generals, soldiers, politicians, and protesters. Edited with a generally liberal slant, although conservative views are represented.
Sandra M. Wittman	*Writing About Vietnam.* Boston: G.K. Hall & Co., 1989. A book-length annotated bibliography listing novels, personal narratives, and teaching materials on the Vietnam War.

Index